The Washington Post

DINING GUIDE

THE DEFINITIVE WORD ON WHERE TO EAT IN AND AROUND THE NATION'S CAPITAL

TOM SIETSEMA

FOOD CRITIC FOR THE WASHINGTON POST

Published by

The Washington Post

1150 15th St. NW
Washington, D.C. 20071

The body copy is set in Filosofia, and the display type is Clarendon Bold.

Printed by Chroma Graphics, Largo, Md., in association with Alan Abrams.

ISBN: 1-930691-03-3

PUBLISHERS: Lionel Neptune and Cecelia Stephens
EDITOR: Kathleen Stanley
BOOK DESIGN & PRODUCTION: Brian Noyes
COPY EDITOR: Jane Clark
RESEARCHER: Jennifer Beeson
ASSISTANT: Karen Hill
MAP ILLUSTRATION: Gene Thorp
ILLUSTRATIONS: Eric Hanson
PHOTOGRAPHS: Chad Dowling

CONTENTS

INTRODUCTION

Who serves Czechoslovakian food? goes one of the many questions I field each day. *Where can I get a nice dinner with a view on the cheap?* someone else needs to know, right now, because he's in love—and broke—and she likes scenery and tomorrow is her birthday.

They come in by e-mail, by phone, from friends and colleagues and on my weekly online chat—more questions than I'll ever have time to respond to. For some, there is no good answer. (Czech food? Not something I've run across in the Washington area—yet.) But answering the questions I can is one of the great satisfactions of my job: telling people about good places to eat, shielding them from lost causes or steering them to solutions to their dining dilemmas, even if it's just to let them know where they can find one of their favorite foods. Having logged more than 2,800 restaurant meals in the past four years, I've tasted a lot of what the Washington area has to offer, and I'm glad to share my research as widely as I can.

Hence this restaurant guide, with star-rated reviews of 200 dining establishments and listings highlighting special features, including family-friendly venues, rooms with interesting views and places that forbid smoking.

In my rating system, zero stars reflects an overall experience that I think is poor. One star stands for a satisfactory experience; two stars means good; three stars is excellent; and four stars is superlative. I base my ratings primarily on the quality of the food but also take into account service and ambience. Just keep in mind, a restaurant review is not an exact science, but rather, an educated opinion.

RATINGS GUIDE

★ Satisfactory
★★ Good
★★★ Excellent
★★★★ Superlative

Restaurants that earn no stars are rated Poor. Ratings are based primarily on food quality but take into account service and ambience.

In the Washington area, restaurants run the gamut, from down-home to upscale, from French to Brazilian to Japanese. It's impossible to compare a pupusa with a curry. Yet those restaurants sharing the same ranking probably have a lot in common. Poor restaurants are generally disappointing on many levels. One-star restaurants are nice to know about if you live or work nearby; they may have only a handful of notable dishes or a single quality (a view, a scene) to distinguish them. Two-star restaurants have a few more frills and generally appealing cooking; they are worth driving across town for. Three-star establishments tend to be rewarding destinations, no matter where you're coming from; they typically blend high-quality cooking with environs and service to match.

To achieve four-star status, a restaurant doesn't have to spend a fortune on flowers or serve food on gold plates. It simply has to do what it does extraordinarily well—to the point of taking your breath away. No restaurant is perfect all the time, but a four-star venue is perfect more often than not. It adds up to an unsurpassed experience.

A few words about how I work: I try to visit restaurants anonymously, making reservations under names other than my own, and my employer pays for all meals and services. A full review in The Washington Post Magazine is the distillation of multiple meals, a personal rule that allows me to see the restaurant at, say, a slow Monday lunch and a bustling Saturday dinner—and maybe again and again, sometimes over the course of several seasons.

As you use this book, remember that restaurants can—and often do—

change. Chefs come and go, menus get rewritten, dining rooms get dressed up (or go drab). The silken pumpkin soup or homey chocolate cake that you read about in these pages may have been replaced by the time you visit their sources. So consider the reviews as jumping-off points rather than dictates engraved in stone.

On the job, I dine out an average of 13 meals a week. This is not the way anyone but a food critic should eat. My advice to most of you is to collect a handful of restaurants you like, and to cultivate a relationship with them; when you get to know the menu, and the staff becomes familiar—when a place begins to feel like an extension of home—you can't help gaining more pleasure from the experience.

A book is a team effort, and I have had the privilege of working with a four-star stable of talent on this project. Here at The Washington Post, Lionel

Neptune and Cecelia Stephens first initiated and then shepherded the idea of a restaurant guide. From start to finish, Cecelia proved to be a gracious conductor and tireless captain. Karen Hill and Jennifer Beeson, assistant photo editor of the Magazine, cheerfully and valiantly oversaw fact-checking—no small task given that restaurants tend to be busy for much of the day and night. Friends from my first tour of duty at this newspaper, design director Brian Noyes and chief editor Kathleen Stanley—two of the most professional, enthusiastic and careful colleagues I've ever sweated deadlines with—went above and beyond the call of duty to shape this book. Their eye for detail and helpful suggestions are evident all over these pages. Thank you for saying "yes" when I asked. And copy editor Jane Clark provided a strong safety net for us all.

I might not be writing these words if it weren't for my mentor, Phyllis C. Richman, who gave a greenhorn his start as her assistant, or Post food editor Jeanne McManus, who later hired me as a reporter. Over the years I've known them, both women have offered indispensable advice and oceans of support. Plus, they make fabulous dinner companions. My current editor, Susannah Gardiner, managing editor of the Magazine, makes my life easy in so many ways. Every writer should be lucky enough to have a boss who cares about his work as much as she does. A source of constant support, my parents, Elwin and Dorothy Sietsema, and my brother, John, remind me that nothing much matters if you don't have a loving family. (But, bro, would you please stop using our name when you make restaurant reservations?) And then there are the many friends and colleagues, too numerous to mention, who willingly go anywhere and everywhere to help me eat my way through the good, the bad and the ugly.

Finally, I'd like to thank my readers. Your tips, your praise, your criticisms—I appreciate and encourage the dialogue. May this book help you to dine better, and may all your meals have stars in them.

TOM SIETSEMA
Food critic for The Washington Post

THE REVIEWS

BIG BOWL: Vegetable pot stickers with plum sauce

A & J

★ ★

1319-C Rockville Pike, Rockville, MD
301-251-7878

OPEN: *M-F 11:30-9, Sat-Sun 10-9* **ENTREES:** *$1.20-$5.50 (small dishes)*
CHINESE BREAKFAST: *Sat-Sun 10-noon* **ENTREES:** *$1.25-$5.40 (small dishes)*
CREDIT CARDS: *No (cash only)* **RESERVATIONS:** *No*
DRESS: *Casual* **CROSS STREET:** *Templeton Place* **PARKING:** *Lot*
METRO: *Twinbrook*

I T WORRIED MY FRIENDS AND ME when the customers seated next to us at A & J received a menu written in Chinese but ours was in English. "It's the same," a waitress reassured us. And sure enough, the soups and dumplings we ordered by number from the all-day dim sum menu matched what our Asian neighbors were eating.

Of the two branches in this restaurant minichain, I prefer the modest panache of the newer Annandale location, with its undulating mural of long-ago China, faux-stone half wall and wooden banquette. The cooking at both is appealing. Picture big bowls of noodle soup brimming with bits of pork and mustard greens; long, fried-pork pot stickers; a plate of sliced smoked chicken; and batons of cucumber invigorated with a tingling-hot garlic sauce. What's too mild, like the steamed vegetable

Picture big bowls of noodle soup brimming with bits of pork and mustard greens.

dumplings, needs only a splash of soy sauce, vinegar or chili sauce to wake up its flavors. And the price is right; dinner here is about what you'd pay for a movie and popcorn.

SECOND LOCATION: *4316-B Markham St., Annandale, VA 703-813-8181*

Addie's

11120 Rockville Pike, Rockville, MD
301-881-0081

LUNCH: *M-F 11:30-2:30, Sat noon-2:30* **ENTREES:** *$9.95-$13.95*
DINNER: *M-Th 5:30-9:30, F 5:30-10, Sat 5-10, Sun 5-9* **ENTREES:** *$18-$27*
CREDIT CARDS: *All major* **RESERVATIONS:** *Recommended* **DRESS:** *Casual*
CROSS STREET: *Edson Lane* **PARKING:** *Lot* **METRO:** *White Flint*

I CAN COUNT A COUPLE OF REASONS why you should really make a reservation at Addie's: One, the former bungalow consists of two snug dining rooms with seats for only 50 (thank goodness there's a patio to help out in warm weather), and second, it's probably the most interesting modern American food currently playing in Rockville.

Chefs have come and gone in the restaurant's seven years, but each has excelled with ingredients from the water. Small surprise, given that Addie's is owned and watched over by chef Jeff Black of the seafood-themed Black's Bar and Kitchen in Bethesda. As always, fresh food and fun continue to serve as themes. Even striptease joints serve calamari these days, but Addie's takes the obvious and runs with it, placing gently grilled squid on a seductive salad of orzo, feta cheese and pine nuts, and then circling every-

Addie's takes the obvious and runs with it, placing gently grilled squid on a seductive salad of orzo, feta cheese and pine nuts, and then circling everything with a nice pesto.

thing with a nice pesto. Mahi-mahi lands on buttery rice and inky black beans, their flavors bridged with a tropical fruit coulis that balances sweet (mango) with heat (chipotle).

Representing the South, meanwhile, might be a grilled pork tenderloin, lapped with a vanilla-scented bourbon sauce and rounded out with wilted chard and spoon bread veined with corn and Smithfield ham.

The cheery yellow walls, whimsical art and old-fashioned design accents lend a homespun note, as does the brownie. Served warm, the dessert gets dressed up with whipped cream and a shower of toffee bits. Like Mom, it is hard to say "no" to.

Addis Ababa   ★

2106 18th St. NW, Washington, DC (Adams Morgan)
202-232-6092

OPEN: *M-Th noon-1 am, F noon-2 am, Sat 11 am-2 am, Sun 11 am-1 am*
ENTREES: *$7.50-$12.50* **BRUNCH**: *Sat-Sun 11-4* **ENTREES**: *$7.50-$12.50*
CREDIT CARDS: *AE, MC, V* **RESERVATIONS**: *Recommended* **DRESS**: *Casual*
CROSS STREET: *Florida Avenue NW* **PARKING**: *Street*
METRO: *Dupont Circle/Woodley Park-Zoo/Adams Morgan*

ONE OF SEEMINGLY SCORES of Ethiopian restaurants in Washington, Addis Ababa is better for its sum than its parts. Modestly dressed with bamboo screens and some colorful paintings, the small dining room isn't much to look at—its pink tablecloths and red carpet have seen plenty of traffic. And while the servers are pleasant enough, there might be only one to handle the lunch crowd.

Of the à la carte choices, I'm partial to kitfo, Ethiopia's nod to steak tartare, seasoned with herbed butter and blazing with red pepper; or the

For the most variety, pick from among the combination plates, a sampling of four dishes averaging less than $12.

tamer doro wat, chicken simmered in a brick-red sauce of onions, chilies and clarified butter and served with a whole cooked egg. For the most variety, pick from among the combination plates, a sampling of four dishes averaging less than $12. These include rustic stews of chicken, lamb and beef, cloaked in earth-colored sauces, plus a vegetable (the best of which are the tangy collard greens and vibrant chopped-tomato-and-onion salad). Lentil dishes tend to be tame, beef dishes tough.

In typical Ethiopian fashion, everything gets served on a plate lined with injera, the pleasantly sour and spongy pancake that also functions as your eating utensil: Just tear a piece off from a floppy roll, wrap it around a morsel of food and bring it to your mouth. Uncertain? Newbies have been known to get hand-fed instruction from the more conscientious waitresses.

Afghan ★

2700 Jefferson Davis Hwy., Alexandria, VA
703-548-0022

OPEN: *Daily 11-11* **ENTREES:** *$8.95-$13.95*
LUNCH BUFFET: *M-F 11-3, $6.95*
CREDIT CARDS: *All major* **RESERVATIONS:** *Recommended*
DRESS: *Casual* **CROSS STREET:** *Calvert Avenue*
PARKING: *Lot* **METRO:** *Crystal City*

THE VIEW FROM THE WINDOWS is mostly highway, and the service can be matter-of-fact. Yet this big restaurant—which almost triples in size when its folding doors are parted, revealing a satellite dining room—manages to conjure Afghanistan with evocative music on the sound system and food that speaks in a nurturing voice.

The flat bread alone warrants a visit. A ubiquitous sight in dining rooms and shop windows in Kabul, here in Alexandria it shows up on seemingly every table: flat ovals more than a foot long, crisp and chewy after doing some time in a clay oven.

At lunch, bargain hunters can round out the bread with a meal composed of a dozen or so chafing dishes on a buffet, all for $6.95. Picture fried eggplant, chicken curry, and Basmati rice threaded with carrots and sweet with plump raisins. At any time, there are à la carte kebabs of deftly seasoned chicken, beef and ground lamb (my pick); luscious crescent-shaped dumplings stuffed with scallions and topped with a zesty yogurt and meat sauce; and vegetable pleasures extending to fried spinach and—one last Afghan touch—sauteed pumpkin.

Picture fried eggplant, chicken curry, and Basmati rice threaded with carrots and sweet with plump raisins.

Agrodolce ★

21030-J Frederick Rd., Germantown, MD
301-528-6150   www.agrodolce.tv

LUNCH: *M-F 11-4* **ENTREES:** *$7-$11*
DINNER: *M-Th 4-9, F 4-10, Sat 11-10, Sun 11-9* **ENTREES:** *$8-$24*
CREDIT CARDS: *All major* **RESERVATIONS:** *Recommended*
DRESS: *Casual* **CROSS STREET:** *Route 27/Ridge Road*
PARKING: *Lot* **METRO:** *No*

THIS PLACE RADIATES GOOD CHEER, beginning with its yellow neon sign, which shines like a beacon from the corner of a shopping center. When you arrive, the staff comes through with friendly service that's reinforced with true knowledge of the menu and attention to your comfort. The treatment would be admirable in most any neighborhood but is especially welcome in this neck of the exurban woods, where fast food is easier to find than spaghettini al pomodoro and veal scaloppine.

"Why not share a wood-fired pizza as an appetizer?" the menu asks, and a lot of guests bite, choosing from a range of possibilities that include the calabrese, the pollo and a white pizza with two kinds of cheese; so far, so good. But Agrodolce needs to work on its pizza crusts, which are thin and blistered but also surprisingly timid in character.

> **More to my taste are the simple, cheese-stuffed ravioli with creamy tomato sauce, an appetizer of he-man dimensions.**

A smoother entry can be found in a plate of light and crunchy calamari, offered with a wicked marinara sauce, or the spinach and arugula salad. The portions are so generous that almost every appetizer could be shared here.

Pastas run from thin linguine with mussels and white garlic sauce to thick gnocchi topped with morel mushrooms, wisps of arugula, walnut sauce and truffle oil. More to my taste are the simple, cheese-stuffed ravioli with creamy tomato sauce, an appetizer of he-man dimensions. From the wood-stoked oven comes a satisfying lasagna, and Agrodolce's fettuccine, cooked to retain some bite and tossed with tender shrimp and flaked crab, is a soothing indulgence.

Desserts tend to be very sweet and sometimes clever, like the chocolate cookie "cigar" poised on a brick size glass ashtray. The joke runs to the tip of the cigar, where spun sugar "smoke" rises from toasted coconut "ashes." There are more traditional Italian closing statements, but I say, go for the laughs instead.

Al Tiramisu

★★

2014 P St. NW, Washington, DC (Dupont Circle)
202-467-4466   www.altiramisu.com

LUNCH: *M-F noon-2:30* **ENTREES:** *$14.90-$17.90*
DINNER: *Daily 5-11* **ENTREES:** *$14.90-$17.90*
CREDIT CARDS: *AE, DC, MC, V*
RESERVATIONS: *Recommended* **DRESS:** *Business casual*
CROSS STREET: *20th* **PARKING:** *$5 valet at dinner*
METRO: *Dupont Circle*

MY REMEDY FOR A BAD DAY is a meal at Al Tiramisu. There are better Italian restaurants and more beautiful Italian restaurants, but none of them makes me feel as happy to be there as this place does, whether I'm sitting alone on a barstool, watching a soccer match with the waiters and winding linguine with baby clams around my fork, or settled in at a table with pals, eating whatever a server has urged us to try.

Often, that means sparkling-fresh fish, simply grilled and expertly filleted. Sweet, head-on prawns, enhanced with herbs and olive oil, are always a treat, as is tender grilled squid, threaded on skewers, dusted with bread crumbs and brightened with lemon. The kitchen also turns out a fine veal chop, some lovely pastas and an unexpected finale: chocolate "salami" fashioned from ganache and ladyfingers. Irresistible. (Just remember to ask about the prices of the recited specials, which cost substantially more than the choices on the printed menu.)

The kitchen also turns out a fine veal chop, some lovely pastas and an unexpected finale: chocolate "salami" fashioned from ganache and ladyfingers. Irresistible.

The man in the dashing chef's jacket, working the joint like he's running for election? That's Luigi Diotaiuti, whose warm smile and playful spirit filter down to his crew. Narrow, low-ceilinged and often crowded, the dining room probably isn't the best place to start a clandestine relationship. Unless, of course, you're lucky enough to find yourself at table No. 15, an alcove booth that offers some privacy and a view of the room to boot.

Amma Vegetarian Kitchen ★

344-A Maple Ave. E., Vienna, VA
703-938-5328

OPEN: *M-F 11:30-2:30, 5:30-9:30 Sat-Sun 11:30-10*
ENTREES *$3.49-$4.99*
RESERVATIONS: *No* **DRESS:** *Casual*
CROSS STREET: *Glyndon Street*
PARKING: *Street* **METRO:** *Vienna/Fairfax-GMU*

A MERE SHOEBOX, this combination carryout-eatery puts its energy into flavors, not frills. So the utensils are plastic, and the cooking packs some punch—enough to keep the dozen or so tables occupied during prime time. It's promising to see so many Indian faces in the mix, though it might help if the staff had a better command of English.

The main attractions on the brief roster are the thin, crisp pancakes called dosas. Their batter, made with rice and lentils, is allowed to ferment and is then fried into a pleasantly tangy round that can be broken off and dipped into coconut chutney or partnered with a filling and gently rolled up (picture an Indian burrito). At Amma, which has a dressier sibling of the same name in Georgetown, the filling choices include variations on potatoes mashed with onion and a bit of cumin. Sambar, a souplike accompaniment made of lentils, okra and other vegetables, is included in the price of each dosa, turning the snack into a meal.

> **The main attractions on the brief roster are the thin, crisp pancakes called dosas.**

A display case next to the counter at the back tempts you with two-bite appetizers—greaseless turnovers stuffed with peas and potatoes, and minced-vegetable "cutlets" animated with black mustard seeds. Dip them into the accompanying sauce of mint and green chilies, and what was good zooms toward greatness. The same holds true for the hot lemon and mango pickles, which you can buy for an extra 50 cents to set off additional fireworks.

Aside from some soft Indian music and a few geometric prints on the walls, Amma puts the plain in Jane. For about the price of a movie ticket and a Big Gulp, though, it's bargain-priced entertainment.

SECOND LOCATION: *3291-A M St. NW, Washington, DC, 202-625-6625*

Andale ★★

401 Seventh St. NW, Washington, DC (Penn Quarter)
202-783-3133   www.andaledc.com

LUNCH: *M-Sat 11:30-3* **ENTREES:** *$8-$15*
DINNER: *M 5-9, Tu-Th 5-10, F-Sat 5-11* **ENTREES:** *$12-$26*
CLOSED: *Sun* **CREDIT CARDS:** *All major*
RESERVATIONS: *Recommended* **DRESS:** *Casual*
CROSS STREET: *D Street NW* **PARKING:** *$8 valet at dinner*
METRO: *Archives-Navy Memorial*

ANDALE IS SPANISH SLANG for "let's go!" and diners have plenty of reasons to take that advice and delve into chef Alison Swope's pleasing Mexican script. On Monday nights, the restaurant offers half-price bottles of wine from a list so inviting, and so fairly priced, it's worth returning to on other days of the week. And you'd be wise not to pack in too much before dessert, for the kitchen offers two notable endings. One is a fluffy cheesecake, showered with toasted pecans and set on a glossy pool of caramel sauce. Another is a plate of churros—crullers served hot from the fryer and crackling with sugar. The pastries are accompanied by a cup of steaming hot chocolate that I intend to revisit on the next snowy afternoon.

While packing her menu with all the right accents, from haunting mole sauce to tortillas made by hand, chef Swope refers to her creation as "contemporary Mexican," perhaps to stave off criticism from diners who might be looking for 100 percent authenticity. The items to seek out are the least elaborate ones, like the snack of roasted peanuts, spiked with garlic and chili powder and spritzed at the table with fresh lime. Throw in a tangy margarita and a little party unfolds on your palate.

> **You'd be wise not to pack in too much before dessert, for the kitchen offers notable endings.**

Ordering queso fundido will bring to your marble-topped table a shallow casserole of liquid cheese and zesty chorizo, strewn with soft strips of poblano chilies and fried onions—a straightforward but luscious appetizer meant to be scooped up with pieces of warm tortilla. And if you need a little something to sustain you through an 8 o'clock show, a soft-crisp empanada stuffed with shrimp, together with a glass of plummy malbec wine from Argentina, is the light way to go.

Artie's

3260 Old Lee Hwy., Fairfax, VA

703-273-7600   www.greatamericanrestaurants.com

LUNCH: *Daily 11:30-4* **ENTREES:** *$9-$18*
DINNER: *Sun-M 4-10, Tu-Th 4-11, F-Sat 4-midnight* **ENTREES:** *$11-$28*
BRUNCH: *Sun 11:30-2* **ENTREES:** *$10-$15*
CREDIT CARDS: *AE, D, MC, V* **RESERVATIONS:** *No*
DRESS: *Casual* **CROSS STREET:** *Arlington Boulevard/Route 50*
PARKING: *Lot* **METRO:** *No*

CORPORATE RESTAURANTS often get a bum rap—and frequently with good reason. In too many of them, the servers are tethered to a strict "smile-and-sell" routine, the cooks working off recipes dictated from some distant office.

There are exceptions, and Artie's, part of the Falls Church-based family of Great American Restaurants, is one of them. From the hostess who sees that you're promptly seated to the waitress who steers you to dishes that she's actually tasted, the service is as chipper and helpful as at Disney World. The dining rooms—one beneath beams and decorated with model boats, another outfitted with windows, a sloping roof and roomy red booths—prove similarly smart and upbeat.

From Artie's kitchen come fresh takes on American favorites: a first-class crab cake shaped with little more than jumbo lump crab; hickory-tickled wild king salmon brightened with mango salsa and bedded on polenta studded with corn kernels; a trembling banana pudding circled with crushed vanilla cookies and decorated with streaks of caramel and chocolate sauces. Salads

Salads speak to the season; side dishes merit blue ribbons (dig that coleslaw); soups pulse with flavor.

speak to the season; side dishes merit blue ribbons (dig that coleslaw); soups pulse with flavor.

Who would expect to find one of the area's best lobster bisques in a suburban shopping complex? A regular at Artie's might.

Ashby Inn

692 Federal St., Paris, VA

540-592-3900   www.ashbyinn.com

DINNER: *W-Sat 6-9* **ENTREES:** *$19-$32*
BUFFET BRUNCH: *Sun noon-2:30* **PRICE:** *$24*
CREDIT CARDS: *MC, V* **RESERVATIONS:** *Recommended*
DRESS: *Business casual* **CROSS STREET:** *Gap Run Road/Route 701* **PARKING:** *Lot*

"**W**HERE WOULD YOU LIKE TO SIT?" can be a tricky question to answer at the Ashby Inn, where the choices include four cozy rooms, each with a distinct personality. Summertime makes the decision a no-brainer, though. Beneath a sloping roof hung with wisteria and flickering lanterns, diners take in a view of distant rolling hills and nearby gardens—plots that show off both flowers and ingredients for the inn's seasonally changing menu.

"The arugula was picked this afternoon," a genial waitress informs me as she delivers a hillock of the biting greens, set off with Parmesan and lemon wedges and dressed at the table with fruity olive oil. While I'm only a short drive from downtown Washington, I feel thousands of miles removed from the bustle of the big city.

There's a new face in the kitchen these days. Christopher Carey arrived this spring from the Clifton Inn in Charlottesville. Following in the footsteps of his predecessors, Carey serves honest food with a minimum of fuss, relying on good ingredients and sensible combinations. Sweet onion, sun-dried tomatoes and

I feel thousands of miles removed from the bustle of the big city.

tiny olives are gathered on a flaky tart that nods to Provence; an entree of spaghetti is tossed with some of those same sunny ingredients plus baby spinach and olive oil. Grilled quail, plump and delicious, rests on a risotto brightened with bits of slender asparagus and intensified with dark brown juices from the poultry. Lamb sliced over tangy lentils is respectable, but the fish choices, including snowy catfish with remoulade, are better.

Much improved from seasons past, the dessert course beckons diners with simple, familiar flavors. Chocolate silk pie is graciously restrained in its sweetness. Fruit figures in other winners, such as the pretty strawberry shortcake and an apple tart distinguished by a buttery, cookielike crust. There's also a satisfying cheese plate, offered with toasted bread and a green-apple-and-onion relish—a pleasant touch in a restaurant that has been offering many in its 19 years.

A.V. Ristorante ★

607 New York Ave. NW, Washington, DC (Mt. Vernon Square)
202-737-0550

OPEN: *M-Th 11:30-10, F 11:30-11, Sat 5-11* **ENTREES:** *$6.50-$16.95*
CLOSED: *Sun* **CREDIT CARDS:** *All major*
RESERVATIONS: *Required for parties of 15 or more*
DRESS: *Casual* **CROSS STREET:** *6th* **PARKING:** *Lot*
METRO: *Gallery Place/Mt. Vernon Square/7th Street-Convention Center*

STUMBLING INTO THIS long-running, family-owned Italian restaurant (and you might, as it's dim as a cave with its soft lights, blood-red banquettes and dark wood paneling), you could easily tag it as the spaghetti house of your dreams.

Unlike some of those Italian-flavored chains that attempt to re-create yesteryear with boat-size portions and kitschy props, A.V. is the real deal. We're talking walls plastered with restaurant reviews dating to 1962 and signed photographs and letters from long-ago VIPs, Hubert Humphrey among them. Tinny opera music (is that Caruso?) only reinforces the sense of nostalgia.

The food *is* apportioned for lumberjacks—why, the pizza is the size of a hubcap —and while none of it will make you swoon, some of it is satisfying. Eggplant Parmigiana is draped in a tangy-sweet blanket of tomato sauce; tender clams ride the rim of a plate of garlicky, white-sauced linguine; and fried artichokes get stuffed with bread crumbs, capers

A.V. is the real deal. We're talking walls plastered with restaurant reviews dating to 1962 and signed photographs and letters from long-ago VIPs.

and olives (the last makes a nice group appetizer). Heavy and bland, meat dishes are best avoided.

A.V.'s assets extend to efficient service and two fun design details: a big, copper-framed hearth inside and a deck replete with a fountain outside. Of course, the tables are covered in red-and-white checks.

Bacchus ★★

1827 Jefferson Pl. NW, Washington, DC (Dupont Circle)
202-785-0734 www.bacchusdc.net

LUNCH: *M-F noon-2:30* **ENTREES:** *$8.75-$11.75*
DINNER: *M-Th 6-10, F-Sat 6-10:30* **ENTREES:** *$14.25-$17.75*
CLOSED: *Sun* **CREDIT CARDS:** *AE, DC, MC, V*
RESERVATIONS: *Recommended* **DRESS:** *Casual*
CROSS STREET: *Connecticut Avenue*
PARKING: *Complimentary valet at dinner* **METRO:** *Dupont Circle*

NO ONE KNOWS APPETIZERS better than the Lebanese, who snack on them at breakfast and build entire buffets around them later in the day. And few local restaurants lavish more attention on mezze, as the spread is called, than Bacchus's two venerable outposts of Lebanese cooking, whose appetizer lists stretch to some 50 choices.

Such exquisite decisions! Will it be cabbage stuffed with rice, mint, onions and parsley, or some aged cheeses tossed with sumac, tomatoes and fiery paprika? Fried smelts with tahini dip, or smoke-singed chicken drumsticks destined for a dunk in garlic paste? I want them all.

It would be easy to fill up on hors d'oeuvres, but the Washington site requires diners to order a main course at lunch. That turns out to be a good thing; it would be a shame to miss out on Bacchus Delight, a generous plate of fish and chicken marinated with garlic and lemon, nicely grilled and arranged on fluffy, almond-strewn rice.

> **Such exquisite decisions! Will it be cabbage stuffed with rice, mint, onions and parsley, or fried smelts with tahini dip? I want them all.**

The Bethesda branch is larger and fancier, with the advantage of an outdoor courtyard in good weather, yet the original downtown restaurant, cozy beneath its tentlike ceiling and watched over by a gracious staff, remains my favorite. Both, thankfully, serve falafel of distinction and lemonade that tastes freshly made—because it is.

SECOND LOCATION: *7945 Norfolk Ave. Bethesda, MD, 301-657-1722*

Bardeo

★ ★

3309 Connecticut Ave. NW, Washington, DC (Cleveland Park)
202-244-6550

DINNER: *M-Th 5-11, F-Sat 5-midnight, Sun 5-10:30* **ENTREES:** *$6.50-$9.95*
CREDIT CARDS: *AE, DC, MC, V* **RESERVATIONS:** *No* **DRESS:** *Casual*
CROSS STREET: *Macomb Street NW* **PARKING:** *$5 valet*
METRO: *Cleveland Park*

PUT A WINE BAR next to Ardeo restaurant and this is what happens: People who don't want to commit to a full three-course meal show up to graze instead, on small plates of pretty food with the options of wines—thoughtfully poured by both the full and half glass—to complement the dishes.

Thus, a luscious chicken-filled lumpia, hot with curry and flanked with a tropical relish, can be savored with a chardonnay, and minty lamb sausage on grilled polenta carries the possibility of a malbec. There are about a dozen dishes in all, and while the script was changing when I encountered it, you can always count on something for every taste. Cheese, anyone? Take your pick from an English Stilton, a Spanish manchego or a lovely bite of goat cheese from California's Laurel Chenel.

> **You can always count on something for every taste.**

Like Spanish tapas, the appetizer-sized food here comes out fast from Bardeo's small open kitchen, and one or two plates lead you to ordering one or two more. The room isn't very big, just a few tables near a window up front, some snug brown booths along a wall and tall stools at the handsome marble bar (attended by a friendly bartender, and my favorite place to linger). The wine theme is stylishly reinforced by walls in shades of burgundy and chardonnay, and cool tunes foster a convivial mood. Bardeo feels like a cocktail party.

Big Bowl ★★

2800 Clarendon Blvd., Arlington, VA
703-875-8925   www.bigbowl.com

LUNCH: *M-F 11:30-4, Sun noon-4* **ENTREES:** *$7.95-$12.95*
DINNER: *M-Th 4-10, F-Sat 4-11, Sun 4-9* **ENTREES:** *$7.95-$12.95*
CREDIT CARDS: *AE, D, MC, V*
RESERVATIONS: *Recommended for parties of 6 or more*
DRESS: *Casual* **CROSS STREET:** *N. Fillmore Street*
PARKING: *Street* **METRO:** *Clarendon*

F EW ARE THE RESTAURANTS that can engage both children and discriminating parents. That alone makes Big Bowl something of a find. Pint-size patrons get a Chinese carryout box of crayons, kiddie chopsticks and a fortune cookie, giving their guardians a chance to read the pan-Asian menu. Vegetable pot stickers with plum sauce? Summer rolls packed with fresh greens, herbs and shrimp? Both are good, and easy to eat. There's chicken in a gentle coconut curry, shrimp in a blaze of ginger and chilies (watch out!) and comforting noodle dishes that put most of Chinatown's to shame.

> **Pint-size patrons get a Chinese carryout box of crayons, kiddie chopsticks and a fortune cookie, giving their guardians a chance to read the pan-Asian menu.**

The delivery is quick, the food fresh; the stocks are made anew each day, and the nose-tingling ginger ale is shot through with real ginger. And I've watched more than a few kids wander up to the open kitchen to check out the enticing display of ingredients, where you can choose your own and turn them over to the stir-fry cooks. Big and beautiful, the restaurant also counts a lively bar scene. Sure, it's a chain. But when's the last time you felt so good about eating fast food?

OTHER LOCATIONS: *11915 Democracy Dr., Reston, VA, 703-787-8852
21100 Dulles Town Center, Sterling, VA, 703-421-9989*

Bistro Bis ★★

15 E St. NW, Washington, DC (Capitol Hill)
202-661-2700   www.bistrobis.com

BREAKFAST: *Daily 7-10:30* **ENTREES**: *$7.75-$14.50*
LUNCH: *M-F 11:30-2:30* **ENTREES**: *$13.25-$23.50*
DINNER: *Daily 5:30-10:30* **ENTREES**: *$19.75-$29.50*
BRUNCH: *Sat-Sun 11-3* **ENTREES**: *$9.50-$17*
CREDIT CARDS: *All major* **RESERVATIONS**: *Recommended*
DRESS: *Businees casual* **CROSS STREET**: *N. Capitol Street*
PARKING: *$5 valet at dinner* **METRO**: *Union Station*

IN A NEIGHBORHOOD short on worthy restaurants, this one, from the owners of downtown's southern-minded Vidalia, heads the class. Its handsome zinc bar with glowing saffron backdrop offers a convivial spot for an after-work Pernod or perfect steak tartare; the car-size leather booths frequently fill with boldfaced names (this is Capitol Hill, after all); and the service runs friendly and helpful. Warm-colored wood and honeyed lighting envelop diners in a cocoon of chic.

Steamed mussels with roasted tomatoes and Provencal herbs suggest a trip to somewhere sunny.

From beyond the glass wall separating you from the kitchen comes some fine French bistro fare. A generous gratin of salt cod mashed with potatoes (brandade) and slathered on grilled bread makes for a lusty introduction; scallops dusted with truffles and poised on a tarragon-scented lobster cream prove more elegant. Steamed mussels with roasted tomatoes and Provencal herbs, meanwhile, suggest a trip to somewhere sunny. Move on to rabbit framed in buttery noodles and a garden of soft-cooked vegetables, everything lapped with an assertive mustard cream, or duck confit flanked with luscious sauteed potatoes. A lighter hand with the salt would be welcome, and desserts need tweaking—the tarte Tatin, alas, is undistinguished.

Otherwise, from the complimentary gougeres (warm cheese puffs) that launch dinner to the all-French wine cellar, Bis sets a Gallic standard of distinction.

Bistro d'Oc ★

518 10th St. NW, Washington, DC (Penn Quarter)
202-393-5444

LUNCH: *M-Sat 11:30-2:30* **ENTREES:** *$8.95-$17.95*
DINNER: *M-Th 5:30-10, F-Sat 5:30-11, Sun 5-8:30* **ENTREES:** *$11.95-$19.95*
PRE-THEATER: *Daily 5:30-7, 3-course prix fixe $19.95*
BRUNCH: *Sun 11:30-4* **ENTREES:** *$8.95-$17.95*
CREDIT CARDS: *AE, MC, V* **RESERVATIONS:** *Recommended* **DRESS:** *Casual*
CROSS STREET: *E Street NW* **PARKING:** *Street* **METRO:** *Metro Center*

"HAVE WE BEEN BEFORE?" a woman wonders aloud as she and her mate check out their surroundings at Bistro d'Oc, whose address previously hosted the all-American Star Saloon and, before that, Mike Baker's 10th Street Grill A waiter brings over a chalkboard listing the specials. Tonight, the options include not only crab-stuffed avocado and veal kidney but also chicken satay with peanut sauce. To anyone who knows the owner, chef Bernard Grenier, this Asian accent on the menu is not unexpected, for his wife and business partner, Thasanee, is Thai.

To put Bistro d'Oc in the context of other bistros around town, the newcomer is neither as formal as Bistro Bis nor as consistently delicious

Almost anything served with french fries here is apt to please.

as Bistrot Lepic. Bistro d'Oc is more like a solid B student, likable and reliable and good to know about if you are in the neighborhood or in need of pre-theater sustenance.

The menu has its charms, too. From France, there are snails in garlic butter and a respectable pâté. Better than the French onion soup, though, is the very American bowl of chowder thick with sweet corn and rich bites of crab, punctuated with crisp bacon.

Almost anything served with french fries here is apt to please, be it the crisp-skinned roast chicken or the thin and flavorful hanger steak. An appealing duck leg confit, rich and crisp, comes with more-ordinary sauteed potatoes.

Some fish are more equal than others here. Sauteed salmon on a bed of cabbage with a thyme-laced red wine sauce is satisfying at dinner, as is a steamed salmon entree at lunch. But the bistro's take on bouillabaisse is a big disappointment, with less-than-prime fish and shellfish sitting in a watery broth vaguely seasoned with garlic and saffron.

Desserts lean toward Gallic crowdpleasers. My favorite way to bid adieu is with crepes suzettes. It's an old-fashioned splurge in a restaurant that wants to be more than a convenience and frequently hits that mark.

Bistro Francais ★★

3124-8 M St. NW, Washington, DC (Georgetown)
202-338-3830   www.bistrofrancaisdc.com

LUNCH: *M-F 11-5*   **ENTREES:** *$7.50-$15.95*
DINNER: *Sun-Th 5 pm-3 am, F-Sat 5 pm-4 am*   **ENTREES:** *$14.95-$21.95*
BRUNCH: *Sat-Sun 11-4, $18.95*
CREDIT CARDS: *AE, D, MC, V*   **RESERVATIONS:** *Recommended*
DRESS: *Casual*   **CROSS STREET:** *31st*
PARKING: *Two hours free at Georgetown Park Mall, F-Sat*
METRO: *Foggy Bottom*

ALL DRESSED UP AND NO PLACE TO GO? That can be an obstacle when it's after midnight and you're hungry for something serious to eat. Cozy in dark wood and mirrors that exaggerate its size, this long-time Georgetown fixture comes to the rescue with all manner of appealing French fare: avocado stuffed with crab; seafood pâté set off with a sharp horseradish sauce; thin-cut lamb steak topped with coins of melting herb butter; even steak tartare, punchy with mustard and served with a beet-flecked salad and a pile of skinny fries.

Always there is a long list of specials, too, perhaps including tender scallops served with egg noodles in a light wash of garlic-perfumed tomato sauce. Local chefs like to gather here after their own kitchens close, and you can taste

This long-time Georgetown fixture comes to the rescue with all manner of appealing French fare.

why with a winner like that. Meanwhile, lunchtime yields a bargain: three courses for $14.95, a deal that includes a glass of wine.

Onion soup? But of course. Eggs? You can pick from a quartet of omelets. The coq au vin may be dry and the desserts uninspired, but it's good to know about a spot that stays open until 3 on weeknights, 4 on weekends—long after official Washington has gone to bed.

Bistrot du Coin ★★

1738 Connecticut Ave. NW, Washington, DC (Dupont Circle)
202-234-6969   www.bistrotducoin.com

OPEN: *Sun-W 11:30-11, Th-Sat 11:30-1 am* **ENTREES:** *$12.95-$21.95*
BRUNCH: *Sat-Sun 11-4* **ENTREES:** *$4.95-$8.95*
CREDIT CARDS: *All major* **RESERVATIONS:** *Recommended*
DRESS: *Casual* **CROSS STREET:** *Florida Avenue NW* **PARKING:** *Street*
METRO: *Dupont Circle*

ANYONE WHO'S SPENT any time in Paris will recognize this people magnet. At night in particular, the yellow lighting, combined with like-colored walls, washes the high-ceilinged room in an eerie, nicotine-stained glow; a long, zinc-topped bar practically commands you to pull up for a kir while you're waiting for friends to arrive. And everything we've been told not to eat—organ meats, uncooked beef, french fries, creme brulee—shows up on a menu that celebrates the rich life. Some tiny type on the bill of fare adds to the decadence: "Cigarettes, Cigars: Oui!"

I confess, it's fun being bad at Bistrot du Coin. Ribbons of smoked duck wind through a salad of warm leeks; baked snails provide an excuse to sop up more melted garlic butter than you should; and steak tartare honors that meaty classic. ("How would you like that done?" a waiter jokes with us when we order it.) Along with big pots of steamed mussels (flavor mine with curry, thanks), meat figures prominently on the menu. I'm partial to the thin, sinewy onglet (hanger steak), flanked by a pile of long golden french fries and sharpened with a thin sauce of shallots

I confess, it's fun being bad at Bistrot du Coin.

and peppercorns. Watch out for the trouble spots, like the watery onion soup, with its timid cover of cheese, and the tartiflette, a vapid side dish of potatoes, bacon, onion and cheese that is not nearly as interesting as that combination sounds.

By meal's end, I'm exhausted. The feeling has nothing to do with the wine or the food but rather with the noise: At full throttle, which is almost always, Bistrot du Coin hums, throbs and booms with music and conversation. As I bid adieu, I feel as if I've just left a Metallica concert. But you can bet I'll be back.

Bistrot Lafayette ★★

1118 King St., Alexandria, VA
703-548-2525   www.bistrotlafayette.com

LUNCH: *M-Sat 11:30-2:30*   **ENTREES:** *$10.95-$15.95, 3-course prix fixe $16.95*
DINNER: *M-Sat 5:30-10*   **ENTREES:** *$17.95-$25*   **CLOSED:** *Sun*
CREDIT CARDS: *All major*   **RESERVATIONS:** *Recommended*   **DRESS:** *Casual*
CROSS STREET: *N. Henry Street*   **PARKING:** *Street*   **METRO:** *King Street*

SMALL AND SPECIAL have always been a part of the repertoire of Keo Koumtakoun, whose work has been on display all over the Washington area in the last 15 years. Born in Laos and self-taught, the chef has cooked at Le Paradis in Gaithersburg, La Provence in Vienna and Saveur in Glover Park in the District. Now he's in Old Town Alexandria, turning out his French-accented food in a tiny dining room, appealing in shades of peach and snug with dark tables and people who appear pleased to be gathered around them.

This tour of duty for Koumtakoun is simple in comparison with his past ventures. He's offering bistro cooking that, except for a few daily specials, is for the most part familiar and comforting, things like French onion soup—a fine-tuned performance of light stock, soft onions and melted cheese on bread with a pleasant smoky char—and rack of lamb lightened with thyme jus and served with mashed potatoes and asparagus.

Much of the food leads us into temptation. Koumtakoun's steak tartare, an entree, is first-rate: fine chopped raw beef ignited with mustard, capers and hot sauce and served with french fries (good ones, which also make an appearance with the steamed mussels). People who

He's offering bistro cooking that is for the most part familiar and comforting.

have sworn off escargots based on encounters with rubber bands posing as snails might reconsider after trying the tender, meaty and richly buttery and garlicky plate served as an appetizer at Bistrot Lafayette. Occasionally, a server might announce a dessert special of tarte Tatin; leap at the chance to try it, warm apple slices atop a buttery crust that melts on the tongue. Like a blue blazer, it comes off as a classic.

Bistrot Lepic

1736 Wisconsin Ave. NW, Washington, DC (Georgetown)
202-333-0111   www.bistrotlepic.com

LUNCH: *Tu-F 11:30-2:30*   **ENTREES:** *$11.95-$18.95*
DINNER: *Tu-Th 5:30-10, F-Sat 5:30-10:30, Sun 5:30-9:30*
ENTREES: *$15.95-$21.95*
CLOSED: *M*   **CREDIT CARDS:** *AE, D, MC, V*
RESERVATIONS: *Recommended*   **DRESS:** *Casual*
CROSS STREET: *S Street NW*   **PARKING:** *Street*
METRO: *Foggy Bottom*

IT'S SMALL AND SNUG and seemingly always busy, a gathering spot for ladies who lunch, dashing retired diplomats and the stray tourist lucky enough to find himself in this sunny dining room in upper Georgetown.

The menu is varied, the cooking sure, the plates attractive. Beets and goat cheese mingle in a lovely little tower served with a chic salad and toasted bread, while duck confit enriches a hearty lentil soup. Look for boudin blanc, a mousselike sausage that is one of my favorite dishes here, paired with sauteed apples and silky potato puree. There is food for light appetites—shrimp with whatever vegetables are in vogue—and food for people who want something more robust, maybe a special of nicely cooked lamb atop a risotto thick with potatoes. A diner can also count on fruit desserts that, in the European fashion, aren't too sweet and a loose French spirit to the service.

> **There is food for light appetites and food for people who want something more robust.**

Upstairs there's an intimate wine bar, where terra-cotta walls, cork tile flooring and low tables with custom-made chairs make a sexy backdrop to a brief menu of what chef-owner Bruno Fortin calls "international tapas": tuna tartare, vegetable terrine, cumin chicken.

Black's Bar and Kitchen ★★

7750 Woodmont Ave., Bethesda, MD
301-652-6278

LUNCH: *M-F 11:30-2:30* **ENTREES:** *$6.95-$13.95*
DINNER: *M-Th 5-10, F-Sat 5-11, Sun 5-9:30* **ENTREES:** *$18-$26*
CREDIT CARDS: *All major* **RESERVATIONS:** *Recommended*
DRESS: *Casual* **CROSS STREET:** *Old Georgetown Road*
PARKING: *Street* **METRO:** *Bethesda*

YOU WALK ACROSS A WOODEN PORCH to get to the screen door that separates a lively bar from the dining room, but that's where the sense of rustic charm yields to urban refinement at one of Bethesda's most appealing restaurants.

Soup here is wonderful, be it pea soup garnished with crab in spring or spicy corn soup garnished with crisp-fried oysters in late summer. Depending on the time of year, you can also reel in soft-shell crabs poised on a mound of jicama, red onion and citrus; seafood stew made from just about anything that ever swam (including duck sausage), in a tomato-y broth; a pair of shrimp tacos, the smoky shrimp sharing room with avocado, poblano chilies and a rousing lime-cilantro vinaigrette. This is all interesting, if sometimes busy, food, prepared by chef David Craig.

Meat and dessert courses are not the reason to visit; gracious service and Gulf shrimp—brassy with sun-dried tomatoes, basil and garlic over linguine—definitely are.

> **Depending on the time of year, you can also reel in soft-shell crabs poised on a mound of jicama, red onion and citrus.**

Black Olive ★★

814 S. Bond St., Baltimore, MD
410-276-7141   www.theblackolive.com

LUNCH: *Daily noon-2:30* **ENTREES:** *$10-$27, 3-course prix fixe $17*
DINNER: *M-Th 5-10, F-Sat 5-10:30, Sun 5-9* **ENTREES:** *$22-$36*
CREDIT CARDS: *All major* **RESERVATIONS:** *Recommended*
DRESS: *Casual* **CROSS STREET:** *Aliceanna Street*
PARKING: *Complimentary valet at dinner* **METRO:** *No*

THE FAMILY-OWNED BLACK OLIVE prepares not only a fine, smoke-tinged rack of lamb and a world-class spinach pie, punctuated with melting feta and wrapped in homemade phyllo, but also seafood that tastes moments removed from the sea.

Forget the ubiquitous Chilean sea bass and the common salmon. Here you get to choose from among whole red snapper, wild turbot, genuine Dover sole, sea bream, sardines from Portugal, maybe whole anchovies from Greece. Forget the menu, too. Part of the joy of dining in this taverna, cheerful in blue-and-white linens, is the chance to window-shop for dinner and take cues from your hosts. "Are you ready for your tour?" a server might ask before he escorts you to the open kitchen, fronted with a display case of ingredients that sparkle from their bed of ice.

The cooks know that these pristine treasures need only a little time on the grill and perhaps a sauce of lemon juice, capers and olive oil to enhance their appeal. A thoughtful wine list keeps pace with the catch of

Part of the joy of dining in this taverna, cheerful in blue-and-white linens, is the chance to window-shop for dinner and take cues from your hosts.

the day, as do the appetizers—don't miss the bread pudding, savory with onions, artichokes and mushrooms. Of course there's baklava. If you think all fruit plates are created equal, you haven't seen Black Olive's glorious arrangement of mangoes, figs, blueberries and cherries, ready for a close-up in *Gourmet* magazine.

Bob Kinkead's Colvin Run Tavern

★ ★ ★

8045 Leesburg Pike, Tysons Corner, VA

703-356-9500   www.kinkead.com

LUNCH: *M-F 11:30-2:30*   **ENTREES:** *$13-$20, 2-to-3-course prix fixe $20.03-$29*
DINNER: *M-Th 5:30-10, F-Sat 5:30-10:30, Sun 5-9*   **ENTREES:** *$24-$39*
CREDIT CARDS: *All major*   **RESERVATIONS:** *Recommended*
DRESS: *Business casual*   **CROSS STREET:** *Towers Crescent Drive*
PARKING: *Complimentary valet*   **METRO:** *Dunn Loring/Vienna*

MAN SHALL NOT LIVE by steak alone. But that's almost all Tysons Corner offered in upscale restaurants before Bob Kinkead sent his No. 2 chef from Washington to Northern Virginia.

Like Kinkead's seafood restaurant in the city, this one serves bountiful plates of spirited food that look to the world for inspiration; unlike Kinkead's downtown destination, the menu here holds as much turf as surf. So there are ravioli stuffed with pumpkin, brushed with brown butter and garnished with fried sage; a cool salad of jicama, chilies and avocado drizzled with buttermilk-lime dressing; grilled pork tenderloin paired with spoon bread and a maple-vinegar sauce; and a Rolls-Royce of a carving cart, under whose dome sits a handsome hunk of beef, pork, venison or rack of veal. From the sea come scallops lapped with a caper-spiked parsley sauce; crisp-roasted cod gilded with a "succotash" of corn, cranberry beans and lobster; and a delicious tour of New England called "Clams Five Ways," which brings together fritters, clams casino, fried clams, stuffed clams and a demitasse of chowder. Some of the dishes would be better with an ingredient or two fewer, and the portions are daunting, but you'll probably want to loosen your belt to accommodate dessert.

You'll probably want to loosen your belt to accommodate dessert.

It's not just the cooking, under the direction of Jeff Gaetjen, or the wine program, orchestrated by ace sommelier Michael Flynn, that impresses me. I love walking in to hear live piano music in the foyer lounge, to spot a big marble bar at which to wait for friends, and to have the choice of four dining rooms, each with a regional theme. The Charleston, sophisticated in shades of gold and black, and the Shenandoah, cozy with a flagstone hearth, are my favorites; avoid, if you can, the bland Nantucket, which offers all the pizzazz of an airport lounge.

Bombay Club ★★

815 Connecticut Ave. NW, Washington, DC (Downtown)
202-659-3727   www.bombayclubdc.com

LUNCH: *M-F 11:30-2:30*   **ENTREES:** *$7.50-$22*
DINNER: *M-Th 5:30-10:30, F-Sat 5:30-11, Sun 5:30-9*   **ENTREES:** *$8.50-$22*
PRE-THEATER: *M-Sat 5:30-6:45, 3-course prix fixe $26.50*
BUFFET BRUNCH: *Sun 11:30-2:30*   **PRICE:** *$18.50*
CREDIT CARDS: *AE, DC, MC, V*   **RESERVATIONS:** *Recommended*
DRESS: *Business casual*   **CROSS STREET:** *H Street NW*
PARKING: *Complimentary valet*   **METRO:** *Farragut West*

ROMANCE WITH AN INDIAN ACCENT—that's Bombay Club, the city's most sumptuous spot for shrimp with mango chutney and chicken tikka. You and your significant other will sit in broad chairs surrounded by pools of space in a large room dressed as if the British raj still held sway, an image reinforced by lazy circling fans, peachy lighting and piano music at dinner. New fabrics make the restaurant even more alluring.

The food, both beautifully presented and refined in flavor, can be just as indulgent. Salmon pulses from a rub of red chilies, ginger and garlic. Calamari is stir-fried with onion, tamarind, curry leaves and what tastes like fire. And every

Anything from the tandoor is apt to please, be it ginger-laced lamb chops or moist whole trout.

bite of the green-chili chicken is followed by delicious waves of coriander and mint. Anything from the tandoor is apt to please, be it ginger-laced lamb chops or moist whole trout. The breads show up hot and blistered from their time in the clay oven (new on the menu: a hot pocket with goat cheese), and the desserts include first-rate versions of kulfi, the slightly chewy Indian ice cream, and carrot pudding, scented with cardamom.

The missteps are thankfully few: dull spinach, tough lamb rogan josh and well-intentioned service that sometimes goes overboard, with too much bowing and scraping. Keep Bombay Club in mind for brunch: A buffet of Indian flavors, presented in silver chafing dishes and accompanied by free-flowing bubbly, is a ticket to India for less than $20.

Bombay Tandoor ★★

8603 Westwood Center Dr., Vienna, VA

703-734-2202   www.bombaytandoor.com

LUNCH: *M-F 11:30-2:30* **ENTREES:** *$7.50-$16.95*
BUFFET: *M-Th $8.95, F-Sun $9.95*
DINNER: *Daily 5:30-10* **ENTREES:** *$7.50-$16.95*
BRUNCH: *Sat-Sun noon-3* **BUFFET:** *$9.95* **CREDIT CARDS:** *AE, MC, V*
RESERVATIONS: *Recommended* **DRESS:** *Casual*
CROSS STREET: *Leesburg Pike* **PARKING:** *Lot* **METRO:** *Vienna*

BOMBAY TANDOOR, a spinoff of downtown Washington's Bombay Palace, delivers plenty of style for the price. Paintings of long-ago maharajahs stare down from the big, sand-colored walls, and acres of blue carpet cushion your walk from foyer to prettily set table. It's an enormous space warmed up with a rosewood bar and lilting Indian music that help you forget you're in a suburban business district.

Some of the cooking has that effect, too. Though the menu embraces all the familiar Indian restaurant staples, the kitchen distinguishes itself from the pack with a vindaloo of lamb or vegetables that should cheer the fire-eater with its blazing sauce of vinegar, chilies and ginger, as well as fluffy Basmati rice dishes (biryanis) with a choice of shrimp, lamb, vegetables or dried fruit.

> **Though the menu embraces all the familiar Indian restaurant staples, the kitchen distinguishes itself from the pack with a vindaloo of lamb or vegetables that should cheer the fire-eater.**

Alas, the breads these days taste routine, the vegetable fritters ordinary. But lamb chops rubbed with the dusky spice blend known as masala and cooked in the tandoor are terrific, and butter chicken in a creamy tomato sauce lives up to its billing. Indian beer makes the best companion to this food, and it's poured into a frosted mug. Nice touch.

Boulevard Woodgrill ★

2901 Wilson Blvd., Arlington, VA
703-875-9663   www.boulevardwoodgrill.com

LUNCH: *M-F 11:30-4* **ENTREES:** *$5.50-$16.95*
DINNER: *M-Th 4-11, F-Sat 4-11:30, Sun 4-10* **ENTREES:** *$9.95-$23.95*
BRUNCH: *Sat 11-3, Sun 10-3* **ENTREES:** *$7.95-$23.95*
CREDIT CARDS: *AE, DC, MC, V*
RESERVATIONS: *No* **DRESS:** *Casual*
CROSS STREET: *N. Fillmore Street* **PARKING:** *Lot*
METRO: *Clarendon*

OWNER RYAN DUNCAN put his wine salesmen on notice as he prepared to open Boulevard Woodgrill, a spinoff of the nearby Faccia Luna pizzeria: "Don't show us anything we can find at Harris Teeter or Fresh Fields." He asked instead for wines that were off the beaten path, affordable and suitable for a menu with a lot of grilled dishes. The result is more than 30 varieties, representing a world of choices, offered by the glass—and nothing more than $7 a pour.

This directive wouldn't be such a big deal in an expense acccount establishment, but it's remarkable for a restaurant whose menu reads like Mom had a hand in developing it. We're talking tomato-edged meat loaf, fish and chips flanked with a sweetly fresh coleslaw, and crab cakes that are satisfying by themselves but better with a heap of hot, hand-cut french fries. The kitchen isn't trying to do somersaults, just to turn out some simple dishes as well as it can (the exception is a bland hamburger patty upstaged by its accessories). Shrimp rolled in Japanese bread crumbs and fried to a gentle shade of gold are as fancy as things get here.

If only you could hear yourself think! Everything about the design of the Boulevard Woodgrill encourages you to bring earplugs, from the hard-

> **The kitchen isn't trying to do somersaults, just to turn out some simple dishes as well as it can.**

wood floors and bare tabletops to the high ceilings and big glass windows. Not to mention the streams of neighbors and others who converge on the place, particularly at night, for cocktails, conversation and a bite to eat from the open, stainless steel kitchen. Thank goodness for those umbrella-shaded tables that ring the exterior. If you're more concerned about refueling than making a connection, dine early; anytime, keep in mind that the Boulevard Woodgrill doesn't accept reservations. That means you'll have time to get to know the top-shelf bartenders, who not only whip up some fine cocktails but also, despite the crowds, remember you from visit to visit.

Breadline ★★

1751 Pennsylvania Ave. NW, Washington, DC (Downtown)
202-822-8900

BREAKFAST: *M-F 7:30-10:30* **ENTREES:** *$1.25-$3.95*
LUNCH: *M-F 10:30-3:30* **ENTREES:** *$4-$7.50*
CLOSED: *Sat-Sun* **CREDIT CARDS:** *AE, MC, V*
RESERVATIONS: *No* **DRESS:** *Casual*
CROSS STREET: *17th* **PARKING:** *Street*
METRO: *Farragut West*

BREAD IS THE STAR OF THE SHOW, and customers waiting in line to order it in some form—as a pizza, a sandwich, an empanada—are the rule at this downtown bakery-cafe, situated an olive roll's toss from the World Bank.

Open and airy, Breadline combines an industrial look—concrete floors and naked light bulbs suspended from the ceiling—with the reassuring aromas of a kitchen that truly cares how you eat. So expect tomatoes only in season and forget Coke (the refrigerator case invites you to try fresh fruit juices and vegetable juices instead).

Yes, the owner is a friend of mine, but I'd be remiss not to tell you about this place. Almost everything that can be made from scratch is, and the ingredients are all prime, which means the prosciutto hails from Parma and the Parmesan is Reggiano. The french fries are amazing, the seasonal soups comforting, the sandwiches all models of their kind (one passion among many is meatballs—soft, minty and shaped from ground Niman Ranch beef).

> **Breadline combines an industrial look with the reassuring aromas of a kitchen that truly cares how you eat.**

The noise drowns out the classical music, and the ordering process remains awkward, but that doesn't stop drop-ins by the powers that be, like the White House speech writer who routinely shows up for some food for thought—and sticks around to pen the president's declarations.

Buck's Fishing & Camping

(too new to assign stars)

5031 Connecticut Ave. NW, Washington, DC (Upper NW)
202-364-0777

DINNER: *Tu-Th 5-10:30, F-Sat 5-11, Sun 5-10* **ENTREES:** *$10.25-$32.50*
CLOSED: *M* **CREDIT CARDS:** *MC, V*
RESERVATIONS: *No* **DRESS:** *Casual*
CROSS STREET: *Nebraska Avenue NW* **PARKING:** *Street*
METRO: *Tenleytown-AU/Van Ness-UDC*

GREENWOOD, THE STYLISH American restaurant named after Carole Greenwood, quietly shuttered its doors this summer. But the veteran chef with three short-lived restaurants behind her staged an immediate comeback at the same address, with a new concept and a new business partner, James Alefantis, who until recently served as general manager at Johnny's Half Shell in Dupont Circle. Their joint production carries the odd title Buck's Fishing & Camping and began serving dinner in October.

Maybe the fourth time will be the charm. In his new role, Alefantis will be restructuring the restaurant, tweaking the way it's been run to "better serve the neighborhood." Brunch is planned, for instance. The dramatic blood-red walls remain, but the seating has been expanded to accommodate 100 diners, including outdoors and at a handsome communal table that stretches nearly the length of the dining room. To reinforce its outdoorsy new name, an aluminum canoe now floats from the ceiling.

As for the menu, fans of the chef's dry-aged prime sirloin and luscious mussels bathed in red wine and rosemary will be pleased to see that Greenwood has not only kept on those signatures but also dropped prices and added homier comforts: chicken

> **To reinforce its outdoorsy new name, an aluminum canoe now floats from the ceiling.**

and (excellent) biscuits, smothered pork chops, a fried-fish basket with hush puppies, and a rib-sticking casserole of duck and sausage. Desserts continue the theme and tap into a vein of nostalgia: Both the chocolate icebox cake and lemon pudding cake are blue-ribbon winners.

Even the owners can't explain the unusual name of their fledgling restaurant, beyond the fact they both like the name Buck. "My only worry," cracked Alefantis during renovation, "is people thinking we carry sporting goods." Sure enough, no sooner did Buck's open than he got a call from a man inquiring about ... a fishing license.

Burma   ★

740 Sixth St. NW, Washington, DC (Chinatown)
202-638-1280

LUNCH: *M-F 11-3* **ENTREES:** *$4.95-$7.95*
DINNER: *Daily 6-10* **ENTREES:** *$4.95-$22*
CREDIT CARDS: *All major*
RESERVATIONS: *Recommended for parties of 6 or more*
DRESS: *Casual* **CROSS STREET:** *H Street NW*
PARKING: *Street* **METRO:** *Gallery Place-Chinatown*

I F YOU'RE NOT FAMILIAR with the cooking style, keep in mind that Burma shares borders with India, China and Thailand. Imagine a reper-toire of pork and seafood, hot and sour, crisp and soft, dried fish and coconut milk, noodles and curries—in all, a seductive marriage of cultures.

Spareribs win raves for their size and their honey-basil glaze; "gold fingers" turn out to be delicious lengths of squash in a light batter, served with a tamarind sauce that unfolds in tangy waves on the tongue. Even better is smoky scored squid tossed with sauteed onions and choice bits of ham. If there's a single dish I'd seek out in this crowd, though, it's the refreshing young ginger salad, subtly hot and interesting with peanuts, cabbage, carrots, crisped shallots and lemon juice.

Even better is smoky scored squid tossed with sauteed onions and choice bits of ham.

The lure here is what's on the plate, not the environs; frills are limited to a few wall hangings and some straw mats on the glass-topped tables. But the food comes out quickly and the service is helpful.

Located on the second floor above a video shop, Burma acts like it wants to be kept a secret. Don't let it.

Cafe Asia ★

1720 I St. NW, Washington, DC (Downtown)
202-659-2696   www.cafeasia.com

OPEN: *M-Th 11:30-11, F 11:30-midnight, Sat noon-midnight, Sun noon-11*
ENTREES: *$7-$27*
CREDIT CARDS: *All major*   **RESERVATIONS:** *Recommended*
DRESS: *Casual*   **CROSS STREET:** *17th*   **PARKING:** *Street*
METRO: *Farragut West*

PART OF A WAVE OF EYE-CATCHING new restaurants in the capital is Cafe Asia, a spinoff of the Arlington restaurant of the same name. A discreet green sign outside of Cafe Asia gives way to a vast vision in white and silver, in the form of a two-story dining area with an atrium that allows people upstairs and down to observe one another.

Like its sibling across the river, Washington's Cafe Asia takes diners on a tour of the Far East with a menu that makes side trips to Thailand and Japan. No one country triumphs here, but a little hunting turns up satisfying possibilities from each contributor.

The spring rolls are a bit greasy, for instance, but tender pieces of chicken splashed with lime juice, then skewered together with vegetables, speak favorably of Vietnam. Hot-and-sour soup is not really either, but Chinese "ravioli"—zestily seasoned pork dumplings—make for a diverting snack. Of the Thai offerings, two of the top draws are ground chicken salad (larb gai) and shrimp draped in a teasing red curry. Noodle dishes are well represented; vermicelli combined with shrimp, bits of roasted pork and carrot threads—curry-redolent "Singapore" noodles—is particularly satisfying.

Knowing that chef Elis Triany is

> **Washington's Cafe Asia takes diners on a tour of the Far East with a menu that makes side trips to Thailand and Japan.**

from Indonesia should lead you to try the dishes from her homeland. Triany's stewlike beef rendang is only gently fiery but still interesting. Even better is nasi uduk, a long platter lined with a small feast of fragrant rice, peanut-sauced chicken satay, airy crackers, pickled vegetables, and a tantalizing toss of tiny dried fish and peanuts. But the Indonesian dish that really ignites the palate is a fish fillet spread with a rough paste of lemon grass, turmeric, basil and more, and swaddled in banana leaves. The stabs of heat and spice, pronounced but not overwhelming, are details that keep you going back for more.

SECOND LOCATION: *1550 Wilson Blvd. Arlington, VA, 703-741-0870*

Cafe Atlantico

★ ★ ★

405 Eighth St. NW, Washington, DC (Penn Quarter)
202-393-0812   www.cafeatlanticodc.com

LUNCH: *M-F 11:30-2:30* **ENTREES:** *$9-$16*
DINNER: *Sun-Th 5-10, F-Sat 5-11* **ENTREES:** *$19-$24, 3-course tasting menu $45*
LATINO DIM SUM BRUNCH: *Sat-Sun 11:30-2:30*
ENTREES: *small dishes $2.50-$9.95, tasting menus $24.95-$34.95*
PRE-THEATER: *Daily 5-6:30, 3-course prix fixe $22*
CREDIT CARDS: *All major* **RESERVATIONS:** *Recommended*
DRESS: *Business casual* **CROSS STREET:** *D Street NW* **PARKING:** *$8 valet*
METRO: *Archives-Navy Memorial*

A MEAL AT CAFE ATLANTICO is like a trip to South America without the jet lag. From the saucer-size pupusas oozing a filling of pork and cheese to the moist red snapper jazzed up with a brassy sauce of tomatoes, olives and lime, the cooking here is both vibrant and delicious. Bored with seviche and guacamole mashed tableside? The kitchen dares you to try something new, maybe a chilled tomato soup sweetened with chunks of watermelon and coconut cream and excited with ginger oil. Or a Latino dim sum, served weekends, that runs to small plates of avocado-stuffed "ravioli" made with sheer slices of jicama, and scallops anointed with orange-flavored oil. Desserts take liberties with traditional recipes, yet they're terrific. Anyone for a pina colada parfait?

The food gets an appropriately cool package. Before you take a bite, your eyes and ears are tickled by the setting, three whimsical dining rooms on three different levels, each with a distinct vantage point. The ground floor has windows that face the street, the middle frames an open kitchen, and the top offers a bird's-eye view of the party below. Vibrant murals and bright-striped banquettes color the scene, as does a bouncy soundtrack that has guys loosening their ties a few songs in.

Before you take a bite, your eyes and ears are tickled by the setting.

Or maybe it's those cocktails that put everyone at ease. Cafe Atlantico pours some of the best tropical libations you're likely to encounter anywhere, including a bracing margarita and a world-class mojito that stirs rum, lime juice and fresh mint into a liquid beach vacation.

Cafe de Paris ★★

8808 Centre Park Dr., Columbia, MD
410-997-3560

BREAKFAST: *M-F 7:30-11* **ENTREES:** *$4.95-$6.75*
LUNCH: *Tu-F 11:30-2:30* **ENTREES:** *$9.95-$12.95*
DINNER: *Tu-Sun 5-9* **ENTREES:** *$15.95-$23.95, 3-course prix fixe, $32.95*
BRUNCH: *Sun 11:30-2:30* **PRICE:** *$19.95*
CREDIT CARDS: *AE, D, MC, V* **RESERVATIONS:** *Recommended*
DRESS: *Casual* **CROSS STREET:** *Route 108* **PARKING:** *Lot* **METRO:** *No*

ERIK ROCHARD throws more of himself into his French restaurant than most of his competition. He sends out cheery newsletters, reminding patrons that his deli case is stocked with French cheeses or fruit tarts. He performs in the restaurant's once-a-month jazz night (he's the flutist). And when a guest complained that she didn't much care for French cooking but loved a good crab cake, he found a bunch of crab cake recipes for his young chef, Benjamin Cattan, to audition—and won the gratitude of the complainer by putting the not-so-Gallic appetizer on the menu.

The best way to experience Cafe de Paris is to order the three-course dinner "formule" for $32.95, which includes your choice of starters, entrees and desserts. One fine path to follow: tender and garlicky snails followed

There's plenty to keep you smiling, including a proper French onion soup, diced lamb and apricots in a gentle curry and very good french fries to accompany a rib-eye steak.

by meaty duck leg confit shored up with buttery mashed potatoes and scattered with chopped mushrooms, and a pear and peach tart, gently sweet, to close.

Not every dish sings—the goat cheese stuffed into a roasted red pepper was stiff and cold the night I tried it, and a fruit soup made with red wine pitted bland berries against astringent broth— but there's plenty to keep you smiling, including a proper French onion soup, diced lamb and apricots in a gentle curry and very good french fries to accompany a rib-eye steak.

Knotty wood floors, scarlet banquettes and walls the color of good mustard wrap diners in a warm embrace. More likely than not, the affable Rochard will drop by the table to say "bon jour" and tell a joke or share a story, like the time a guy came in and announced he was boycotting French wine and asked the host what he could drink.

Without missing a beat, Rochard replied, "Chinese beer?"

Cafe Divan ★★

1834 Wisconsin Ave. NW, Washington, DC (Georgetown)
202-338-1747   www.cafedivan.com

LUNCH: *Daily 11-3:30* **ENTREES:** *$6.50-$16*
DINNER: *M-Th 3:30-10:30, F-Sun 3:30-11* **ENTREES:** *$6.95-$18*
CREDIT CARDS: *AE, DC, MC, V* **RESERVATIONS:** *Recommended*
DRESS: *Casual* **CROSS STREET:** *34th* **PARKING:** *Street*
METRO: *No*

ANOTHER TURKISH RESTAURANT in the Washington area warrants a bulletin. There aren't very many such purveyors around, and Northern Virginia claims most of them. Rarity alone shouldn't elevate a cuisine, however. At its most seductive, the cooking of Turkey is an edible tapestry.

The latest arrival, Cafe Divan, celebrates that notion and does so in a lovely corner location in Georgetown. Wrapped in windows, its main room sports a modern look warmed by walls of flagstone or painted in tones of pomegranate and mustard.

One of the most enticing entry points is the mezze platter, an attractive sampler that includes squares of chalk-white feta cheese; moist grape leaves stuffed with sweetly spiced rice, pine nuts and currants; a dab of chickpea dip; pencils of fried pastry oozing hot cheese; and smoky pureed eggplant. Thoughtfully, the tour is offered not just for a group but for the solo diner, too (for a manageable $4.95 at lunch, a dollar more at dinner).

Most Turkish restaurants limit serving doner kebab, a combination of lamb and veal pressed on a spit, to weekends, when they're busiest. Steady requests from fans of the dish persuaded the owner to offer doner kebab every day of the week, and at lunch as well as dinner. I'm a huge fan of this classic, in which the meat is marinated overnight in olive oil, onions and cumin, and carved to order in thin slices that are crisp on the edges and succulent throughout. But the meat is only half the equation; the folds are arranged on a savory cushion of bread draped in yogurt and enlivened with tomato and hot green pepper. It's one of the best one-dish meals around.

At its most seductive, the cooking of Turkey is an edible tapestry.

From the kitchen's oak-burning oven slide satisfying pizzas known as pides, which can be topped more than a dozen ways. A meal as full-flavored as at Cafe Divan is best followed with Turkish coffee, as bracing as it gets.

Cafe 15   ★★

806 15th St. NW, Washington, DC (Downtown)
202-730-8800

BREAKFAST: *Daily 6:30-10:30* **ENTREES:** *$12*
LUNCH: *M-F 11:30-2* **ENTREES:** *$19-$26*
DINNER: *Daily 6-10:30* **ENTREES:** *$26-$34*
CREDIT CARDS: *All major* **RESERVATIONS:** *Recommended*
DRESS: *Business casual* **CROSS STREET:** *H Street NW* **PARKING:** *$7 valet*
METRO: *McPherson Square*

NEWS THAT ANTOINE WESTERMANN—chef of Restaurant Buerehiesel in Strasbourg, France, which has the ultimate Michelin rating of three stars—was hired as a consultant to this elegant hotel in 2002 got the city's food cognoscenti wondering: Would it be a trailblazer? Or just another fancy place to drop some serious money?

I could argue the point either way, sometimes both sides at the same meal. Some dishes are superlative, like Westermann's signature, an appetizer of frog's legs and ravioli: A cluster of small, meaty and buttery legs looks like a bunch of lollipops, on a plate shared with pasta filled with sweet, almost melting onions. The extraordinarily succulent meat and the light-as-air ravioli washed with chervil sauce are a storybook match; at once refined and rustic, the dish shows its Alsatian origins. Every bit as starworthy: medallions of tuna accented with shimmering tomato paste, olives and onion and sandwiched between delicate pastry, and any dessert involving fruit or chocolate. Vegetables are inevitably transformed into something luxe and luscious. But seed-crusted salmon is ordinary, scallops with parsley cream are cooked too long and duck confit finds itself in a dull sort of shepherd's pie.

The extraordinarily succulent meat and the light-as-air ravioli washed with chervil sauce are a storybook match.

The airy dining room is small and smart, with high ceilings and big windows set with planters of lush grass, a fresh contrast to the earth tones and moody purples that otherwise dominate the interior. The chairs are broad and the tables mahogany; the gleaming Guy Degrenne silverware is lined up on its edges next to Bernardaud china. Under the watchful eye of restaurant manager Nicolas Sangros, a veteran of the esteemed Jean Georges and Lespinasse in New York, the service, too, is impressive.

Daring and delicious, but also earthbound and uneven—Cafe 15 is some of the former and too much of the latter.

Cafe Milano ★

3251 Prospect St. NW, Washington, DC (Georgetown)
202-333-6183   www.cafemilano.net

LUNCH: *M-Sat 11:30-4* **ENTREES:** *$10-$36*
DINNER: *Daily 4-1* **ENTREES:** *$15-$36*
BRUNCH: *Sun 11:30-4* **ENTREES:** *$10-$36*
CREDIT CARDS: *All major* **RESERVATIONS:** *Recommended* **DRESS:** *Casual*
CROSS STREET: *Wisconsin Avenue NW* **PARKING:** *$9 valet at dinner*
METRO: *Foggy Bottom*

AUTHORS, ACTORS, SOCIALITES, POLS—Cafe Milano attracts them all to its several stylish dining rooms (and one of the busiest outdoor patios in the city). Sometimes the Italian restaurant feeds them well, too. Tuna carpaccio makes a nice introduction, as does a racy salad of white anchovies and fennel. Spring delivers a fine asparagus puree, accessorized with thin shards of Parmesan that slowly melt into the hot green soup.

Moving deeper into the menu, diners can find a proper veal Milanese, pounded nearly as thin as paper and set off with a fluff of arugula, and whole sea bass, carefully cooked, deftly filleted at the table and arranged on the plate with glossy grilled vegetables. But gnocchi draped with a bland crumble of sausage and bitter rapini is a bust, and the pizza is decent, nothing more. The prices at Cafe Milano don't leave room for many slips.

Does anyone care, though? As the lights go down at night, the energy level shoots up. The scene at this famous Georgetown address is always irresistible: Servers who look like they stepped out of an Armani ad, cute young things attached to their cell phones, a famous face or fat bank account at seemingly every other table all make for delicious stories tomorrow. Cafe

The scene at this famous Georgetown address is always irresistible.

Milano is as much a club as a place to refuel. You know where you stand here by where you're seated and what comes your way: Favorite guests might ease in with a complimentary fried squash blossom, while biscotti and a shot of something potent might precede your server's saying "ciao."

Cafe Salsa   ★

808 King St., Alexandria, VA

703-684-4100   www.cafesalsarestaurant.com

LUNCH: *Daily 11:30-4* **ENTREES:** *$9.95-$12.95*
DINNER: *Sun-Th 4-10, F-Sat 4-11* **ENTREES:** *$14.95-$19.95*
BRUNCH: *Sun 11-3* **ENTREES:** *$7.95-$9.95*
CREDIT CARDS: *All major* **RESERVATIONS:** *Recommended*
DRESS: *Casual* **CROSS STREET:** *N. Columbus Street* **PARKING:** *Street*
METRO: *King Street*

C AFE SALSA IS THE MOST RECENT REMINDER I've had of a general restaurant truth: More often than not, appetizers are better than entrees.

The crowd gathered on just about any night at this colorful Latin American destination suggests that it can be whatever a visitor wants: a place where one can drop by with friends after work, or to get the family together for a quick refueling, or to break the ice with someone new. Things look promising when you and your pals are fighting over the last of the long, crisp plantain chips and dusky salsa that launch every meal, listening to some salsa music in the background and being looked after by attentive servers.

One of the most introductions is a pair of pretty fluted empanadas, filled with luscious shredded beef and served with a macho green dip that shocks the palate. Puerto Rico, home to the chef, is represented by exceptional alcapurrias, their thin, crisp casing of mashed green bananas hiding a stuffing of ground meat seasoned with cilantro and garlic and boosted with a little cup of jalapeno sauce for dunking. Seafood appetizers are no less appealing. Tiny white scallops and ivory squid mingle with corn, red onion and lime juice in a sprightly seviche.

Puerto Rico, home to the chef, is represented by exceptional alcapurrias.

All that said, it's frustrating when you depart from the first two pages of the menu. Did the cooks go home early? It can taste that way. Cafe Salsa has only half a dozen entrees, give or take a few specials, and honestly, there's not one I'd return for.

For the most fun, head upstairs. That's where you'll find half-priced starters, weekdays from 4 to 7 p.m. The second-floor bar also pours fine margaritas, mojitos and Latinopolitans—a twist on the standard cosmopolitan, and breezy with mint.

Cantina Marina ★

600 Water St. SW, Washington, DC (SW Waterfront)
202-554-8396   www.cantinamarina.com

OPEN: *M-Th 11:30-10, F-Sat 11:30-11, Sun 11:30-9 (seasonal)*   **ENTREES:** *$12-$20*
MEXICAN BRUNCH: *Sat-Sun 11:30-2:30*   **ENTREES:** *$5.95-$7.95*
PRE-THEATER: *Tu-Sun 5-7, 3-course prix fixe $19.95*   **CREDIT CARDS:** *AE, MC, V*
RESERVATIONS: *Pre-theater only*   **DRESS:** *Casual*   **CROSS STREET:** *7th Street SW*
PARKING: *Street*   **METRO:** *Waterfront-SEU*

INDING EVEN DECENT FOOD in a restaurant with a view tends to be an elusive goal—why not try being first in line at the DMV while you're at it? Yet every now and then a restaurant surfaces to reward a diner's efforts.

Exhibit A turns out to be Cantina Marina, overlooking the Southwest waterfront. Not only is this small eatery situated in a part of the city with too few satisfying places to eat but also it was brought to life by two cooks with some experience under their belts—Christy Velie and Tom Przystawik, both late of Cafe Atlantico—and a popular veteran restaurateur, Nick Fontana.

Bouncy music plays in the octagon-shaped dining area, a second-floor tower painted in a South Beach palette. An expansive covered patio outside serves as a stage for live music on Friday. Together, these spaces strike just the right chord for a meal that might begin with an entree of fried catfish tucked inside soft tortillas and conclude with a tangy Key lime pudding.

Louisiana influences much of the small menu. In addition to those fish tacos, there are very good wraps filled with golden shrimp, a po' boy stuffed with juicy tomato slices and crunchy oysters, and a muffuletta that does justice to that New Orleans-style classic. Two of you could easily **It's a messy meal, but plenty good.** split a tostada, layered with black beans, chopped tomato and generous amounts of either chopped beef or pulled chicken.

It's a messy meal, but plenty good. Asian Cajun spareribs are a bust, though; their meat is tough and tasteless. I'd erect a stop sign before the gumbo, too, a one-note swamp of rice and dull seasonings. But it's full speed ahead with the shrimp cocktail.

You should know that the service at Cantina Marina is beach-casual, and so are the utensils. And the decibel level shoots up, up and away as the after-work crowd elbows its way inside. The upside to all the informality: a chance to gaze at a fleet of boats on the Potomac.

Carlyle
★★

4000 S. 28th St., Arlington, VA

703-931-0777   www.greatamericanrestaurants.com

LUNCH: *M-Sat 11:30-4* **ENTREES:** *$10-$19*
DINNER: *M-Th 4-11, F-Sat 4-midnight, Sun 3-11* **ENTREES:** *$13-$23*
BRUNCH: *Sun 10:30-2:30* **ENTREES:** *$10-$19*
CREDIT CARDS: *AE, D, MC, V* **RESERVATIONS:** *No*
DRESS: *Casual* **CROSS STREET:** *Quincy Street* **PARKING:** *Lot*
METRO: *No*

SINCE ITS $4 MILLION FACE-LIFT, there are fresh reasons to check out the Carlyle. Notice the expanded foyer? The new red-leather banquettes and globe-shaped lights fashioned from bronze and alabaster? The ground-floor bar is more handsome than ever, thanks to some mirrors and a soaring wall of frosted glass.

As always, the staff throws out a big welcome mat, and the American cooking is both familiar and interesting. Among just the appetizers, egg rolls adopt a Tex-Mex accent with their zesty fillings of smoked chicken, roast corn and black beans; creamy-centered crab fritters show up in spiky coats of shredded wheat; and each day gets a soup of its own (Saturday finds a glorious clam chowder).

The kitchen acts as if it doesn't want any taste to feel left out. So it offers meaty beef ribs with a tangy barbecue sauce plus maca-

Egg rolls adopt a Tex-Mex accent with their zesty fillings of smoked chicken, roast corn and black beans.

roni and cheese for the dedicated carnivore, and trout showered with spiced pecans and bedded on Parmesan potatoes for the fish fancier. The breads are baked right next door at the restaurant's own bakery (it even makes biscuits for your pooch), and from the bar comes a sidecar that reminds you of why the classic cocktail is back in vogue. Desserts run to old-fashioned comforts like deep-dish apple pie and, in season, a mile-high shortcake with a garden of fruit and a cloud of whipped cream.

Not everything scores—one night's roast pork tenderloin is marred by an overdose of salt—but the hits far outnumber the misses. From the partylike atmosphere to the sleek design, the Carlyle is a model neighborhood restaurant.

Cashion's Eat Place

1819 Columbia Rd. NW, Washington, DC (Adams Morgan)
202-797-1819   www.cashionseatplace.com

DINNER: *Tu 5:30-10, W-Sat 5:30-11, Sun 5:30-10* **ENTREES:** *$19-$28*
BRUNCH: *Sun 11:30-2:30* **ENTREES:** *$7.50-$11.50*
CLOSED: *M* **CREDIT CARDS:** *AE, MC, V* **RESERVATIONS:** *Recommended*
DRESS: *Business casual* **CROSS STREET:** *18th* **PARKING:** *$5 valet at 6:30*
METRO: *Woodley Park-Zoo/Adams Morgan*

ONE OF WASHINGTON'S best practitioners of modern American cooking, and one of the city's most conscientious cooks, period, Ann Cashion shops to precisely reflect the time of year, then turns what she finds into dishes of real personality. So spring finds diners scraping the bottom of their bowls to retrieve every drop of a vibrant pea soup, its flavor broadened with rosemary oil.

Unlike too many other chefs, Cashion is content to let good ingredients stand on their own. She knows that a simple wash of sauce best suits whatever fresh fish she is serving; that a zesty salsa can stand up to a crusty-edged pork shoulder; and that honest desserts—lemon chiffon cake, sugar cookies perfumed with lavender, coffee-scented custard—create lasting impressions. Her food is by turns rustic (nubbins of crisp pork belly scattered over soft polenta) and refined (light and airy, one night's shrimp and vegetable tempura, served with a racy dipping sauce, rivals that of the city's best Asian practitioners).

> **Cashion is content to let good ingredients stand on their own.**

Recently spruced up, Cashion's is where you'll see serious food lovers mingling with the occasional boldface name and others who just want to catch up with pals or better get to know a date; the lighting is flattering, the wine list holds some treasures, the slips (dry sliced leg of lamb with ordinary broccoli) are few.

Caspian House of Kabob ★

19911-C N. Frederick Rd., Germantown, MD
301-353-0000

OPEN: *M-Sat 11-10, Sun noon-9* **ENTREES**: *$5-$15.95*
CREDIT CARDS: *D, MC, V* **RESERVATIONS**: *No*
DRESS: *Casual* **CROSS STREET**: *Middlebrook Road*
PARKING: *Lot* **METRO**: *Shady Grove*

"**W**E MAKE EVERYTHING HERE," says Fahimeh Shirazi, who owns this Persian fast feeder with her husband, Ali. "Nothing is frozen, nothing is fried." The cooking sure tastes that way, we think to ourselves as we dab pieces of pita bread into tangy bowls of yogurt with chopped cucumber and a smooth, garlicky chickpea dip. The pleasures continue with the crusty lamb chops, succulent Cornish hen and juicy, onion-laced ground beef kebab meals made more generous with pillows of Basmati rice garnished with grill-striped tomatoes. Want to kick up your pick a notch? Just ask for it "spicy" and watch mild turn wild (with chili pepper, that is).

> **The pleasures continue with the crusty lamb chops, succulent Cornish hen and juicy, onion-laced ground beef kebab meals.**

The restaurant's name might ring a bell for locals: Caspian House of Kabob turns out to be a bigger, prettier spinoff of the late Caspian Cafe. The new venue, brightened with blue sconces and a handsome painting of the Caspian Sea, doesn't serve alcohol, but you can wash back your food authentically with fresh carrot juice, Persian tea or the frothy yogurt drink called dough.

Planning a party? The kitchen also caters.

Caucus Room

401 Ninth St. NW, Washington, DC (Penn Quarter)
202-393-1300   www.thecaucusroom.com

LUNCH: *M-F 11:30-2:30* **ENTREES:** *$16-$25*
DINNER: *M-Sat 5:30-10:30* **ENTREES:** *$24-$36*
CLOSED: *Sun* **CREDIT CARDS:** *All major*
RESERVATIONS: *Recommended* **DRESS:** *Business casual*
CROSS STREET: *D Street NW* **PARKING:** *$5 valet at dinner*
METRO: *Archives-Navy Memorial*

A FEW YEARS BACK, I ate through more than 20 Washington-area restaurants in search of The Perfect Steakhouse. I spent a lot of money and a lot of time and felt as if I had left no filet mignon or sirloin unsliced in my quest for the best.

It turned out there wasn't a single place that excels in all that I want from such a restaurant—great meat, great service, great wine, great sides—though some purveyors came closer to that ideal than others. The Caucus Room was one of the finalists.

To start, I adore its chopped salad with blue cheese and bell peppers, or the big, creamy crab cakes, followed by a thick, juicy porterhouse or some fine lamb, always cooked just the way I ask. Invariably, I'll get a side of horserad-ish-spiked mashed potatoes, or creamed spinach (more vegetable than dairy, thank goodness), and I like to tap the waiter for good ideas from the extensive wine list.

Always, I save room for the warm pecan pie; it's as thick as a phone book, with a high nuts-to-caramel ratio. (Then again, it has stiff competition from the fabulous, mile-high coconut cake.) Ask to sit in the main dining room, handsome in chocolate-colored booths and regal blue carpet. To get to it, guests stroll down a long, broad hall, past an impressive wine display and a gallery's worth of black-and-white photographs recalling the personalities of Washington past. (Check out the rare sight of FDR in a wheelchair.)

> **To start, I adore its chopped salad with blue cheese and bell peppers, or the big, creamy crab cakes.**

Ceiba

(too new to assign stars)

701 14th St. NW, Washington, DC (Downtown)
202-393-3983   www.ceibarestaurant.com

LUNCH: *M-F 11:30-2:30*   **ENTREES:** *$11-$16*
DINNER: *M-Sat 5:30-11*   **ENTREES:** *$17-$26*
CLOSED: *Sun*   **CREDIT CARDS:** *All major*
RESERVATIONS: *Recommended*   **DRESS:** *Casual*
CROSS STREET: *G Street NW*   **PARKING:** *$5 valet at dinner*
METRO: *Metro Center*

ROM THE GUYS WHO GAVE THE CAPITAL a new way to think of seafood at DC Coast followed by a fresh twist on things Asian at TenPenh comes this lively tour of Latin America. Ceiba takes its name from an umbrella-shaped tree indigenous to that part of the world and said to have mystical significance.

Early on, at least, signs at this newcomer (pronounced SAY-bah) are promising. The seviches—well, most of them—sparkle. Conch chowder bursts with savor thanks in part to the tiny pitchers of sherry and rum that accompany the bowl. Empanadas come fat with shredded duck and raisins, and the rosy grilled skirt steak gets a kick out of its brassy chimichurri sauce. The mojitos take you to Havana with every sip, and the silken flan, treated to a drift of caramel cream, tastes like comfort food gone to finishing school. Spoiling the fun, though, are gluey crab fritters and salmon foisted on a dull broth of tomato and cumin.

The mojitos take you to Havana with every sip.

Rich wood, bright carpets, a sea of votives and a semi-open kitchen make a nice package for Ceiba's exuberant cooking. And the servers prove to be expert guides. But bring your earplugs to this party, or learn to read lips. At full throttle, the place is deafening.

C.F. Folks

✔ *Critic's Pick*

★ ★

1225 19th St. NW, Washington, DC (Dupont Circle)
202-293-0162   www.cffolks.com

LUNCH: *M-F 11:45-2:30* **ENTREES:** *$5.75-$10.95*
CLOSED: *Sat-Sun* **CREDIT CARDS:** *All major*
RESERVATIONS: *No* **DRESS:** *Casual*
CROSS STREET: *Jefferson Place*
PARKING: *Street* **METRO:** *Dupont Circle*

"DID YOU PAINT?" a customer asks the owner. "The entry looks brighter." Art Carlson scans his tiny domain—11 green stools lined up at a Formica counter—in mock seriousness before delivering the punch line: "No, we must have mopped the floor."

While other restaurants bend like contortionists to please their patrons, Carlson lets his audience know it's his way or the highway, Bub. News-hounds (and there are plenty in this crowd of lawyers and journalists) have to settle for no TV; Carlson prefers opera and public radio. C.F. Folks is open only on weekdays and only for lunch because that's how much the owner wants to work—period.

C.F. Folks is open only on weekdays and only for lunch because that's how much the owner wants to work—period.

The printed menu is mostly salads and sandwiches, and good as the almond chicken salad is, you'd miss the point of eating here if you didn't take your cue from the small blackboard on the wall. That's where you'll find the five or so specials each day. Monday showcases Louisiana with red beans and rice and chunks of andouille, Wednesday detours to Italy (and maybe a fine pasta Bolognese) and Friday it's "Something from the Middle East."

Charleston

1000 Lancaster St., Baltimore, MD

410-332-7373   www.charlestonrestaurant.com

DINNER: *M-Th 5:30-10, F-Sat 5:30-11*
ENTREES: *$26-$36, 6-7-course prix fixe $70-$79*
CLOSED: *Sun*   **CREDIT CARDS:** *All major*
RESERVATIONS: *Recommended*   **DRESS:** *Business casual*
CROSS STREET: *Exeter Street*   **PARKING:** *Complimentary valet*

WE'VE BARELY BEEN SEATED when our waiter launches into a lengthy spiel about the restaurant's chef, Cindy Wolf, that is so thorough, it sounds like an A&E "Biography" profile.

"Her technique is French, but you'll notice a lot of local ingredients and a southern flair," he says, pointing out such signature dishes as Wolf's "sandwich" of crisp fried green tomatoes, lobster and lump crab. "She recently visited Argentina, where she picked up some new ideas," he continues, plugging grilled sweetbreads splashed with lemony butter. Wolf directs the action in the open kitchen while her husband, Tony Foreman, watches over the the trio of dining rooms, one of which displays the restaurant's impressive inventory of wine and another that looks as if it had been airlifted in from South Carolina. From the Italian linens to the gleaming silver, every detail speaks of high standards.

What to order? I'm partial to dishes that hail from the water, like pan-roasted grouper with lemon beurre blanc, poised over a hash of Vidalia onions. Nothing against the pepper-edged venison strip loin, but its lusty frame of crowder peas, lima beans and black-eyed peas upstages the meat.

> **I'm partial to dishes that hail from the water, like pan-roasted grouper with lemon beurre blanc, poised over a hash of Vidalia onions.**

To wrap it up, there are nice ice creams, a distinguished chocolate cake and a cheese trolley, just like you might see in the fancy restaurants of New York or Washington but very much at home here in Baltimore.

Charlie Palmer Steak ★★

101 Constitution Ave. NW, Washington, DC (Capitol Hill)
202-547-8100   www.charliepalmer.com

LUNCH: *M-F 11:30-2:30*   **ENTREES:** *$17-$31, 3-course prix fixe $29*
DINNER: *M-F 5:30-10, Sat 5-10:30*   **ENTREES:** *$21-$39*
PRE-THEATER: *M-Sat 5:30-6:30, 3-course prix fixe $35*
CLOSED: *Sun*   **CREDIT CARDS:** *AE, DC, MC, V*
RESERVATIONS: *Recommended*   **DRESS:** *Business casual*
CROSS STREET: *First Street NW*   **PARKING:** *$5 valet M-Sat dinner*
METRO: *Judiciary Square*

WHEN THE RESTAURANT made its debut on the Hill in May 2003, Charlie Palmer himself described the latest addition to his empire as "not a traditional steakhouse." The New York chef, best known for Aureole and its spinoffs, makes a strong case. There's an abundance of surf to compete with the turf on the menu. And the vast dining room forgoes the usual meat-market design for something fresh. Its clean lines, blue-and-silver color scheme and floor-to-ceiling windows give it the sleek appearance of an ocean liner.

Palmer recruited Bryan Voltaggio to take charge of the kitchen here, and Voltaggio has much to be proud of, though early on, entrees outperformed appetizers. Meat connoisseurs can slice into a thick and savory pork loin chop crowned with candied fruits in a mustard syrup; a fine dry-aged rib-eye (hold the sweet sauce, please); or a rosy porterhouse built for two (minus the bone, alas). And to enhance the à la carte entrees are some terrific side dishes: Gnocchi melts on the tongue, broccoli rabe gets a pleasing garlic punch, and risotto—gilded with fragrant shavings of truffle—is as creamy as you would hope.

Charlie Palmer Steak has invested in a serious wine program, bringing in a master sommelier and placing a glass-wrapped wine "cellar"—suspended over a lighted moat of water and stones—in the middle of its dining room. Guests can order the traditional way, from a thick book of selections, or from a hand-held computer, an e-Winebook. Geeks love that $2,000 toy, which allows them to bookmark choices they might want to discuss with the sommelier, get on a mailing list or even send a note to the chef.

> **Meat connoisseurs can slice into a thick and savory pork loin chop crowned with candied fruits in a mustard syrup.**

Chicken on the Run ★

4933 St. Elmo Ave., Bethesda, MD
301-652-9004

OPEN: *M-Sat 11-9, Sun noon-8* **ENTREES**: *$5.50-$8.95*
CREDIT CARDS: *MC, V* **RESERVATIONS**: *No*
DRESS: *Casual* **CROSS STREET**: *Norfolk Avenue*
PARKING: *Lot* **METRO**: *Bethesda*

AS THE NAME IMPLIES, Chicken on the Run specializes in rotisserie birds available for carryout. This fledgling business, located in the Woodmont Triangle, packs a lot of style in a small space. Cheery in yellow, its walls are further brightened with handsome Peruvian ceramics, and five indoor tables beckon those of us who can't wait to get home to eat lunch or dinner (the eatery is open daily for both meals).

From Chicken on the Run's two brick ovens come flavorful entrees massaged with cumin and oregano and served, as at any number of Latin American purveyors, with a razor-sharp green sauce of pureed jalapeno and green chili peppers. Also offered: chicken soup with rice and vegetables, and "chop chop," pulled chicken and black beans over a bed of rice with salsa on the side. Fresh-tasting cole slaw and fried yuca are among the choice accompaniments.

> **From Chicken on the Run's two brick ovens come flavorful entrees massaged with cumin and oregano and served with a razor-sharp green sauce of pureed jalapeno and green chili peppers.**

Cho's Garden ★

9940 Lee Hwy., Fairfax, VA
703-359-9801

LUNCH: *Daily 11-2:30* **ENTREES:** *$7.95-$39.95*
LUNCH BUFFET: *M-F 11:30-2* **PRICE:** *$11.99*
DINNER: *Sun-Th 2:30-11, F-Sat 2:30 pm-2 am* **ENTREES:** *$7.95-$39.95*
CREDIT CARDS: *All major* **RESERVATIONS:** *Recommended*
DRESS: *Casual* **CROSS STREET:** *Rabel Run* **PARKING:** *Lot*

ALREADY, NORTHERN VIRGINIA is home to more Korean restaurants than Joan Rivers has had face-lifts, and if you were only to read the menu at Cho's Garden, one of the newest additions, you might wonder why it gets so crowded. Like many of the others, it has a sushi bar that's nothing special by Japanese standards. The Korean dishes listed in the handsomely bound bill of fare—noodles, seafood pancakes and grilled meats—don't sound like anything out of the ordinary, either.

More than most, however, Cho's Garden knows how to keep its guests entertained. It celebrates Monday through Thursday with happy-hour specials and Wednesday night with karaoke. Its waitresses tend to smother you with attention—which is not always the case in Korean eateries. Repeat customers are sometimes greeted with a gratis nosh.

There are several dishes you shouldn't miss. One is the classic bibim bap, a mound of warm rice served in a thick clay bowl and colorfully decked out with lean beef, threads of carrot and radish, a fried egg and acorn curd.

Some like it hot, and for them, there is much to investigate. Spicy octopus, for instance, teams the main ingredient— unusually tender, in this case—with carrots

Cho's Garden knows how to keep its guests entertained.

and onions, everything slathered in a wicked chili paste. And barbecue fans will find happiness in garlicky marinated grilled beef ribs (kalbi), cooked to a crisp-soft texture and accompanied by bundles of lettuce leaves, warm rice and chili paste—the makings of a savory Asian taco of sorts.

One of the better bargains in the area is the lunch buffet, priced at $11.99 a person. Set up in the lounge area of the restaurant, the spread is both pretty and varied.

Circle Bistro ★★

1 Washington Circle NW, Washington, DC (Foggy Bottom/West End)
202-293-5390   www.circlebistro.com

BREAKFAST: *M-F 7-10, Sat-Sun 8-10:30* **ENTREES:** *$8.50-$11*
LUNCH: *M-Sat 11:30-2:30* **ENTREES:** *$12-$21*
DINNER: *Sun-Th 5-10, F-Sat 5-11* **ENTREES:** *$15-$23*
PRE-THEATER: *Daily 5-7, 3-course prix fixe $28*
BRUNCH: *Sun 11:30-2:30* **ENTREES:** *$9-$14*
CREDIT CARDS: *All major* **RESERVATIONS:** *Recommended*
DRESS: *Casual* **CROSS STREET:** *New Hampshire Avenue NW*
PARKING: *Complimentary valet* **METRO:** *Foggy Bottom*

WHAT WAS ONCE the West End Cafe has been transformed into a soothing vision in orange and yellow and a nice spot to know about before a show (the Kennedy Center is just a short cab ride away). This being a hotel restaurant, chef George Vetsch offers the expected Caesar salad and steak but broadens his menu's appeal with choices that show a sense of adventure, beginning with the very first taste: Diners are welcomed not with a bread basket, but with paper cones of fritto misto—in this case, cleanly fried potatoes, squid, chicken and zucchini with a quartet of enticing dips.

Not everything succeeds, but the Swiss native's selections pack in plenty of personality, like gently poached oysters, presented in their shells and moistened with a warm splash of horseradish cream. Entrees tend to be better than first courses. One strong performer brings together luscious bites of veal cheeks, pillows of lemony rice, a gentle curry and slices of grilled tropical fruit. Another dish I'd like to try again is guinea hen, served with crisp haricots verts mixed with soft onions and bits of bacon.

> **One strong performer brings together luscious bites of veal cheeks, pillows of lemony rice, a gentle curry and slices of grilled tropical fruit.**

Fresh herbs and butter, slipped beneath skin roasted to a gentle crisp, make for a hen to remember. A rib-eye bursts with savor from its marinade of juniper berries, lemon and bay leaf.

Vetsch's cooking gets a worthy companion in the restaurant's wine list. Instead of foisting marquee names and hefty prices on customers, the way so many hotels do, this small, French-leaning selection includes wines that not only pair well with the food but also are priced to encourage testing: For $26, why not try a bottle from Uruguay? The bar, with its communal table and fireplace in one corner, makes an especially cozy destination for exploring the possibilities.

Colorado Kitchen

✔ *Critic's Pick*

★ ★

5515 Colorado Ave. NW, Washington, DC (Brightwood)
202-545-8280   www.mmmmbetter.com

LUNCH: *F 11-2* **ENTREES:** *$5.95-$9.25*
DINNER: *W-Sat 5-10, Sun 5-9* **ENTREES:** *$10.95-$18*
BRUNCH: *Sat-Sun 11-3* **ENTREES:** *$5-$15.50*
CLOSED: *M-Tu* **CREDIT CARDS:** *AE, D, MC, V*
RESERVATIONS: *No* **DRESS:** *Casual*
CROSS STREET: *Kennedy Street NW* **PARKING:** *Street* **METRO:** *No*

IT LOOKS THE PART of the neighborhood joint, with a pressed-tin ceiling, a black-and-white-tile floor and chrome chairs with cherry red seats.

"The kitchen makes just about everything from scratch, and it's all fresh," the menu brags—and the cooking supports the claim. The light biscuit that shows up at brunch with an order of fried catfish, all crackling batter and snowy flesh, tastes like the effort of a southern grandmother, while the herb gravy that comes with a dinner of roast chicken, mashed potatoes and summery green beans is so good you wish it were sold by the jar. Sharing space with the lineup of American all-stars might be flat-iron steak with a puree of white beans, and monkfish paired with roasted tomatoes and polenta.

> **The light biscuit that shows up at brunch tastes like the effort of a southern grandmother.**

From her semi-open kitchen, chef Gillian Clark performs a one-woman show, spooning up soup and flipping first-rate hamburgers (available, fans know, only at Friday lunch and on Thursday and Sunday nights). Think of it as refined comfort food, and be patient: The service in this storefront eatery can be slow and forgetful. A slice of pineapple upside-down cake, though, goes a long way toward making up for any lapses.

Corduroy

Four Points by Sheraton Hotel, 1201 K St. NW, Washington, DC (Downtown)
202-589-0699 www.corduroydc.com

LUNCH: *M-F noon-2:30* **ENTREES:** *$10-$17*
DINNER: *M-F 5:30-10:30; Sat 5-11* **ENTREES:** *$18-$27*
CLOSED: *Sun* **CREDIT CARDS:** *AE, D, MC, V*
RESERVATIONS: *Recommended* **DRESS:** *Business casual*
CROSS STREET: *12th* **PARKING:** *Hotel parking validated*
METRO: *Metro Center*

WITH ITS MOSS-COLORED CARPET, beige chairs, saucer lights and generic art, Corduroy looks more like an airport lounge than a high-end dining room. And the service in this second-floor hotel restaurant, located off the beaten track downtown, tends to be on the restrained side.

Still, here is where I send people looking for peace and quiet—and good cooking—and, inevitably, those are the qualities they end up praising. "Just right for my meeting," said one. "Really nice lunch," said another. Chef Tom Power once cooked at Michel Richard Citronelle, and that experience shows in his fetching presentations and food free of gimmicks.

> **Chef Tom Power once cooked at Michel Richard Citronelle, and that experience shows in his fetching presentations and food free of gimmicks.**

An elegant cauliflower soup bolstered with shavings of Parmesan swells with far more flavor than one might expect of such a lowly vegetable. Goat cheese is bound in spindly fried potato and set on a pool of roasted red pepper sauce. There might be crisp-skinned salmon paired with garlicky spinach, succulent chicken breast surrounded by a fine savoy cabbage slaw, and (oops) boring steak redeemed somewhat by a pile of terrific french fries. A decadent finish: warm chocolate tart sided by slices of caramelized banana and topped with chocolate ice cream.

With food like this, I don't need a lot of ambiance.

Costa Verde ★★

946 N. Jackson St., Arlington, VA
703-522-6976   www.costaverderestaurant.com

OPEN: *M-Th 11-10, F 11-11, Sat 10 am-11 pm, Sun 9 am-10 pm*
ENTREES: *$8.95-$15.95* **CREDIT CARDS:** *AE, D, MC, V*
RESERVATIONS: *No* **DRESS:** *Casual*
CROSS STREET: *Wilson Boulevard* **PARKING:** *Lot*
METRO: *Virginia Square-GMU*

LESS THAN FIVE MILES from downtown Washington, this Peruvian restaurant whisks its guests to another continent faster than you can say, "Make mine a pisco sour." (And you should: The cocktail is at once refreshing with whipped egg white and bracing with brandy, a nice companion to the crunchy corn nuts that show up as you're seated, along with a violent green dip.)

Spanish is the language of choice, salsa music provides a festive backdrop, and potatoes—boiled, roasted, fried—show up in more guises than Mike Myers in an Austin Powers flick.

Soft chunks of sweet potato round out a big platter of squid, octopus, shrimp, fish and mussels, garnished with lime and red onion, while fried potatoes make an appearance with the mixed grill of pork, chicken and beef. No mere side-kicks, tubers star on their own in such appetizers as papa rellena—mashed potatoes stuffed with chopped meat and fried.

The menu is half seafood, half meat, thoroughly homey and generous.

The menu is half seafood, half meat, thoroughly homey and generous. I prefer the surf side: Whole fried trout is delicious, as are the seviche (colorful with sweet potatoes) and the shrimp chowder.

The open room isn't much to look at, though frilly curtains help dress up the place, and weekend nights are enlivened by a musician.

Crisp & Juicy

4540 Lee Hwy., Arlington, VA
703-243-4222

OPEN: *M-Sat 11-9:30, Sun 11-9*
ENTREES: *$2.55-$8.95 (platters $5.99-$24.99)*
CREDIT CARDS: *All major* **RESERVATIONS:** *No*
DRESS: *Casual* **CROSS STREET:** *N. Upton Street*
PARKING: *Lot* **METRO:** *Ballston*

TRUE TO ITS TITLE, this Latin American rotisserie-chicken chain turns out birds of distinction, their meat always succulent and their skin always crisp (and nicely smoky from time spent in a wood-fired cooker). Sauce seems unnecessary, though Crisp & Juicy's tingling pink and garlicky green moisteners make irresistible additions to any order.

There's more to applaud: lusty black beans, crunchy yuca fries, soothing plantains. While the flan is stolid, the white cookies sandwiched with soft caramel nearly melt on the tongue. Some chicken and some sides add up to a memorable Latino picnic; indeed, a lot of the faces in the inevitable lines that snake out of one of Crisp & Juicy's four area locations appear to be people looking for a taste of home. And finding it, of course.

> **Some chicken and some sides add up to a memorable Latino picnic.**

Carryout is the way to go, for the settings are small and spare. (The narrow Arlington branch offers a brick-paved porch enclosed in glass whose tables go fast at peak hours.) But you've come to Crisp & Juicy to eat great chicken, not drink in the scenery, right?

OTHER LOCATIONS: *913 W. Broad St., Falls Church, VA, 703-241-9091*
3800 International Dr., Silver Spring, MD, 301-598-3300
1331 Rockville Pike, Rockville, MD, 301-251-8833

Cuban Corner

825 Hungerford Dr., Rockville, MD
301-279-0310

OPEN: *M-Th 11-9, F-Sat 11-10* **ENTREES:** *$6.69-$15.99*
CLOSED: *Sun* **CREDIT CARDS:** *AE, D, MC, V*
RESERVATIONS: *Recommended* **DRESS:** *Casual*
CROSS STREET: *Ivy League Lane* **PARKING:** *Street* **METRO:** *Rockville*

IS IT A PLACE TO EAT or a shrine? At first glance, it's hard to tell. One wall is tiled with a who's who of Cuban Americans and their achievements; another displays the namesake island outlined in colorful neon and surrounded by painted palm trees and travel posters. Salsa music—and more conversations in Spanish than English—underscores the community-center feel.

The aroma of garlic, beef and onions wafting from the tiny kitchen of this small storefront reveals the Cuban Corner's real mission: to deliver a taste of the old country to the masses. This goal is accomplished with thin braided empanadas lined with onion-laced ground beef, fried green plantains stuffed with shrimp, red snapper in tomato-y vinaigrette, and my favorite entree, morsels of pork sauteed with green olives and pimentos ("montuno cubano" on the menu). Add some oiled white rice, inky black beans and soft, sweet plantains and you've got a meal to remember.

Don't come here expecting a group hug: Your food is apt to come out quickly, and your interaction with the staff will probably lean toward the matter-of-fact, unless you're a regular.

Don't come here expecting a group hug: Your food is apt to come out quickly, and your interaction with the staff will probably lean toward the matter-of-fact, unless you're a regular. Most of the passion comes to the table by way of the upbeat music and the cooking. Even so, lunch finds a steady stream of office workers stopping in to refuel; as afternoon fades to black, the clientele shifts to couples and families. (Note to parental units: There's a children's menu for kids 10 and younger.)

The well-documented Cuban sweet tooth surfaces at dessert, most winningly with a slice of tres leches, or three-milk cake. Out comes a square of white cake drenched in a syrup of sweetened condensed milk, whole milk and evaporated milk. If I could vote to expand the honor roll at this mom-and-pop eatery, that cake would get a tile of its own on the wall listing Cuban wonders.

Cubano's   ★★

1201 Fidler Lane, Silver Spring, MD
301-563-4020

LUNCH: *Daily 11:30-3* **ENTREES:** *$7.95-$18.95*
DINNER: *Sun-W 3-10, Th-Sat 3-11* **ENTREES:** *$9.95-$18.95*
CREDIT CARDS: *All major* **RESERVATIONS:** *Recommended*
DRESS: *Casual* **CROSS STREET:** *Georgia Avenue*
PARKING: *Lot* **METRO:** *Silver Spring*

O NE OF MY LITMUS TESTS for a good Cuban restaurant is black bean soup, and a bowl at the family-run Cubano's never fails to pass with flying colors. Unlike all the one-note competitors out there, this soup pulses with cumin, bay leaf, garlic and oregano, each seasoning marching in lock step with the other for a meal to remember.

There are more such crowdpleasers on the long menu: fried green plantains with a snappy dip of tomato, garlic and lime; pork marinated in bitter oranges and roasted to a soft collapse; and shredded beef (ropa vieja, or "old rags") laced with red pepper strips and rich with tomato. Cubano's quiet service is balanced by room after small room of tropical cheer, in the form of bouncy music and bright paintings of beaches and other island scenes.

Cubano's quiet service is balanced by room after small room of tropical cheer.

A little more space between the tables would be welcome—you can't help but eavesdrop on your neighbor—and the kitchen might overcook the occasional entree.

But the gripes are minor in light of the details that make dining here such a pleasure. The mojitos pack a nice rum-and-mint punch, the meat-and-cheese-stuffed Cuban sandwich is the real deal, and if you need a sugar fix, the solution is found in a moist slice of "drunken cake."

Hate making decisions? Use a trick that inevitably works for me and pick those dishes that have someone's name linked to their descriptions: "Olga's favorite traditional turnovers" – stuffed with beef or chicken—turn out to be some of mine, too.

David Greggory ★ ★

2030 M St. NW, Washington, DC (Foggy Bottom/West End)
202-872-8700   www.davidgreggory.com

LUNCH: *M-F 11:30-2:30*   **ENTREES:** *$10-$18*
DINNER: *M-W 5:30-10:30, F-Sat 5:30-11*   **ENTREES:** *$10-$28*
CLOSED: *Sun*   **CREDIT CARDS:** *All major*
RESERVATIONS: *Recommended*   **DRESS:** *Business casual*
CROSS STREET: *21st*   **PARKING:** *$6 valet at dinner*
METRO: *Foggy Bottom*

AFTER YEARS OF TALKING ABOUT IT, David Hagedorn, who made a name for himself as the chef of the innovative but now-closed Trumpets, and Greggory Hill, who bade farewell to the Latin American restaurant Gabriel after a delicious nine-year run, finally opened a place of their own in the city's West End this spring.

Hoping to capitalize on their joint brand, the business partners christened the space David Greggory; trying not to step on each other's toes, they split up the chores. Hagedorn put himself in charge of the dining room, an airy L shape. Hill presides over the kitchen, cooking up a menu that bears very little resemblance to what he's done before.

You could invite the United Nations here and everyone would find something to eat.

You name it, Hill serves it. Moving through the myriad possibilities, you'll find steak frites for meat eaters and a tuna burger with fennel chips for seafood fanciers. Vegetarians will applaud their many options, including a nicely chewy-crisp pizza strewn with leeks, garlic, shaved truffles and cheese. The chef alludes to India with grilled salmon partnered with Basmati rice and terrific curried spinach. And Japan gets a nod with skate in miso broth plus seaweed and shiitake chips. Appetizers like empanadas and seviche remind us that Hill was an early pioneer of nuevo Latino cuisine in Washington. Why, you could invite the United Nations here and everyone would find something to eat.

Meanwhile, every dessert tells a joke. Presented in a little black skillet, buttermilk panna cotta topped with gingery apricot halves looks exactly like a couple of fried eggs—right down to the wafer-thin "bacon" cookie. Alas, it's more clever than it is delicious.

Fueled by fun, David Greggory has much to offer: enthusiastic service, terrific cocktails, lovely biscuits in its bread basket and more choices than Baskin-Robbins. It just needs to learn to stop while it's ahead.

DC Coast ★★★

1401 K St. NW, Washington, DC (Downtown)
202-216-5988   www.dccoast.com

LUNCH: *M-F 11:30-2:30* **ENTREES:** *$14-$19*
DINNER: *M-Th 5:30-10:30, F-Sat 5:30-11* **ENTREES:** *$19-$33*
CLOSED: *Sun* **CREDIT CARDS:** *All major* **RESERVATIONS:** *Recommended*
DRESS: *Casual* **CROSS STREET:** *14th* **PARKING:** *$5 valet M-Sat dinner*
METRO: *McPherson Square*

THERE'S NOTHING SUBTLE about DC Coast. The ceilings of this bustling, Art Deco tribute soar. Massive oval mirrors dress up its curved bar. An abundance of good tables—the place seats 200—shrugs off any suggestion of Siberia; I'm just as fond of a seat along the glass-wrapped balcony, with its bird's-eye view of the action below, as I am of a perch center stage, in a booth shaped like a Tilt-A-Whirl that looks into the exhibition kitchen.

What a party!

The food shares that sense of expansiveness. Silky diced raw tuna splashed with coconut milk, ginger, jalapenos and fish sauce shows up in a coconut shell, tricked out with slivers of lime, red onion and fresh cilantro. Lobster bisque tastes like the distillation of 1,000 crustaceans and floats a mushroom-filled won ton. The crab cakes are tall and mostly crabmeat, while the fried oysters dress up as

> **DC Coast's bestseller—chef Jeff Tunks' Chinese-style smoked lobster—deserves its popularity.**

"Buffalo" oysters with shaved fennel, crumbled blue cheese and a ring of hot-sauce-laced butter. DC Coast's bestseller—chef Jeff Tunks' Chinese-style smoked lobster—deserves its popularity: Framed in a wreath of deep-fried spinach leaves are soft, sweetly fresh lobster chunks, the meat enhanced with a paste of Vietnamese chili sauce, ginger and garlic and a quick trip in a smoking-hot skillet. Stick around for dessert and you'll be rewarded with the likes of a trembling milk chocolate souffle, a fig tart lapped with orange cream, and sorbets that all taste true to their fruits.

Now and then, the kitchen sends out a loopy salad or an overcooked piece of fish, and some plates can get as busy as the Beltway. More frequently, DC Coast offers coastal encounters of the best kind.

The Diner ★

2453 18th St. NW, Washington, DC (Adams Morgan)
202-232-8800   www.trystdc.com/diner

OPEN: *Daily 24 hr.* **ENTREES:** *$4.95-$14.95*
CREDIT CARDS: *MC, V* **RESERVATIONS:** *No* **DRESS:** *Casual*
CROSS STREET: *Columbia Road NW* **PARKING:** *Street*
METRO: *Woodley Park-Zoo/Adams Morgan*

HERE'S A WASHINGTON RESTAURANT that stays open not only after "news, weather and sports," but 24/7. There are too few kitchens that do so, and fewer still that offer the range that the Diner does; here, it's no problem if one of you wants French toast with a side of corned beef hash and someone else wants penne pasta or a turkey sandwich.

Carved from the former J&O Auto Parts, the Diner looks like what you'd expect of a place with that title, only bigger and more Restoration Hardware than Route 1. The pressed-tin ceiling hovers 15 feet above the white-and-black-tile floor, and there are two counters to accommodate customers who like that option.

Omelets in the a.m. are fine, but I prefer the Diner later in the day, for grazing. The onion rings are a bit greasy, but chances are you won't leave one sweet, golden slice uneaten. A Caesar salad shows spunk in its creamy dressing, and the spicy chicken wings are tamed by a plunge into their cool dip, invigorated with mint and cilantro. If you spring for the cheese and bacon, a hamburger goes from plain to satisfying, and the fries that come with it are hot, crisp and habit-forming. Pass on the shrimp-and-crab dip, though, which tastes mostly of creamy binder.

If you spring for the cheese and bacon, a hamburger goes from plain to satisfying, and the fries that come with it are hot, crisp and habit-forming.

Among the entrees billed as "homemade dinners" you can find a big, soft slab of meat loaf shored up with a small mountain of very good mashed potatoes.

If you want something sweet, splurge on a shake or a malt in the comforting flavors of chocolate, strawberry or vanilla (my pick). Any extra is served next to your glass in a tall metal container. If you're anything like me, you won't stop until you've hit bottom.

Dish ★★

924 25th St. NW, Washington, DC (Foggy Bottom/West End)
202-338-8707 www.dishdc.com

BREAKFAST: *M-F 7-10, Sat-Sun 8-10* **ENTREES:** *$6.40-$10*
LUNCH: *M-F 11:30-2:30* **ENTREES:** *$9.95-$12.95*
DINNER: *Daily 5-11* **ENTREES:** *$15.95-$22.95, 3-course prix fixe $30 (W only)*
CREDIT CARDS: *AE, D, MC, V* **RESERVATIONS:** *Recommended* **DRESS:** *Casual*
CROSS STREET: *I Street NW* **PARKING:** *Complimentary valet at lunch, $5 at dinner*
METRO: *Foggy Bottom*

IS RON REDA HAVING FUN? It certainly looks that way at Dish, where the chef appears to spend as much time chatting up guests in the small dining room as he does in the kitchen dreaming up new ways to serve some of America's favorite flavors.

Buttermilk fried chicken comes to the table with a no-holds-barred red sauce and a rolled-up paper napkin, the latter a hint that it's perfectly okay to eat with your fingers. Mozzarella and tomato salad is rearranged with a wink: The whole tomato is sliced vertically, each slit holding a shard of balsamic-edged mozzarella. And what looks like a shore picnic—a heap of seafood steamed with snappy andouille sausage and sweet corn on the cob—is presented beneath a billowing tent of tinfoil.

Another restaurant near the Kennedy Center is a welcome sight, but Dish is not a particularly attractive or comfortable spot. Fifty seats are crammed into a room with low ceilings and a fat marble column, intrusive as an elephant in this tiny space. A single piece of art lends panache, though, and it's endearing: A sepia-toned photograph by William Wegman depicts a handsome dog in repose.

His excellent apple pie shouts U.S.A. all the way.

Reda's frequently whimsical food competes with that photograph for the eye's attention. In one of his best lunch dishes, crisp shrimp are slipped between slices of pillowy ciabatta in a blimp-size BLT that gets a nice kick from some jalapeno mayonnaise. Shrimp returns in several other good ideas, including an appetizer of fried shrimp offered with a habanero sauce that turns out to be the taste equivalent of 76 trombones: brassy. A diner will also find as many side-dish options as at a steakhouse but priced at a more budget-friendly $3 each.

As with so much here, Reda sticks close to home for dessert. His excellent apple pie shouts U.S.A. all the way, while rice pudding goes upscale with fat grains of Arborio rice and plump cranberries. The brownie looks and tastes like a Hostess cupcake, only from the right side of the tracks.

Dukem ★

1114-8 U St. NW, Washington, DC (U Street Corridor)
202-667-8735   www.dukemrestaurant.com

OPEN: *M-F 9 am-1 am, Sat-Sun 9 am-2 am*   **ENTREES**: *$8.25-$19.95*
CREDIT CARDS: *AE, D, MC, V*   **RESERVATIONS**: *Recommended*
DRESS: *Casual*   **CROSS STREET**: *12th*
PARKING: *Street*   **METRO**: *U Street/African Amer Civil War Memorial/Cardozo*

YOU DON'T GET FORKS OR KNIVES; as is typical of Ethiopian dining, the food at Dukem is eaten with fingers and pieces of injera, the slightly sour crepe that also stands in for a plate.

If you're a novice, be advised: No staff member I encountered at this corner dining room spoke much English, if any. But pointing and enlisting the help of native Ethiopian customers, who seem to treat this as a gathering spot as much as a place to eat, can land you some pleasant memories to take back home.

One signature is kitfo, a mound of raw ground beef blended with house-made cottage cheese, herbed butter and hot red pepper. Imagine steak tartare mixed with fire. You don't have to be a carnivore to eat well, though. Follow the lead of seemingly every other table and request the vegetable combination: Out comes a floppy round of injera, dolloped with a variety of earth-toned selections, from chopped greens and yellow lentils to a tomato salad sparked with jalapenos.

You don't have to be a carnivore to eat well. Follow the lead of seemingly every other table and request the vegetable combination.

Afternoon soap operas and CNN on TV yield to live Ethiopian music onstage Thursday through Monday evenings.

Eat First

★★

609 H St. NW, Washington, DC (Chinatown)
202-289-1703

LUNCH: *Daily 11 am -3 pm* **ENTREES:** *$3.95-$14.95*
DINNER: *Daily 3 pm -3 am* **ENTREES:** *$7.95-$24.95*
CREDIT CARDS: *AE, MC, V* **RESERVATIONS:** *Recommended*
DRESS: *Casual* **CROSS STREET:** *6th* **PARKING:** *Street*
METRO: *Gallery Place-Chinatown*

I T'S NOT MUCH TO LOOK AT, this sparsely dressed Cantonese restaurant. Pink table covers seem to be the lone attempt at offering frills. But what it lacks in dining-room flair is more than compensated for by much of what comes from the kitchen.

An active fish tank and a flock of roasted ducks hanging near the kitchen's window should be your cue to sample Eat First's fresh shrimp, fried whole flounder or crisp-skinned roast duck. Seasonal suggestions might highlight pink, mousselike slabs of shrimp cake with gently cooked Chinese broccoli and a light wash of ginger sauce, or a verdant bundle of sweet-potato shoots. The menu descriptions frequently underplay the repertoire; an order of "sauteed oyster in shell with black bean sauce," for instance, brings six fresh, brick-size bivalves to the

> **Seasonal suggestions might highlight pink, mousselike slabs of shrimp cake with gently cooked Chinese broccoli and a light wash of ginger sauce, or a verdant bundle of sweet-potato shoots.**

table—leaving fellow diners wide-eyed at the sight of the plump giants.

Eat First's epic menu is bigger still for the numerous specials, printed in Chinese on colored strips of paper that hang from the mirrored walls. With luck, your server can decipher the possibilities and let you know that frogs and snails also await your consideration. A bland duck soup here or a greasy eggplant dish there are infrequent disappointments in a restaurant that aims to deliver only delights.

88

★ ★

1910 18th St. NW, Washington, DC (Dupont Circle)
202-588-5288   www.grille88.com

DINNER: *Tu-Th 5:30-10:30, F-Sat 5:30-11, Sun 5:30-10:30* **ENTREES:** *$14-$24*
BRUNCH: *Sun 11-3* **ENTREES:** *$8-$20*
CLOSED: *M* **CREDIT CARDS:** *AE, DC, MC, V*
RESERVATIONS: *Recommended* **DRESS:** *Casual*
CROSS STREET: *Florida Avenue NW* **PARKING:** *Street* **METRO:** *Dupont Circle*

"GRILLE" HAS DISAPPEARED from its title, as have the appetizers once billed as "halfnotes." This neighborhood restaurant no longer beats you over the head with nonstop references to the 88 keys of a piano, though it does continue to serve up live music every night. The performances tend to be worth tuning in to—much like the cooking these days.

In winter there are savory beef short ribs, the rich meat topped with crisp vegetables and bedded on creamy polenta, likely eaten in the oh-so-blue dining room off the lounge. Summer brings such fish as halibut, nicely cooked and wreathed in oyster mushrooms and a delicate mustard cream, which you can enjoy on the front patio. Brunch includes a nice omelet with blue cheese and sauteed portobellos but goes beyond breakfast staples to include herb-threaded crab cakes and mashed-potato-stuffed taquitos, ignited with a fiery salsa.

> **Summer brings such fish as halibut, nicely cooked and wreathed in oyster mushrooms and a delicate mustard cream, which you can enjoy on the front patio.**

Service, alas, runs hot and cold. At one meal I'm ready to nominate my server to a waiter's hall of fame for her enthusiasm and smarts; the next visit I get someone who ignores me until she brings appetizers and entrees all at once.

Bargain hunters, take note: By-the-bottle wine prices are slashed in half on Tuesday and Wednesday.

El Chalan

★★

1924 I St. NW, Washington, DC (Downtown)
202-293-2765   www.elchalanrestaurant.com

LUNCH: *M-F 11:30-3* **ENTREES:** *$9-$14*
DINNER: *M-F 5:30-10:30, Sat 1-11, Sun 1-9* **ENTREES:** *$12-$18*
CREDIT CARDS: *All major* **RESERVATIONS:** *Recommended* **DRESS:** *Casual*
CROSS STREET: *20th* **PARKING:** *Street* **METRO:** *Farragut West*

PATRONS LEAVE WASHINGTON AT THE DOOR when they enter the small English basement that for nearly three decades has housed this Peruvian restaurant. Listen: Most of the conversations around you unfold in Spanish. Look around: The low ceilings, carved chairs, tile floors and religious paintings suggest a faraway sanctuary in Lima.

Now taste: The fish seviche, colorful with corn and sweet potatoes, pulses with lemon, chilies and red onion. Bony but tender chunks of goat dominate a main-course stew that's tangy with vinegar and beer and balanced with soft-cooked white beans. Peruvians love their potatoes, and you will, too, after a taste of potatoes mashed with fish, then chilled, sliced and served with a cilantro-laced salad of red onions. And regulars know that the little white dish of salsa picante, a wicked condiment here, is meant to be slathered on the bread that precedes your meal. (Ouch! More!)

> **Regulars know that the little white dish of salsa picante, a wicked condiment here, is meant to be slathered on the bread that precedes your meal.**

Shredded chicken in a light blanket of peanut sauce is merely decent, and the seating is so tight, you get to hear all the juicy details about your neighbor's new job or last date whether you care to or not. Service is indifferent; the beef hearts, spunky from their marinade of lemon, vinegar and paprika, are anything but.

El Golfo

★★

8739 Flower Ave., Silver Spring, MD
301-608-2122

LUNCH: *Daily 11-2:30* **ENTREES:** *$5.95-$15.95*
DINNER: *Sun-Th 2:30-10, F-Sat 2:30-11* **ENTREES:** *$7.95-$15.95*
CREDIT CARDS: *All major* **RESERVATIONS:** *Recommended*
DRESS: *Casual* **CROSS STREET:** *Piney Branch Road*
PARKING: *Lot* **METRO:** *Silver Spring*

I F YOU SAMPLED NOTHING BUT SOUP at this Salvadoran-Mexican charmer, you'd leave happier than when you arrived, for every bowl tastes as if someone's generous mama had a hand in its creation. Meaty short ribs and soft cabbage dominate one recipe, its beef broth bolstered with chunks of yuca and plantain and a wedge of lemon. Rich slivers of chicken swim in another bowl, thick with bright-colored carrots and celery and pungent with cilantro.

They are among several good beginnings to be had in the two rosy dining areas, which are set off with arches, mirrors and Mexican paintings of sunny beaches and quiet alleys—thoughtful alternatives to the usual tourist posters. The tamales, stuffed with shredded chicken or studded with corn kernels, play hot nosh off the cool tang of sour cream, while yuca con chicharron—a little feast of tender pork and crisp, starchy yuca—gets invigorated by a sharp salsa.

Despite the water-themed name, meat selections remain El Golfo's strong suit.

Despite the water-themed name, meat selections remain El Golfo's strong suit. Two standouts are carne asada, a thin but succulent and surprisingly juicy grilled beefsteak, and lomo saltado, a rustic toss of beef strips, green pepper chunks, sliced potatoes and red onion moistened with a light, tomato-y sauce and flanked by oiled white rice. A pitcher of sangria, holding an orchard's worth of chopped apples, goes down well with this fare; nondrinkers might opt for the gently sweet, almond-flavored beverage known as horchata.

For the most part, this is food, homey and bountiful, that leaves you satisfied even as you undo your belt and vow to reacquaint yourself with the gym.

Ella's Wood Fired Pizza ★★

901 F St. NW, Washington, DC (Penn Quarter)
202-638-3434 www.ellaspizza.com

OPEN: *M-Sat 11-11* **ENTREES**: *$7.95-$12.95*
CLOSED: *Sun* **CREDIT CARDS**: *All major*
RESERVATIONS: *Recommended* **DRESS**: *Casual*
CROSS STREET: *9th* **PARKING**: *Street*
METRO: *Gallery Place-Chinatown*

THE LAST SEVERAL YEARS have seen a Starbucks-like explosion in the number of pizza joints around Washington, as established players like Pizzeria Paradiso in Dupont Circle have spawned new location, and newcomers, including Matchbox in Chinatown, have introduced more than just pies to the genre.

Named after the owner's young daughter, Ella's represents a pizza parlor for today. Thus your Chianti is served in a thin-lipped glass, the better to savor the wine. What isn't painted cherry red or pale yellow is handsome fieldstone; modern art and slim mirrors punctuate those walls. As for the signature dish, the crust is lightly crisp and nicely chewy—well, most of the time—with a fine yeasty aftertaste and toppings that reveal a good buyer. (Over summer, the specials included proscuitto di Parma with plump figs, and sweet cherry tomatoes in two colors, plus ricotta and fresh oregano.)

Named after the owner's young daughter, Ella's represents a pizza parlor for today.

There are fine salads—greens tossed with Parmesan and an anchovy-mustard dressing, orange and beets with toasted walnuts—to precede a pizza and nostalgia-inducing desserts—chocolate pudding, warm cookies, (too-sweet) lemon bars—to follow.

A blizzard of fanny packs and maps reminds you how close you are to the Mall and other tourist attractions, but there are enough ties, briefcases and security tags in the dining room to make Ella's feel like a hangout for locals, too.

El Manantial ★★

12050-A N. Shore Dr., Reston, VA
703-742-6466

LUNCH: *M-F 11-3* **ENTREES:** *$7.95-$14.95*
DINNER: *M-Sat 5-10, Sun 3-8* **ENTREES:** *$13.95-$25.95*
BRUNCH: *Sun 11-3* **ENTREES:** *$6.95-$11.95*
CREDIT CARDS: *All major* **RESERVATIONS:** *Recommended*
DRESS: *Casual* **CROSS STREET:** *Wiehle Avenue* **PARKING:** *Lot* **METRO:** *No*

ITS SPANISH TITLE REFERS TO AN OASIS, and a welcome sight this restaurant is—once you look beyond the generic façade. Inside this shopping-strip denizen there's an entire wall painted to persuade diners that they're overlooking an Italian courtyard, amber lights that resemble falling stars and a brand-new tapas bar, enclosed in honeyed wood and glass windows.

Ten members of the Fuentes family work in this handsome European restaurant, and they make an ace team, whether it's in the dining room, introducing you to a fresh treat like Parmesan sticks, or in the kitchen, turning out pretty salads and lovely soups.

The food nods to Spain, France, Italy and points beyond. From the standing menu there are buttery snails, shrimp sauteed with tomatoes and garlic, and crackling fried oysters with pickled red onions to open a meal, and zesty blackened tilapia, a good roast veal chop and, from the massive stone oven, one of several

Ten members of the Fuentes family work in this handsome European restaurant and they make an ace team, whether it's in the dining room or in the kitchen.

delectable pizzas to move on to. One night's special of rack of lamb is ordinary eating, and vegetable accompaniments might be limp from oversteaming, but more often than not, this is careful cooking with personality.

Made on site, the desserts are big and showy; stick with anything featuring fruit, whether it's a banana napoleon or a tarte tatin. The latter is as big as a dome, served piping hot with ice cream—and likely gone within minutes of its arrival on your table.

Elysium

★★★

116 S. Alfred St., Alexandria, VA
703-838-8000   www.morrisonhouse.com

BREAKFAST: *M-F 7-10, Sat-Sun 8-10* **ENTREES:** *$8-$15*
DINNER: *Tu-Sat 6-9:30* **PRICE:** *6- to 7-course prix fixe, $67*
CREDIT CARDS: *AE, DC, MC, V* **RESERVATIONS:** *Recommended*
CLOSED: *Sun-M* **DRESS:** *Jacket suggested*
CROSS STREET: *King Street* **PARKING:** *Complimentary valet* **METRO:** *King Street*

AN AUSTRIAN CHEF has replaced an Italian in the kitchen at Elysium, but the restaurant's signature recipe remains the same: Guests continue to order dinner not from a written menu but after consulting with the man in charge, who spends the first few minutes of the evening detailing what ingredients he has on hand, and what you might like, before returning to the kitchen and whipping up a series of surprises.

"Tell me what you want," a sous-chef told my friend and me after reciting the available fish, fowl and meats, "and I'll fill in the blanks."

"Sea scallops," my pal answered. Minutes later, he was spooning up a clear tomato juice centered with sweet seared seafood. Light and elegant. Moist, pan-roasted guinea fowl, nicely arranged with shaved fennel, fingerling potatoes and baby beets, followed, as did a surf and turf of salmon and pork, presented

> **Regulars are known to challenge the chef with special requests, even calling ahead to ask for favorite recipes.**

with celeriac puree and velvety chanterelles. On a previous evening, the kitchen demonstrated a flair for fish (I can still taste the crisped butterfish and fried artichokes accented with sherry cream and paprika oil) and game (wild boar, which the chef served simply with veal jus and the nutty grain quinoa).

And so a typical dinner unfolds, one small plate after another—and beautifully partnered with appropriate wines, if you wish. The actual number of dishes varies depending on your appetite, but the portions are scaled down to accommodate up to seven courses. (Regulars are known to challenge the chef with special requests, even calling ahead to ask for favorite recipes.)

The room whispers romance, with fresh flowers, an abundance of flickering candles and classical music, and walls that suggest spun gold. Tapestries, oil paintings and thick linens further contribute to a sense of the good life—as does the elegant shared dessert platter, arranged with bite-size temptations.

Equinox

✔ *Critic's Pick*

★ ★ ★

818 Connecticut Ave. NW, Washington, DC (Downtown)
202-331-8118   www.equinoxrestaurant.com

LUNCH: *M-F 11:30-2* **ENTREES:** *$16-$24*
DINNER: *M-Th 5:30-10, F-Sat 5:30-10:30, Sun 5-9* **ENTREES:** *$24-$32*
TASTING MENUS: *$60-$80 (with wine $80-$105)*
CREDIT CARDS: *All major* **RESERVATIONS:** *Recommended*
DRESS: *Business casual* **CROSS STREET:** *H Street NW*
PARKING: *$4 garage validation* **METRO:** *Farragut North/West*

I ALWAYS LOOK FORWARD to a meal at Equinox. Its chef-owner, Todd Gray, serves seasonal American food that is very much to my taste, reflecting an imagination grounded in classical training. In Gray's pastas, I can taste the years he spent cooking at Galileo; his local ingredients and stylish arrangements remind me that he was taught well by a few of southern California's culinary masters, too. If you are tired of gimmicks and looking for an honest plate of food, Equinox is where you want to be.

A welcoming nibble from the kitchen—say, crab fritters with a dab of anchovy mayonnaise—gets a meal off to an elegant start, and what follows is no less special: Recent fond memories have been made from sweet scallops on a puddle of polenta, robust venison lapped with a racy "fondue" of olives and tomatoes, and brioche-crusted cod enlivened with (surprise!) diced pineapple and caper butter.

Aside from a charming wine room in the back and two cozy rear booths, though, the interior remains one of downtown Washington's lesser sights for the price; the glass-enclosed front room, with its sloping floor and skylights, feels too much like an unfinished solarium. And the tables for two are small fits for large frames.

Yet the staff is so attentive, such true believers in what they're feeding you, that all I can do is look the other way—at the fine wine in my glass, a perfect side dish, or one of pastry chef Lisa Scruggs's quietly inspired desserts.

> **A welcoming nibble from the kitchen—say, crab fritters with a dab of anchovy mayonnaise—gets a meal off to an elegant start.**

Famous Luigi's   ★

1132 19th St. NW, Washington, DC (Downtown)
202-331-7574   www.famousluigis.com

LUNCH: *M-Sat 11-3, Sun noon-3*   **ENTREES:** *$6.50-$14*
DINNER: *M-Sat 11 am-midnight, Sun noon-midnight*
ENTREES: *$10.75-$17.75*
CREDIT CARDS: *All major*   **RESERVATIONS:** *Recommended for parties of 5 or more*
DRESS: *Casual*   **CROSS STREET:** *M Street NW*   **PARKING:** *Street*
METRO: *Dupont Circle/Farragut North*

I N THE SAME SPACE since 1943, this is the kind of spaghetti house that's become increasingly hard to find, with red-and-white-check table covers and not a whiff of truffle oil to be sniffed. Picture lasagna and pizza as opposed to beef carpaccio and braised baby octopus.

"Inside or out?" a waiter might ask, nodding first to the glass-enclosed front room, then to the darker interior that houses Luigi's bar. Beneath whirling overhead fans, both spaces are crammed with tables set with shakers of red pepper flakes and grated Parmesan. Sometimes friendly, other times curt, the service invariably leans to the quick and efficient—a good thing, too, since the restaurant is particularly popular with groups, who show up in streams at lunchtime.

Head for whatever looks homey on the menu. Vegetable soup yields a Mom-like bowl of golden broth brimming with peas, celery, tomatoes, big soft chunks of carrot and more. Just the ticket on a cold winter's day. A brick-size slab of lasagna soothes its takers with layers of noodles, cheese, cubed beef and pleasantly sweet tomato sauce.

Head for whatever looks homey on the menu.

And fans of carbonara will find happiness in the version here, a steaming turban of spaghetti showered with crisp bacon bits and enough cream sauce to moisten but not overwhelm the pasta. Nothing too fussy, everything doled out as if a friend were feeding you—Famous Luigi's hits the spot.

Faryab ★

4917 Cordell Ave., Bethesda, MD
301-951-3484

DINNER: *Tu-Sun 5-10* **ENTREES:** *$10.95-$17.95*
CLOSED: *M* **CREDIT CARDS:** *AE, MC, V*
RESERVATIONS: *Recommended* **DRESS:** *Casual*
CROSS STREET: *Old Georgetown Road* **PARKING:** *Street*
METRO: *Bethesda*

PRETTY IN CHALK-WHITE WALLS and prints from afar, Faryab gets the best-dressed award among the area's small collection of Afghan restaurants. As for the food, first courses are particularly appealing: The crackling turnovers of scallions and herbs (bulanee) and beef-filled dumplings draped in tangy yogurt (mantu) are quiet comforts. Succulent lamb kebabs and fresh-tasting vegetable dishes, including stewed pumpkin and onion-laced spinach, are all habit-forming.

Too bad the sullen staff doesn't play along. My last two visits were less pleasant thanks to servers who barely acknowledged my friends and me, leaving us to pour our own wine (too warm, by the way) and never bothering to inquire if we needed anything but the check.

> **Succulent lamb kebabs and fresh-tasting vegetable dishes, including stewed pumpkin and onion-laced spinach, are all habit-forming.**

Desserts—rose-water-perfumed rice pudding, fried dough dusted with pistachios and powdered sugar—helped sweeten those evenings, but frankly, I wished Faryab were a carryout so I could minimize my time with the people who work here.

15 ria ★★

1515 Rhode Island Ave. NW, Washington, DC (Logan Circle)
202-742-0015   www.15ria.com

BREAKFAST: *Daily 6:30-10:30*   **ENTREES:** *$6.50-$12.95*
LUNCH: *M-F 11:30-2:30, Sat noon-4 (bar menu)*   **ENTREES:** *$14-$18*
DINNER: *M-Th 6-10:30, F-Sat 6-11:30, Sun 6-10*   **ENTREES:** *$16-$28*
BRUNCH: *Sun 11-4*   **ENTREES:** *$6-$17*
CREDIT CARDS: *All major*   **RESERVATIONS:** *Recommended*
DRESS: *Casual*   **CROSS STREET:** *15th*   **PARKING:** *$5 valet*
METRO: *McPherson Square*

I F IT'S WEDNESDAY, and you're at 15 ria, it must be roast suckling pig. This hotel restaurant, named for its Rhode Island Avenue address, is distinguished in part by nightly specials that appear to have been designed in consultation with Mom. A case in point is that pig, decorated with a mahogany pane of crackling skin and so utterly comforting, you'll want to note its once-a-week appearance in your PalmPilot.

This is not to slight the other days of the week. Tuesday evening, for instance, brings braised short ribs. The molasses-braised meat, scattered with homey diced vegetables, practically falls from the bone and swells with an old-fashioned savor. The "Meat & Two" deal includes a choice of two sides (among the picks might be sauteed greens, roast squash and marinated beets).

Nor should the rest of the menu be overlooked. Executive chef Jamie Leeds, a veteran of such notable New York restaurants as Tribeca Grill and Union Square Cafe, seems to know just what we're hungry for these days and, better, how to turn common meals into appealing memories. Her chicken salad with diced preserved lemons and arugula sparkles; her salmon might be massaged with chilies and maple syrup and treated to a corn pudding ignited

The executive chef seems to know just what we're hungry for these days

with jalapenos. Bring a program from church or synagogue to Sunday brunch and you're rewarded with a free basket of scones, biscuits and more.

This very appealing food gets a setting that looks both back and forward. The geometric fabric on the tall chairs echoes the flagstones of the fireplace, lending a subtle retro touch to the space, while the shimmery copper-colored curtains could almost pass for sculpture. But if the weather cooperates, the place you want to be tucking into a good crab cake or fresh ricotta with brandied cherries is 15 ria's lovely outdoor courtyard.

Firefly ★★

1310 New Hampshire Ave. NW, Washington, DC (Dupont Circle)
202-861-1310   www.firefly-dc.com

BREAKFAST: *Daily 7-10* **ENTREES:** *$2.75-$3.50, $13 for continental*
LUNCH: *M-F 11:30-2:30* **ENTREES:** *$10-$15*
DINNER: *Sun-Th 5:30-10:30, F-Sat 5:30-11* **ENTREES:** *$13-$23.50*
BRUNCH: *Sat-Sun 11-2:30* **ENTREES:** *$7.50-$12.50*
CREDIT CARDS: *All major* **RESERVATIONS:** *Recommended* **DRESS:** *Casual*
CROSS STREET: *N Street NW* **PARKING:** *$5 valet at dinner, Tu-Sat*
METRO: *Dupont Circle*

WHETHER ON A BANQUETTE below yellow walls lined with birch logs or an ostrich-leather stool at the bar, I am always happy to find myself in this small and cozy restaurant. Distinguished with a faux tree whose branches dangle with tiny lanterns, it's the most recent boutique hotel to claim John Wabeck as its chef (he's the boyish-looking fellow you can see through the kitchen window).

Fried oysters excited with a chipotle-spiked tartar sauce as well as creamy risotto threaded with dill and zucchini make better introductions than the stodgy gnocchi or a chorizo tart that overemphasizes caramelized onions (a sweet fistful obscures everything else). With a few exceptions, this is the rare restaurant whose entrees outperform its appetizers. Meat dishes are particularly good: Thick and succulent steak treated to onion sauce and a paper cone of french

> **With a few exceptions, this is the rare restaurant whose entrees outperform its appetizers.**

fries, and grilled lamb steak scattered with fresh rosemary, garlic and summery cherry tomato slices are just the right mood enhancers after a tough day at the office. The fish known as wahoo (firm of flesh and mild in flavor) sits in a tangy clear lime broth with a colorful dice of avocado and sweet potato; it's pleasant despite the undercooked sweet potatoes. Roast chicken lapped with a sherry-laced mushroom cream is elevated comfort food.

Desserts don't raise the bar, but the small and thoughtful wine list does. And I never fail to be charmed by the presentation of the bill, which shows up in a mason jar—a friendly touch in a fine neighborhood destination.

Four & Twenty Blackbirds

✔ *Critic's Pick*

★★

650 Zachary Taylor Hwy., Flint Hill, VA
540-675-1111

DINNER: *W-Sat 5:30-9* **ENTREES:** *$24-$32*
BRUNCH: *Sun 10-2* **ENTREES:** *$10.95-$15.95*
CLOSED: *M-Tu* **CREDIT CARDS:** *MC, V*
RESERVATIONS: *Recommended* **DRESS:** *Casual*
CROSS STREET: *Crest Hill Road (Route 647)* **PARKING:** *Lot*
METRO: *No*

I T'S JUST WHAT YOU WANT after a lulling drive from city to country: a cozy room, an interesting plate of food, perhaps some wine from a vineyard that isn't all that far from where you're dining.

The cooking at Four & Twenty Blackbirds is a reflection of what people really want to eat and where maitre d' Vincent Deluise and chef Heidi Morf have traveled. Thus you may find a thick pork chop braised with local apple cider or wild rockfish arranged with succotash—as well as shrimp jambalaya and a napoleon of Thai-style vegetables. Morf's eclectic menu changes frequently, so there's no tiring of anything—and much to anticipate: The fall months, for instance, might bring savory pumpkin waffles topped with goat cheese and seasonal mushrooms. Desserts are restrained in their sweetness and tend to be homey. Picture a plum tart, apple-spice cake or baby doughnuts paired with

The fall months, for instance, might bring savory pumpkin waffles topped with goat cheese and seasonal mushrooms.

tangy buttermilk ice cream. The quibbles—salty biscuits in the bread basket, a chewy duck satay—are minor.

Dinner takes place in two small rooms, one cheerful with lace curtains, another wrapped in stone walls and wood beams. Service is soothing, and some nights are graced with live music. When's the last time you got a harp with your halibut? Four & Twenty brims with such thoughtful details.

Gabriel

(too new to assign stars)

Radisson Barcelo Hotel, 2121 P St. NW, Washington, DC (Dupont Circle)
202-956-6690

BREAKFAST: *Daily 7-10:30* **ENTREES:** *$8-$12.50*
DINNER: *Tu-Th 5:30-10, F-Sat 5:30-10:30* **ENTREES:** *$8.75-$28.95*
BUFFET BRUNCH: *Sun 11-3* **PRICE:** *$26.75*
CREDIT CARDS: *All major* **RESERVATIONS:** *Recommended*
DRESS: *Casual* **CROSS STREET:** *21st* **PARKING:** *Complimentary valet*
METRO: *Dupont Circle*

THEY'VE KEPT THE NAME and the design intact, but otherwise, it's a brand-new way to eat at Gabriel, the handsome underground dining room that reopened in the Radisson Barcelo Hotel after a short hiatus.

In moving from a modern Latin American menu to a contemporary American bill of fare, chef Antonio Burrell says he and his staff talked about how they prefer to eat. Everyone liked appetizers and everyone sought out a variety of flavors. So the choices at the revamped restaurant fall under the headings "Fields," "Sea," "Farm" and "Market," and the majority of the plates pass for either generous appetizers or scaled-back entrees.

Burrell is hoping for "people to share and get a lot of different tastes" during dinner. The 27-year-old chef spent three years as a sous-chef at Vidalia and also cooked at the innovative but now-closed Swedish restaurant Aquavit in Minneapolis.

Among the plates I'm eager to try again: seared scallops, velvety mushrooms and fingerling potatoes lapped with thyme-scented cream.

Among the plates I'm eager to try again: seared scallops, velvety mushrooms and fingerling potatoes lapped with thyme-scented cream; smoked duck breast sliced over grilled peaches and Swiss chard; and fried snapper and juicy rock shrimp bedded on succotash. On the other hand, fried green tomatoes trapped in an armor of cornmeal and served with a baseball-size dollop of remoulade are a surprise, given the chef's time at the southern-themed Vidalia. And a trio of oysters perched on coins of yellow melon and splashed with white balsamic mignonette is a waste of good bivalves.

Burrell follows chef Greggory Hill, who left the hotel restaurant after nine years to open David Greggory in Washington's West End. A bit of his handiwork remains behind: One dish Burrell plans to keep on his brunch menu, at least for the near future, is Hill's signature roast suckling pig.

Galileo ★★

1110 21st St. NW, Washington, DC (Downtown)
202-293-7191   www.galileodc.com

LUNCH: *M-F 11:30-2:15* **ENTREES**: *$14-$22*
DINNER: *M-Th 5:30-10, F-Sat 5:30-10:30, Sun 5-10* **ENTREES**: *$24-$35*
CREDIT CARDS: *AE, D, MC, V* **RESERVATIONS**: *Recommended*
DRESS: *Business casual* **CROSS STREET**: *L Street NW*
PARKING: *Complimentary valet after 6*
METRO: *Foggy Bottom/Farragut North*

ONE FORKFUL of Roberto Donna's meatballs, shaped from pork and soft as custard, and I'm hooked on his (lunch-only) bar menu. Much as I might enjoy the Italian chef's truffles and flourishes in Galileo's dining room, I like a bargain even better. Where else in town am I going to find a meal like this—three plump meatballs set on a soothing puddle of polenta, ringed with vibrant tomato sauce—for just under $7? Throw in a marble counter or a cushy sofa in a light-filled setting, and you've got a delicious deal.

There are plenty of other excuses to show up for lunch at the bar. No one around makes a finer ribollita, Tuscany's classic soup of leftover bread cooked to a savory mush with vegetables, white beans and Parmesan, its surface brightened with fruity olive oil and sprigs of fresh basil. This is home cooking raised to glory. In a second dish, a winy

This is home cooking raised to glory.

minced beef punched up with fresh rosemary is draped over a swirl of feathery fettuccine. Each of these gently priced plates—there are 16 in all—could stand as a meal by itself.

As for the more formal dining room, my meals over the years there have been hit-or-miss. One night I might get first-class service with an extraordinary plate of thinly sliced veal tongue draped in a creamy herb sauce; another evening the agnolotti tastes not all that different from my neighborhood Italian place, and everyone gets the wrong plates. The most engaging flavors tend to be from whatever Italian region—Tuscany, Donna's native Piedmont— the kitchen happens to be highlighting. Few restaurants feed as many VIPS as does this one, though. Even ordinary agnolotti goes down better when it's eaten in view of a visitor like Catherine Zeta-Jones.

Gerard's Place ★★★

915 15th St. NW, Washington, DC (Downtown)
202-737-4445

LUNCH: *M-F 11:30-2:30* **ENTREES:** *$24.50-$52.50, 3-course prix fixe $29.50*
DINNER: *M-Th 5:30-9, F-Sat 5:30-9:30*
ENTREES: *$28-$52.50, 5-course prix fixe $85*
CLOSED: *Sun* **CREDIT CARDS:** *AE, DC, MC, V* **RESERVATIONS:** *Recommended*
DRESS: *Jacket and tie required* **CROSS STREET:** *K Street NW*
PARKING: *Street* **METRO:** *McPherson Square*

THE WOMAN AT THE NEXT TABLE lets out a little gasp, and having eaten the same appetizer as she is savoring, I understand: Chef Gerard Pangaud's scallops have the ability to transport diners from here to heaven. The plate is elegant in its simplicity—four sweet coins of crisp-edged scallops on a shimmering green pool of parsley sauce, enhanced with a garlic flan that's as soft as a whisper—and a star-filled introduction to dinner.

There's much more where that came from. An extraordinary mushroom tart brims with "the first cepes of the season," the chic hostess announces as the earthy dish is brought out. Sauteed foie gras, paired with caramelized mango,

Sauteed foie gras, paired with caramelized mango, cuts like soft butter at the mere touch of a knife.

cuts like soft butter at the mere touch of a knife. Baby lamb is staged on a large plate and divided into quarters, each of which displays a different exquisite treatment (my favorite: roasted tenderloin with chanterelles). And a crisp square of cod stars in a "bouillabaisse" whose near-melting ribbons of sweet peppers and subtly tangy broth won't let you stop eating them.

Desserts are made to order and take time; your patience is rewarded with every bite of a souffle of tropical fruit and a fragile tart arranged with wine-soaked pears and walnut cream. Pangaud's work in his native France resulted in two Michelin stars; a decade after opening Gerard's Place in Washington, he's cooking as confidently as he ever has.

Food is not all, however. People paying for first-class should also expect service that is more polished ("Where did my waiter disappear to?") and a dining room with more panache. Cozy as it is with its red walls and tentlike ceiling, Gerard's Place looks as if Pottery Barn had a hand in dressing it. And the plain white plates are right out of a college cafeteria. Pangaud's art deserves a finer frame.

Green Papaya ★★

4922 Elm St., Bethesda, MD
301-654-8986

LUNCH: *M-F 11:30-2:30* **ENTREES:** *$7.95-$21.95*
DINNER: *M-F 5-10, Sat 12:30-10, Sun 5-9:30* **ENTREES:** *$8.95-$21.95*
CREDIT CARDS: *All major* **RESERVATIONS:** *Recommended*
DRESS: *Business casual* **CROSS STREET:** *Woodmont Avenue*
PARKING: *Street* **METRO:** *Bethesda*

EVERYWHERE YOU LOOK in this Vietnamese restaurant there's something to catch the eye: handsome wall hangings, a tall banana tree fashioned from wood, mammoth vases, even a wall of water running over turquoise tiles in the bar. Softly lighted and backed by an eclectic soundtrack, the room would be an impressive place to seal a deal or woo a partner, though the prices are gentle enough to make Green Papaya a habit.

The kitchen can encourage return engagements, too. Settle in with squid salad tossed with green papaya and red onion and sparked with fresh herbs, maybe, or grilled quail, better after a dip in the accompanying sauce, which prickles with black pepper. And from the list of specials might come a light roll of Vietnamese sausage, chestnuts and dried shrimp bound in rice paper and served with black

Settle in with squid salad tossed with green papaya and red onion and sparked with fresh herbs.

plum sauce. It would be easy to compose a little feast from just the appetizers, yet that would mean forgoing such pleasures as bo luc lac, a rib sticker of stir-fried beef, onions and potato.

The waiters in their smart orange jackets are unfailingly pleasant but can also be inattentive—Some water, please? The bill?—and the flavors in the food tend to be less bright, the cooking techniques less polished than at the area's best Vietnamese restaurant, Huong Que in Falls Church. But the occasional overcooked rack of lamb with limp snow peas is balanced by thin cigars of ground beef wrapped in vine leaves and dusted with fried onions and crushed peanuts. The odds are in your favor.

Guajillo ★★

1727 Wilson Blvd., Arlington, VA
703-807-0840   www.guajillogrill.com

LUNCH: *Daily 11-5* **ENTREES:** *$6.50-$10*
DINNER: *Daily 5-11* **ENTREES** *$9-$16*
BRUNCH: *Sun 11-3* **ENTREES:** *$8-$12*
CREDIT CARDS: *AE, D, MC, V* **RESERVATIONS:** *No*
CROSS STREET: *Rhodes Street* **PARKING:** *Lot*
METRO: *Rosslyn/Courthouse*

TACOS, FAJITAS, BURRITOS—you can find all the usual Mexican restaurant standbys at this family-run storefront tucked into a small shopping strip. But concentrate on the daily list of specials for a taste of what's best at Guajillo. On any given day it might yield big, tender scallops invigorated with rosemary, wine and a touch of habanero pepper; pork marinated in garlic sauce and roasted in a banana leaf; or delectable crab cakes shaped with cilantro and served with chipotle cream sauce.

Guajillo, which takes its name from a burgundy-colored chili pepper, is graciously free of clichés. Forget cheese-heavy dishes and mariachi music. Here patrons sink into deep chairs of cowhide and wood to drink fruity sangria and bracing mojitos and to dip into dusky salsas, soothing pinto beans and one of the spunkiest seviches around.

Concentrate on the daily list of specials for a taste of what's best at Guajillo.

Sound perfect? It's not. Guajillo's haunting mole of ground pumpkin seeds, plantains, nuts and chocolate is wasted on blank-tasting chicken; the service tends to be slow and hesitant; and the room gets noisy at prime time. So dine early if you want some peace with your carne asada.

Hakuba ★

706 Center Point Way, Gaithersburg, MD
301-947-1283

LUNCH: *M-Sat 11:30-2:30* **ENTREES:** *$6.75-$12.95*
DINNER: *Sun-Th 5-9:30, F-Sat 5-10:30* **ENTREES:** *$8.95-$27.95*
CREDIT CARDS: *AE, MC, V* **RESERVATIONS:** *Recommended* **DRESS:** *Casual*
CROSS STREET: *Great Seneca Highway* **PARKING:** *Lot*

S EVERAL YEARS AFTER IT OPENED on a busy corner of Kentlands' Market Square, this Japanese restaurant continues to provide neighborly service and a sleek spot for eating sushi. As diners settle in with their menus, a little treat shows up, maybe tofu splashed with soy sauce and vinegar. Wavy aluminum panels float above the chic bar, and a cushioned banquette in earth tones runs the length of the airy dining room.

Following a change of owners over the summer, though, the cooking here is less of a sure thing. While the sushi is respectable and the shrimp dumplings melt on the tongue, the seaweed salad with sesame oil dressing shows up in a frozen clump. Beef teriyaki yields bland meat in a pool of candy-sweet brown sauce, and vegetable tempura produced yawns from my tablemates.

Wavy aluminum panels float above the chic bar, and a cushioned banquette in earth tones runs the length of the airy dining room.

A glimmer of what Hakuba used to be shows up in a special, like spicy tuna bound in a wispy tempura; the roll is at once soft and crisp, while the fish tastes as if it had been lit with a firecracker. Too bad there aren't more such hits.

Han Sung Oak ★★

6341 Columbia Pike, Falls Church, VA
703-642-0808

OPEN: *Daily 11-11* **ENTREES:** *$8.95-$23.95*
CREDIT CARDS: *AE, MC, V*
RESERVATIONS: *Recommended* **DRESS:** *Casual*
CROSS STREET: *Ashwood Place* **PARKING:** *Street*
METRO: *Falls Church*

T HE AROMA OF GRILLED MEAT, garlic and chilies greets diners right at the door. But the welcome to this handsome restaurant continues with the blue-uniformed waitresses, as pleasant and engaging as you will meet in any local Korean restaurant.

The women are quick to smile, eager to steer you to dishes you might like and happy to demonstrate the tabletop grills almost everyone ends up using. Squid, tripe, pork, beef short ribs—the flames take on those and other marinated ingredients, which are then served with steamed rice and crisp lettuce leaves for bundling.

To begin, though, there are fried dumplings, meat-stuffed green peppers and a savory "pancake" veined with red and green, slivers of squid and oysters. As is customary in Korean restaurants, half a dozen or so little taste treats, or panchan, precede the main event, crowding the large table; each snack dish is different

The women are quick to smile, eager to steer you to dishes you might like and happy to demonstrate the tabletop grills almost everyone ends up using.

and delicious, be it chewy marinated soybeans, cucumber salad, strings of lightly pickled radish or the chili-stoked cabbage known as kimchi, so prized a dish that it merits a museum back home in Seoul.

Harris Crab House ★★

433 Kent Narrows Way N., Grasonville, MD
410-827-9500   www.harriscrabhouse.com

OPEN: *Daily 11-10*   **ENTREES:** *$9.50-$22.50*
CREDIT CARDS: *MC, V*   **RESERVATIONS:** *No*
DRESS: *Casual*   **CROSS STREET:** *Route 50*
PARKING: *Lot*   **METRO:** *No*

BIG, WELCOMING—and far from thoughts of the office. That's Harris Crab House, one of the worst-kept secrets on the Eastern Shore. No problem: The restaurant has 400 seats, including some on a dock outside.

For two decades now, people have been pulling up to Harris' brown-paper-covered tables for the chance to get down and dirty with some steamed hard-shell crabs, sold in four sizes and stinging with paprika, mustard and salt. You don't have to lift a mallet for a sweet taste of crab if you don't want to, though; the crab imperial and the crab cakes are made with choice lump crabmeat.

> For two decades now, people have been pulling up to Harris' brown-paper-covered tables for the chance to get down and dirty with some steamed hard-shell crabs.

Beyond crab, think steamed or fried oysters, shrimp, mussels and clams. The platters arrive with a choice of two sides, the best of which are the mustardy potato salad and creamy slaw. Of course you'll have a Bud with that. And for sure you've saved room for a Nutty Buddy. Covered in chocolate and nuts, that locally dipped ice cream novelty is practically a draw in itself.

Harry's Tap Room ★★

2800 Clarendon Blvd., Arlington, VA
703-778-7788   www.harrystaproom.com

LUNCH: *M-F 11:30-4* **ENTREES:** *$7.95-$18.95*
DINNER: *M-Sat 5:30-11, Sun 5:30-10* **ENTREES:** *$9.95-$23.95*
BRUNCH: *Sat-Sun 10-3* **ENTREES:** *$7.95-$19.95*
CREDIT CARDS: *AE, D, MC, V* **RESERVATIONS:** *No* **DRESS:** *Casual*
CROSS STREET: *N. Fillmore Street* **PARKING:** *Garage*
METRO: *Clarendon*

BEGINNING WITH ITS NAME, Harry's Tap Room wants us to think it's a casual alternative to the tried-and-true steakhouse recipe, and on the surface it is: The bar pours nearly 30 different beers, and the menu includes such saloon staples as fried calamari and hamburgers. But it doesn't take a card-carrying member of Mensa to see that this suburban offshoot of Sam & Harry's in Washington is more like the kid who leaves the nest and ends up outshining his parents.

The newcomer is a knockout. Its ground floor entices guests with an airy lounge that looks as if it had been transported from some tony resort out West. A winding staircase takes you to another dining room, where faux-leather padded walls and gem-colored acrylic panels add luxurious accents.

Fans of beef Wellington will be cheered to see a modified version of that classic here, tucked among the appetizers. For lighter appetites, there are several fine salads and a sparkling shrimp seviche that's good enough to compete in any solid Latino kitchen.

Harry's makes a big deal of its twin beef tenderloin filets and pots of steamed mussels. I'm a guy who prefers a bone and a bit of fat with his steak, so the filet is a waste of time for me. And while I'm passionate about steamed mussels, I'm not so crazy about eating them at Harry's, where more than once I've found them to be scrawny and even a bit off-tasting.

Fans of beef Wellington will be cheered to see a modified version of that classic here.

Fortunately, there's lots more to focus on. When in the mood for meat, I'm apt to gravitate to the roasted pork tenderloin, crisped on the grill just before serving. And keep Harry's in mind for brunch. You won't find a more dashing spot in Arlington for tender pancakes or lusty corned beef hash.

Heritage India

★★★

2400 Wisconsin Ave. NW, Washington, DC (Glover Park)
202-333-3120   www.heritageindia.biz

LUNCH: *Sun-F 11:30-2:30* **ENTREES:** *$6.95-$10.95*
DINNER: *Sun-Th 5:30-10:30 F-Sat 5:30-11* **ENTREES:** *$8.95-$23.95*
CREDIT CARDS: *All major* **RESERVATIONS:** *Recommended*
DRESS: *Business casual* **CROSS STREET:** *Calvert Street*
PARKING: *$5 valet at dinner* **METRO:** *Tenleytown-AU*

D OWNTOWN WASHINGTON'S Bombay Club has a lock on the best service among area Indian restaurants, but when it's a fiery lamb vindaloo or a refined vegetable curry I'm after, I make a beeline for Glover Park and Heritage India.

The kitchen, under the direction of chef Sudhir Seth, rarely wavers. The stuffed breads are always hot and delicious; the tandoori prawns are consistently big, sweet and smoky; the black lentils appear to be a union of silk, earth and midnight; sauteed calamari with coconut teases the palate with jolts of lemon. Elsewhere, the fried pastries called samosas can be dull and heavy; here, they turn up light and cardamom-scented. At Heritage India, even such a standard as pureed spinach tastes like a new dish, colorful with kernels of corn. Slips like overcooked lamb chops prove rare.

Elsewhere, the fried pastries called samosas can be dull and heavy; here, they turn up light and cardamom-scented.

The catch? The staff. Diners are just as likely to be rushed into placing an order, or overordering, as they are to be seduced by the host's detailed description of the menu. Excellent cooking helps smooth over some of those annoyances, as does a handsome backdrop of green-and-gold banquettes, romantic sepia-toned photographs and thin-lipped stemware, which is brought out even for beer.

Hollywood East Cafe

2312 Price Ave., Wheaton, MD
301-942-8282 www.hollywoodeastcafe.com

LUNCH: *Daily 11-3* **ENTREES:** *$4.50-$27.95*
DINNER: *Sun-Th 3 pm-1 am, F-Sat 3 pm-2 am* **ENTREES:** *$7.95-$27.95*
CREDIT CARDS: *All major* **RESERVATIONS:** *Recommended*
DRESS: *Casual* **CROSS STREET:** *Ennalls Avenue/Route 193* **PARKING:** *Lot*
METRO: *Wheaton*

I HAVE A BIG PROBLEM with this menu: It's simply too large. I could stay here until closing time (and Hollywood East Cafe is open late, until 2 a.m. Friday and Saturday nights and 1 a.m. during the week) and still not sample a fraction of the several hundred choices—let alone the many specials, handwritten in Chinese on bright strips of paper that decorate the walls.

Luckily, the staff is composed of helpful tour guides, who take the time to point out major attractions while suggesting detours to whatever is new. Among the many draws, I'd count crisp roasted pork, flavorful from its marinade of five-spice powder and hoisin, as well as dumplings stuffed with shrimp and pork and set off by house-made XO sauce—brassy with minced Smithfield ham, dried scallops, chilies and soy sauce. Fried shrimp tossed with honeyed walnuts and lemony mayonnaise has become a recent bad habit of mine, but I balance it out with the more virtuous steamed rockfish, strewn with ginger, garlic and scallions.

> **The staff is composed of helpful tour guides, who take the time to point out major attractions while suggesting detours to whatever is new.**

Fresh scallops in black bean sauce and lobster casserole with vermicelli will have to wait for next time—but not an almond cookie, prepared by owner Janet Yu from her mother's recipe. "You can't try everything in one visit!" she reminds us as we finally leave, stuffed yet eager to return.

Huong Que (Four Sisters)

✓ *Critic's Pick*

★★★

6769 Wilson Blvd., Falls Church, VA
703-538-6717

OPEN: *Sun-Th 10:30-10, F-Sat 10:30 am-11 pm* **ENTREES:** *$5.25-$24.95*
CREDIT CARDS: *AE, MC, V* **RESERVATIONS:** *Recommended*
DRESS: *Casual* **CROSS STREET:** *Arlington Boulevard/ Route 7*
PARKING: *Lot* **METRO:** *East Falls Church*

THE LAST TIME I DROPPED BY, instead of ordering what experience had taught me was good from the mile-long Vietnamese menu, I requested to speak with one of the four sisters from whom this gracious restaurant gets its unofficial title. "Just bring me a few of your favorite dishes," I asked Le Lai, who introduced herself as "Sister No. 2."

She seemed thrilled at the prospect, and within a few minutes I was eating some of the best food I'd had in recent memory. The treasures began with delicately crisp spring rolls, which she told me to wrap in the accompanying fresh herbs and dip in the sparkling fish sauce. Next came tender baby clams and chopped pork tossed with onions and cilantro and brightened with lime juice. "This is popular in central Vietnam," she offered, demonstrating with her hands how to eat the salad: Scoop it up with a piece of sesame cracker. What a delicious geography lesson!

Within a few minutes I was eating some of the best food I'd had in recent memory.

Succulent grill-striped beef followed, along with a crisp sea bass fillet enhanced with black bean sauce. "You have to have some vegetables, too," said the waitress as she brought a glistening plate of snow peas and bias-cut asparagus fragrant with garlic slivers. The nonstop pampering was impressive, but all around me, Le Lai and staff were lavishing similar attention on everyone else, too.

Il Pizzico ★★

15209 Frederick Rd., Rockville, MD
301-309-0610

LUNCH: *M-F 11-2:30* **ENTREES:** *$9.95-$16.95*
DINNER: *M-Th 5-9:30, F-Sat 5-10* **ENTREES:** *$10.95-$19.95*
CLOSED: *Sun* **CREDIT CARDS:** *AE, MC, V* **RESERVATIONS:** *No*
DRESS: *Casual* **CROSS STREET:** *Gude Drive*
PARKING: *Lot* **METRO:** *Rockville*

FROM THE STREET, Il Pizzico ("The Pinch") looks nondescript, the kind of restaurant, tucked in a tiny shopping strip, that you'd drive right past on your way to dinner—someplace else.

That would be a mistake. The plain façade gives way to two cozy dining rooms, sunny in yellow paint and charming with frescoes, plus a menu of Italian favorites that frequently rises above standard issue. All the pastas can be ordered in half portions, and a lot of them are made in-house, including the bucatini and rigatoni; try the latter with smoked prosciutto and sage. Meat dishes—thin slices of veal, lamb chops—trump the fish options, which can run to a damp fillet of sole or thin and mushy grilled swordfish (but kudos to the kitchen for the tasty vegetables that accompany them).

> **All the pastas can be ordered in half portions, and a lot of them are made in-house.**

Service lags at prime time, when diners are kept waiting at the host stand and food is doled out to whichever person responds to "Who gets the penne?" Still, the moderate prices and fluffy tiramisu help level those bumps.

Opened by Enzo Livia, a Sicilian native, just as the Gulf War began in 1991, this neighborhood destination spawned a more elegant dining room in downtown Washington, Spezie, just a decade later—on September 11, 2001, to be exact.

India Palace ★

19743 Frederick Rd., Germantown, MD
301-540-3000

LUNCH BUFFET: *M-F 11:30-2:30* **PRICE:** *$7.95*
DINNER: *Daily 5:30-10* **ENTREES:** *$6.95-$16.95*
BRUNCH BUFFET: *Sat-Sun noon-3* **PRICE:** *$9.95*
CREDIT CARDS: *AE, D, MC, V* **RESERVATIONS:** *Recommended*
DRESS: *Casual* **CROSS STREET:** *Middlebrook Road*
PARKING: *Lot* **METRO:** *Shady Grove*

IT'S THE ACCUMULATION OF DETAILS that sets this shopping center restaurant apart: friendly service, an enticing daily lunch buffet, and a big room furnished with carved wooden chairs, scene-setting murals and transporting music.

The familiar Indian introductions—lentil soup, vegetable fritters—are all gathered here, but my inclination is to jump ahead to the main dishes. The seasonings are right on the mark: Lamb vindaloo roughs up the palate, as it should, with its vinegar and red chili punch, while butter chicken is enveloped in a smooth cloak of tomato, cream and sweet herbs. A gentle but fragrant curry enhances a bowl of fresh-tasting vegetables, one of more than a dozen meatless options.

Not everything succeeds, though. On a recent visit, I found the shrimp in the shrimp tandoori cooked to rigidity and the coconut chutney served ice-cold with my otherwise delicious masala dosa. But there's more to applaud than to argue with—just try

Lamb vindaloo roughs up the palate, as it should, with its vinegar and red chili punch.

not to fill up on the piping-hot stuffed breads, and keep an eye out for the occasional special menus that celebrate regional Indian cooking.

Indique ★★

3512-14 Connecticut Ave. NW, Washington, DC (Cleveland Park)
202-244-6600   www.indique.com

LUNCH: *Daily noon-3* **ENTREES**: *$8-$11*
DINNER: *Sun-Th 5:30-10:30, F-Sat 5:30-11* **ENTREES**: *$10-$19*
PRE-THEATER: *Sun-Th 5:30-7, 3-course prix fixe $18*
CREDIT CARDS: *All major* **RESERVATIONS**: *Recommended*
DRESS: *Casual* **CROSS STREET**: *Ordway Street NW*
PARKING: *$5 valet Th-Sun dinner* **METRO**: *Cleveland Park*

MARRY "INDIA" WITH "UNIQUE" and this is what you get: a restaurant eager to satisfy its guests with a menu of gently priced small plates, beautiful arrangements and service that is anything but ordinary.

Patrons can ease into a meal with a margarita spiked with tamarind, one of several chic cocktails, while they peruse the long menu. Potatoes, chickpeas and fried flour chips are blended with cilantro, yogurt and chutney for a snack to remember, and tapas fans will applaud the crepelike dosa, cut down in size but not in flavor, from the usual log length. Garlic, tomato, coconut milk and more make a great bath for steamed mussels, and among the curries is Cornish game hen in a searing paste of curry leaves and hot peppers. Vegetable dishes like spinach with corn and fenugreek charm us with their deft preparation and careful seasoning; the breads leave the tandoor crisp and chewy. Desserts caused me to rethink Indian sweets. The slips—chewy squid, tame salmon cakes, a boring vegetable skewer with Indian cheese—are few.

> **Garlic, tomato, coconut milk and more make a great bath for steamed mussels.**

Spread over two floors, Indique opens with a cozy bar and a kitchen visible behind glass and continues up a flight of carpeted stairs with two dining areas separated by an atrium and beautiful carved marble fences. Indique appeals to the eye as much as the palate.

Inn at Easton

28 S. Harrison St., Easton, MD
410-822-4910   www.theinnateaston.com

DINNER: *W-Sun 5:30-9:30* **ENTREES:** *$24-$32*
CLOSED: *M-Tu* **CREDIT CARDS:** *AE, MC, V*
RESERVATIONS: *Recommended* **DRESS:** *Business casual*
CROSS STREET: *Route 50/Ocean Gateway* **PARKING:** *Street*

UPSTAIRS, YOU CAN FIND 406-thread-count linens in the guest rooms of this Eastern Shore destination. Downstairs awaits another luxury: contemporary Australian cooking, translated here as fresh ingredients with nods to the Mediterranean and Southeast Asia.

Like many talented chefs, Andrew Evans changes his menu frequently, so there's no way of predicting what might be offered at any time, but his is a personal style that rarely misses. The four-course dinner always begins with a savory snack from the kitchen—maybe crab bisque topped off with mushroom foam—before moving on to trembling vegetable souffles, enticing fish preparations, sometimes even kangaroo filet.

The four-course dinner always begins with a savory snack from the kitchen before moving on to trembling vegetable souffles, enticing fish preparations, sometimes even kangaroo filet.

There is warm bread, a refreshing salad to bridge the first course and entree, charming service, and sweet reminders that Evans actually spent considerable time cooking down under (don't miss the scrumptious sticky fig and ginger pudding).

The light-filled dining room of this 200-year-old property is at once spare and rich, a mere 35 seats surrounded by paintings that would look at home in a fine gallery. And a topnotch wine list showcases super Australian labels that encourage exploration.

Inn at Little Washington ★★★

Middle and Main Streets, Washington, VA

540-675-3800

DINNER: *M, W-Th 6-9:30 (last seating), F 5:15-9:30, Sat 5:15-9:15, Sun 4-8*
ENTREES: *4-course prix fixe M-Th $118, F $128, Sat $158*
CHEF'S TABLE: *Nightly 7-course tasting menus $158*
CLOSED: *Tu (July-August, December-March)* **CREDIT CARDS:** *MC, V*
RESERVATIONS: *Recommended* **DRESS:** *Business casual*
PARKING: *Complimentary valet* **METRO:** *No*

"IS IT REALLY WORTH IT?" people ask when I tell them I've been to the Inn at Little Washington. They've heard about hard-to-get reservations and lofty tabs and want to know if the experience could possibly live up to the restaurant's voluminous raves.

Then I tell them about the last time I visited, and my reception at the door: "Would you like to relax in the lounge before being seated for dinner?" a gentleman asked in the most soothing of voices, and we accepted. A minute later, we were sipping champagne cocktails and munching on nuts from a silver dish in a room that swallowed us in cushioned comfort. Later we were ushered to plush seats in a dining room every bit as richly textured as you'd expect of a space created by a stage set designer. The lighting flatters. Service is formal but hardly stuffy. Trays of nibbles show up—a bite-size biscuit with local ham, a gold marble of risotto, a salmon pinwheel—and while they're scrumptious, they seem not to change much from year to year.

No one should miss plump squab bedded on garlic-perfumed polenta and sweetened with blackberry sauce.

Chef and co-owner Patrick O'Connell's witty American menu makes decisions difficult. No one, after all, should miss plump squab bedded on garlic-perfumed polenta and sweetened with blackberry sauce or herb-crusted lamb chops framed in a glorious garden of infant Brussels sprouts, braised leeks and gingery stewed tomatoes. They are among the many dishes, fine on their own, made more delicious by the jewel box in which they are offered.

Admittedly, hairline cracks sometimes appear: an appetizer of rouget might be cooked a few seconds too long, and the dessert course could use some new notions. Still, I'm invariably tickled to revisit "Seven Deadly Sins," a wicked sampler of the pastry kitchen's handiwork, described by a server as "a kinder, gentler version" of the infamous offenses it's named after.

In answer to the question: If you've never been before, absolutely.

Islander Caribbean ★★

1201 U St. NW, Washington, DC (U Street Corridor)
202-234-4955 or 4971 www.islander-restaurant.com

LUNCH: *Tu-Sun noon-4:30* **ENTREES:** *$8-$14*
DINNER: *Tu-Th 5:30-10:30, F-Sun 4:30-midnight* **ENTREES:** *$10.95-$27.50*
CLOSED: *M* **CREDIT CARDS:** *D, MC, V* **RESERVATIONS:** *Recommended*
DRESS: *Casual* **CROSS STREET:** *12th* **PARKING:** *Street*
METRO: *U Street/African Amer Civil War Memorial/Cardozo*

A GLASS OF GENTLY SWEET And delicately floral Christmas-red sorrel juice gets a meal off to a tropical start at this modest corner storefront along the U Street corridor. Accras—piping-hot cod fritters partnered with a creamy pink dip—enhance the mood.

Just about everything that comes out of the kitchen of chef Addie Green, a native of Trinidad, makes the islands appear very close to where you're eating. I'm partial to the tender (if bony) goat curry and the "calypso chicken," braised and cloaked in a tantalizing sauce of onions, pimentos and basil—two of a dozen or so dishes that diners can pick from to create their own sampler. But just as appealing are Green's peppery mango chicken wings—move over, Buffalo—and moist whole red snapper served beneath a tangle of soft-cooked bell peppers and cabbage. The Islander is also a rare city source for roti, the unleavened bread tucked around generous and mild curried fillings of fish, vegetables, beef or shrimp; wrapped in waxed paper, these hefty pockets average $8 and amount to a meal on their own. In all, this is confident, comforting and spirited cooking (if you think all ginger ale tastes the same, you haven't tried the drink here, which packs a refreshing wallop).

> **Just about everything that comes out of the kitchen makes the islands appear very close to where you're eating.**

Alas, the pace can be a little too authentically tropical (it's slooooow), but a greeting from the raspy-voiced Green, who has a habit of checking in on her charges in the dining room, smooths over any bumps. "I might sit down and eat with you," she is known to tease her guests.

Jaleo

480 Seventh St. NW, Washington, DC (Penn Quarter)

202-628-7949

LUNCH: *Daily 11:30-5* **ENTREES:** *$6.50-$12.95* **TAPAS:** *$3.25-$7.95*
DINNER: *Sun-M 5-10, Tu-Th 5-11:30, F-Sat 5-midnight*
ENTREES: *$12.95-$15.50* **TAPAS:** *$3.25-$7.95*
BRUNCH: *Sun 11:30-3* **TAPAS:** *$4.25-$6.25*
CREDIT CARDS: *All major* **RESERVATIONS:** *Recommended for lunch;*
pre-theater (5-6:30) only for dinner **DRESS:** *Casual*
CROSS STREET: *E Street NW* **PARKING:** *$8 valet at dinner M-Sat*
METRO: *Gallery Place-Chinatown*

 MALL PLATES OF APPETIZERS continue to be what many of us like to eat in restaurants, which explains why the Spanish notion of tapas has spawned American, Middle Eastern and even Japanese imitators.

Still, there's no place like Jaleo, which lives up to its spirited name with flamenco dancers on Wednesday nights and a menu of tapas as long as "Stairway to Heaven." Fried potatoes with aioli, eggplant flan in a red pepper sauce, grilled chorizo, vinegary mussels—the mouthwatering snacks come to the table in no particular order but almost always quickly.

> **There's no place like Jaleo, which lives up to its spirited name with flamenco dancers on Wednesday nights and a menu of tapas as long as "Stairway to Heaven."**

Just be careful: With the sangria flowing and everyone caught up in the fun, it's easy to rack up a big tab in no time. The convivial original location, near the Shakespeare Theatre and the MCI Center, seems always to play to SRO crowds; the Bethesda branch, bigger and more beautiful, is its gustatory equal.

SECOND LOCATION: *7271 Woodmont Ave., Bethesda, MD, 301-913-0003*

Jimmy Cantler's ★★

458 Forest Beach Rd., Annapolis, MD
410-757-1311 www.cantlers.com

OPEN: *Daily 11-11* **ENTREES**: *$7.50-$20.99 (crabs $25-$75/dozen)*
CREDIT CARDS: *All major* **RESERVATIONS**: *No*
DRESS: *Casual* **CROSS STREET**: *St. Margaret's Road*
PARKING: *Lot*

THERE REALLY IS A JIMMY and he lives near his scrappy namesake, which pulls in legions of crab eaters who don't mind tap-tap-tap-ping their way through a meal of hard-shells with wooden mallets. On a beautiful weekend afternoon, their Volkswagens and BMWs form a line that can stretch 20 cars long.

Fans will tell you that you want to show up early for the best seats (outside, overlooking lazy Mill Creek) and the biggest crabs (offered in five sizes, from small to super jumbo, and dumped before you on paper-covered tables).

Here's what else you should know: The potato salad and coleslaw take their cues from a southern church social. The shell-on shrimp are good, the big crab cakes are even better. And the service runs young, sweet and helpful.

Cantler's big, dark dining room smells distinctly of sea and beer; the porch, heated in cool weather, brings you closer to the action on the water. After an hour or so of feasting, you may find yourself littered with bits of shell. Thank goodness for the tub-size washbasin out back.

Cantler's big, dark dining room smells distinctly of sea and beer.

Joe's Noodle House

★ ★

1488-C Rockville Pike, Rockville, MD

301-881-5518   www.joesnoodlehouse.com

LUNCH: *M-F 11:30-3, Sat-Sun 11-3* **ENTREES:** *$4.95-$10.95*
DINNER: *Daily 3-10* **ENTREES:** *$6.95-$10.95* **CREDIT CARDS:** *MC, V*
RESERVATIONS: *Recommended for parties of 6 or more* **DRESS:** *Casual*
CROSS STREET: *Templeton Place* **PARKING:** *Lot* **METRO:** *Twinbrook*

THERE'S NO LONGER A JOE, but there are plenty of noodles at this spare storefront Chinese restaurant. Some noodles are thick and white, like the "drunken" rice noodles topped with crumbled beef and crisp slivers of green bell pepper; other noodles are thin and glassy, like the ones in a big bowl of soup, blazing with red chilies and teeming with soft pieces of fish. These and hundreds of other dishes are yours by ordering from a counter in the rear, taking a number sign to your table and waiting for the goods to be delivered whenever they happen to be ready. (Translation: Entrees might arrive before appetizers.)

Regulars pick up a paper menu at the front door and make their decisions before getting to the cashier-hostess; they know they can't miss with fried baby smelt tossed with peanuts, pleasantly chewy baby conch laced with basil, squid paired with tangy cabbage and pungent garlic or delectable, head-on "salty and crispy" shrimp. Ah, but then there are all the specials

> **Regulars pick up a paper menu at the front door and make their decisions before getting to the cashier-hostess.**

posted behind the counter, too! Of course those who know Joe's want to add a plate of hot-and-sour fish to their order. On the other hand, vegetable lo mein is a bit oily, the Chinese beer is served too warm, and gingery pork dumplings are weighed down with too-thick wrappers.

A sign that you've come to the right place: lots of Asian faces in the small mirrored dining room. Even more promising were the words of the Taiwanese native who generously shared his table with a friend and me during a weekend lunch rush. "This food reminds me of home."

Johnny's Half Shell

2002 P St. NW, Washington, DC (Dupont Circle)
202-296-2021   www.johnnyshalfshell.net

LUNCH: *M-Sat 11:30-5* **ENTREES:** *$11.95-$21.95*
DINNER: *M-Th 5-10:30, F-Sat 5-11, Sun 5-10* **ENTREES:** *$15.95-$22.95*
CREDIT CARDS: *AE, MC, V* **RESERVATIONS:** *No*
DRESS: *Casual* **CROSS STREET:** *20th* **PARKING:** *Street*
METRO: *Dupont Circle*

EATING OUT FOR WORK a dozen times a week doesn't leave much time for play, but when I want to kick back from the routine, chances are here's where you'll find me.

The cool marble counter with its pretty aquarium is a great place for a glass of wine and glistening raw oysters or a shrimp po' boy at lunch, though I'm also drawn to the wooden booths in the rear. The remaining tables, on the other hand, are parked so close together that you have no choice but to listen in on your neighbors' office gossip or romantic woes. The low ceiling and tile floors only exaggerate the noise problem.

But the cooking makes up for a lot of that. If it's a first-class crab cake or a distinguished piece of fish you want to catch, here's where to find it. Rich with tomatoes, potatoes and tender clams, the Manhattan chowder beats anything I've tried in New York, while a plate of sweet shrimp, fresh peas and feathery fettuccine rivals the work of Washington's best Italian kitchens.

> **If it's a first-class crab cake or a distinguished piece of fish you want to catch, here's where to find it.**

And spring means the arrival of simply battered soft-shell crabs, paired with a homey corn custard. Don't leave without ordering dessert: A slice of buttermilk pie served with a crisp ginger cookie or chocolate angel food cake with caramel sauce does what a shrink can do and for a whole lot less.

Kabob Palace

2315 S. Eads St., Arlington, VA
703-486-3535

OPEN: *Daily 11 am-midnight* **ENTREES**: *$5.50- $12.95*
CREDIT CARDS: *D, MC, V* **RESERVATIONS**: *No*
DRESS: *Casual* **CROSS STREET**: *Jefferson Davis Highway*
PARKING: *Street* **METRO**: *Crystal City*

S HOW ME A TASTE OF HOME, I once challenged a Washington cab-driver. Without hesitation, he steered me to this personable eatery and carryout, where he and his fellow drivers, people of many stripes, assemble for skewer-cooked meat washed back with conversation.

Chunks of marinated lamb, chicken and ground beef line a glass display, awaiting a turn on the grill. Each option is succulent. Lamb is juicy. Chicken, reverberating with garlic, turmeric and red chilies, comes off the flames lightly crusty yet moist. And the ground sirloin is seasoned with fresh cilantro—which you can accent further with onions or a spritz of lemon from the counter.

The kebabs turn into small feasts when you order them as combination plates, replete with warm-from-the-clay-oven pita bread, Basmati rice, a small lettuce salad and a choice of vegetables (the zesty yellow lentils are particularly good).

Chicken, reverberating with garlic, turmeric and red chilies, comes off the flames lightly crusty yet moist.

Neighbors and others drop by to take food home, but I'm content to stay put. Sure, the mirrored room is too bright, but the Afghan owner has made the most of the modest space, slipping colorful fabric beneath glass on the tables and hanging fringed curtains to set off an alcove. A folksy Middle Eastern market scene dominates one wall; the mural seems animated by the air, perfumed with cumin and onion and echoing of distant languages.

Kaz Sushi Bistro

1915 I St. NW, Washington, DC (Downtown)
202-530-5500   www.kazsushi.com

LUNCH: *M-F 11:30-2* **ENTREES:** *$9.25-$16.50*
DINNER: *M-Sat 6-10* **ENTREES:** *$13.75-$24.50*
CLOSED: *Sun* **CREDIT CARDS:** *All major*
RESERVATIONS: *Recommended* **DRESS:** *Casual*
CROSS STREET: *19th* **PARKING:** *Street*
METRO: *Farragut West*

I T WAS 95 DEGREES the last time I dropped by Kaz Sushi Bistro, where I knew I could count on some sparkling sushi and chilled sake to revive me on one of Washington's blistering summer days. What I hadn't anticipated was finding a colorful jumble of sashimi—scallops, salmon, tuna—in a deep white bowl of gazpacho, its orange liquid as cool as ice and teasing with rice wine vinegar. A lunch-hour revelation, it was as elegant a soup as has ever crossed my lips.

Then again, chef Kazuhiro Okuchi has long treated his audiences to Japanese food that goes beyond the familiar and frequently dips into the fabulous. Originally trained to be an artist, he has a keen eye for picking ingredients—the finest rice, pristine fish—and making them sing on the wood block. Tuna tartare has become a restaurant cliche, but the dish tastes new and different here, where Okuchi swaps diced tuna for

Chef Kazuhiro Okuchi has long treated his audiences to Japanese food that goes beyond the familiar and frequently dips into the fabulous.

ribbons of fish and presents it with feathery greens from his own garden and jellylike cubes of carrot.

The best way to explore his range is to ask for a tasting menu or focus on the daily specials; either might showcase flounder sashimi with plum sauce, cold sliced beef tongue anointed with a zippy miso sauce, or a shot glass of warm broth with sweet baby clams. Divine! To sweeten your stay, there's lovely service, fine sake and yuzu ice cream—a cool, fruity and elegant way to return to reality.

Kinkead's ★★

2000 Pennsylvania Ave. NW, Washington, DC (Foggy Bottom/West End)
202-296-7700   www.kinkead.com

LUNCH: *Sun-F 11:30-2:30*   **ENTREES:** *$16-$23*
DINNER: *Daily 5-10*   **ENTREES:** *$25-$34*
CREDIT CARDS: *All major*   **RESERVATIONS:** *Recommended*   **DRESS:** *Casual*
CROSS STREET: *20th*   **PARKING:** *$5 valet after 5:30*   **METRO:** *Foggy Bottom*

C REDIT WHERE CREDIT IS DUE: Bob Kinkead raised the local standard for fish houses when he launched his eponymous restaurant a decade ago, and plenty of cooking talent has sprung from his kitchens over the years, including his much-missed 21 Federal.

But have you dined at Kinkead's restaurant lately?

The voice on the other end of the reservation line sounds as if she really can't be bothered. The hosts at the door can be rude. And if you're not known as a friend of the house, you might be led to some of the least appealing tables in any upscale Washington restaurant, seemingly miles away from the open kitchen and roomy booths on the second floor to what looks like a service hallway (upstairs) or a suburban food court (downstairs).

Still, the place remains busy. Good food has a way of filling (even bad) seats, and there's plenty to admire on

If you are looking for pristine oysters on the half shell, classic fried clams, a first-class grilled swordfish or a lovely banana cream pie, this is the spot.

this menu. If you are looking for pristine oysters on the half shell, classic fried clams, a first-class grilled swordfish or a lovely banana cream pie, this is the spot. But sharing the menu might also be a muddy-tasting whole fried sea bass, a dish with 10 ingredients too many and a snooze of a cheese plate. And as much as wine mavens applaud the list here, it's disappointing to ask your waiter for guidance only to be told that what you're considering is nothing more than "nice."

Like *Cats*, this popular show has no problem pulling in takers, but times are changing, fresh faces are popping up left and right, and Kinkead's seems content to march in place.

Kuna

★★

1324 U St. NW, Washington, DC (U Street Corridor)
202-797-7908

DINNER: *Tu-Th 6-10, F-Sat 6-11* **ENTREES:** *$10.95-$15.95*
CLOSED: *Sun-M* **CREDIT CARDS:** *MC, V* **RESERVATIONS:** *Recommended*
DRESS: *Casual* **CROSS STREET:** *U Street NW* **PARKING:** *Street*
METRO: *U Street/African Amer Civil War Memorial/Cardozo*

WHEN I SHOW UP AT KUNA before my friends, the host waves me to the tiny bar in the rear of the shoebox and encourages me to sample a gratis glass of wine—or two—from a half-dozen open bottles on display at the counter. "I wanted people to feel like this is our house," explains owner Mark Giuricich, a host with the most. "And I don't just hand them bread when they come in the door."

That kind of hospitality extends to the rest of the two-story restaurant, which specializes in "Italian farmhouse cooking," or generous portions of robustly seasoned food that smacks of a home kitchen. Grilled asparagus served with lashings of cheese and spicy chickpeas makes a good start, as do bruschetta decked out with salami and bright green fava beans or a warm risotto "pancake" topped with smoky provolone and cool tomato salsa. A half-dozen or so pastas follow; if they're offered, don't miss linguine with dabs of sea urchin roe and toasted bread crumbs, or fettuccine tossed with a racy lamb ragu and fresh mint. There are always several dinner salads, too, which might team a haunting smoked pork chop and mushrooms with a nest of pleasantly bitter greens.

Don't miss linguine with dabs of sea urchin roe and toasted bread crumbs.

This is food with spirit, served with friendly efficiency in small rooms dressed with chocolate brown walls and not much else. Yes, the prices have crept up since Kuna opened—but so has the quality of the cooking.

Laboratorio del Galileo

★★★★

1110 21st St. NW, Washington, DC (Downtown)
202-331-0880   www.galileodc.com

DINNER: *M-Sat 7:30 (one sitting only)*
PRICE: *10-to-12-course prix fixe, $98 (M-Th) to $110 (F-Sat)*
CLOSED: *Sun* **CREDIT CARDS:** *AE, MC, V*
RESERVATIONS: *Required* **DRESS:** *Business casual*
CROSS STREET: *L Street NW* **PARKING:** *Complimentary valet at dinner*
METRO: *Foggy Bottom/ Farragut West*

THERE ARE THREE DELICIOUS REASONS to keep Galileo in your Blackberry. One is the bargain lunch menu served in the bar on weekdays—meatballs on polenta from a famous chef for $7! Another is the dining room behind it, the source of dishes like smoky octopus set on corn puree and Barolo-sauced venison.

If I'm feeling flush (*really* flush) or want to toast a special occasion, however, I make a reservation at the small and handsome Laboratorio del Galileo in the back. As its name suggests, the space is chef Roberto Donna's showcase for whatever is in season and whatever he's inclined to cook. He and his crew scour the market to see what looks good in the morning and return to Laboratorio's exhibition

The ever-changing menu stretches to include an amazing 12 courses.

kitchen in the afternoon, where they spend the rest of the day thinking up ways to keep you well-fed through the night. The ever-changing menu stretches to include an amazing 12 courses.

One recent night those courses included roasted duck liver with peach sauce; celery root soup poured over a bowl decorated with blood sausage, garlic chips, pancetta and crisped onions; tiny and delicate ravioli filled with sausage and apple, the pasta lapped with veal jus; extraordinary risotto crowned with sweet diver scallops — and those were just for starters. During the show, Donna welcomes guests to come forth and see what he's working on, never mind that he is cranking out pasta or removing the salt crust from a baked branzino. Everything about dinner here is carefully orchestrated, from the intelligent wine service to the first-class cheese trolley. And only one detail ever gets repeated, swears the chef: It's bomboloni (fried doughnut balls), arriving just before the check, to send you home on a high.

La Fourchette ★

2429 18th St. NW, Washington, DC (Adams Morgan)
202-332-3077

LUNCH: *M-F 11:30-3* **ENTREES:** *$13.95-$24.95, 3-course prix fixe $16.95*
DINNER: *Daily 3-10:30* **ENTREES:** *$13.95-$24.95*
PRE-THEATER: *M-Th 11:30-6:30, 3-course prix fixe $19.95*
BRUNCH: *Sat 11-3, Sun 10-3* **ENTREES:** *$5.95-$9.50*
CREDIT CARDS: *AE, DC, MC, V* **RESERVATIONS:** *Recommended*
DRESS: *Casual* **CROSS STREET:** *Belmont Street NW* **PARKING:** *Street*
METRO: *Woodley Park-Zoo/Adams Morgan*

O LD MEN IN TWEED COATS are deep in conversation, but it's not so serious that they don't stop to appreciate the buttery, garlic-scented baked mussels before them. Nearby, a reunion of three friends is in progress, so it's champagne all around. A clutch of young men file through the front door of this long, narrow, brick-walled dining room, whose outsize mural of cafe denizens appears to mirror the actual inhabitants. In French, one of the arrivals requests a table for six from the blonde hostess who has greeted and seated here forever.

Is this the Left Bank or Adams Morgan? La Fourchette would fit well in either locale. Season in and season out, this long-running, well-worn cafe pulls me back with its simple, satisfying French cooking: onion soup, tender veal tongue with boiled potatoes and green beans, plump medallions of pork draped in mustard cream sauce, floating island for dessert. A dry coq au vin or less than prime bouillabaisse is the price you pay for a menu that offers more than a dozen daily specials (hope for a

Season in and season out, this long-running, well-worn cafe pulls me back with its simple, satisfying French cooking.

roseate veal chop with whipped potatoes) and a savory deal: a three-course lunch for only $16.95, served from 11:30 a.m. to 6:30 p.m. Just be warned: That innocent-looking carafe of wine you order might change your plans to return to the office. C'est la vie.

L'Auberge Chez Francois ★★

332 Springvale Rd., Great Falls, VA
703-759-3800   www.laubergechezfrancois.com

DINNER: *Tu-Sat 5:30-9:30, Sun 1:30-8* **ENTREES:** *6-course prix fixe $50-$59*
CLOSED: *M* **CREDIT CARDS:** *All major*
RESERVATIONS: *Recommended* **DRESS:** *Jacket preferred*
CROSS STREET: *Beach Mill Road* **PARKING:** *Lot*
METRO: *No*

AT A TIME when not much in life is certain, it's comforting to know that some things around us never change. For nearly half a century—beginning in 1954 in Washington, then moving in 1976 to Great Falls—L'Auberge Chez Francois has been one of the region's most popular places to celebrate a graduation, toast an anniversary or bring together the family.

Inside, the four dining areas evoke a postcard-perfect Alsatian village. There are old beams overhead, stained glass in the windows and pressed white linens embroidered with tiny flowers.

It might be 90 degrees outside, but I still find myself drawn to the restaurant's four-course menu, and I can still muster interest in choucroute, a narrow bed of tangy sauerkraut piled with plump white and pink sausages, smoked pork loin and spiced apple. It's a strapping and immensely satisfying plate. Rack of lamb is patted with herbs and surrounded with a wreath of traditional turned carrots, zucchini, roast potatoes and even figs. As for innards, veal kidneys are particularly good; dense and tender, they show up beneath a mustardy cream sauce. There are lighter moments, too. Of the fish entrees, I'm partial to the fresh rainbow trout, scattered with slivered almonds and choice bites of crab.

Inside, the four dining areas evoke a postcard-perfect Alsatian village.

It would be easy to let nostalgia excuse the underachievers here. The truth is, some of the cooking is merely okay. Yet food is only part of the equation. The Old World service at L'Auberge is as impressive as anything on the menu.

Take a cue from the dessert display and order a slice of the plum tart; heaped with what appears to be a small orchard of soft, ripe fruit, it's a long-time signature. A meal isn't finished, though, until the golden tuiles and dark chocolates arrive on a small tray. Just as they always have.

L'Auberge Provencale

★★★

13630 Lord Fairfax Hwy., White Post, VA

540-837-1375 or 800-638-1702   www.laubergeprovencale.com

DINNER: *W-Sat 6-10:30, Sun 5-9* **ENTREES:** *5-course prix fixe, $72*
BRUNCH: *Sun 11:30-2:30* **ENTREES:** *$14.95-$22*
CREDIT CARDS: *All major* **RESERVATIONS:** *Recommended*
DRESS: *Jacket recommended* **CROSS STREET:** *Route 340* **PARKING:** *Lot*

IF YOU'RE NOT FEELING HAPPIER about life after a meal here, you haven't got a pulse. Almost everything about the restaurant in this French country inn, opened more than two decades ago by Alain and Celeste Borel, conspires to win your affection.

First, there's the idyllic backdrop of the Blue Ridge Mountains. Second, the dining rooms (one is sunny in oranges and yellows, another more sedate in blue) are watched over by servers who clearly are glad to see you. But most significantly, the kitchen, under the watch of chef Jeff Wood, is turning out some of the loveliest food around.

A veteran of the esteemed Jean Georges in Manhattan, the 29-year-old chef seamlessly weaves the traditional with what's modern. Crisp buttons of sweetbreads are treated to a lemony moistener; a salad of sweetly fresh crab comes with ele-

> **The kitchen, under the watch of chef Jeff Wood, is turning out some of the loveliest food around.**

gant cumin wafers; little towers of seared yellowfin tuna get a fetching sidekick of sliced potatoes, garlic and radishes; and duck is deftly seasoned with pepper and paired with plump and flavorful figs. The garden and fruit orchard outside provide inspiration for a lot of what comes to the table, from the baby arugula and tomatoes to the cherries that land in a delicate summertime savarin. Those are among some of the many seductions on the five-course dinner, which begins with a bite-size treat from the chef (maybe stone crab nestled in sheer pasta and glistening with sturgeon roe) and punctuated with a refreshing sorbet (perhaps hyssop splashed with sparkling wine).

The nitpicks are minor: The wine list deserves finer stemware and the staff is by turns too quiet or too chatty.

An evening as special as one here encourages lingering; thank goodness there are 14 bedrooms nearby for those who plan ahead.

Layalina

★★

5216 Wilson Blvd., Arlington, VA

703-525-1170   www.layalinarestaurant.com

OPEN: *Tu-Th 11:30-10, F-Sat 11:30-10:30, Sun 2-9:30* **ENTREES:** *$11.95-$18.95*
CLOSED: *M* **CREDIT CARDS:** *All major*
RESERVATIONS: *Recommended* **DRESS:** *Casual*
CROSS STREET: *N. Florida Street* **PARKING:** *Street*
METRO: *Ballston*

NO ONE FUSSES OVER HER CUSTOMERS quite like Rima Kodsi. One minute the Syrian native is at the door, greeting regulars as if they were friends coming to her home for dinner, the next she's bringing free tastes of her latest creations for newcomers to try. Her summer was a busy one: She spent the season rethinking her food.

Thus Layalina's already long menu of Syrian and Lebanese dishes has grown even longer—and more appealing. Hummus now can be had in a rainbow of flavors (red pepper packs a zesty punch), and salads have been expanded to include an irresistible mash of feta cheese, fresh herbs, olives

Layalina's already long menu of Syrian and Lebanese dishes has grown even longer— and more appealing.

and tomatoes—a sneaky way, Kodsi will tell you, of getting a cheese-fearing daughter to eat dairy. Altogether, there are more than 20 new plates, including a brassy appetizer of pickled eggplant stuffed with chopped walnuts, red pepper and garlic, and a main dish of marinated chicken served beneath a blanket of cooked tomatoes, chickpeas and mushrooms, everything enhanced with a pomegranate sauce.

Here comes her husband to pour our wine, followed later in the meal by one of two daughters, curious to see how we like her mother's cooking. Oh, the pita bread tastes as if it comes out of a bag, and the wine list is pedestrian. Meats sometimes are cooked too long. But those quibbles are smoothed over by a room made cozy with soft cushions and colorful rugs and the sort of pampering you expect from your mom, not a stranger.

Le Mannequin Pis

18064 Georgia Ave., Olney, MD
301-570-4800

DINNER: *Sun-M 5-9, Tu-Th 5-9:30, F-Sat 5-10* **ENTREES:** *$14.50- $25*
CREDIT CARDS: *MC, V* **RESERVATIONS:** *Recommended*
DRESS: *Casual* **CROSS STREET:** *Route 108 (Olney-Bladensburg Road)*
PARKING: *Lot* **METRO:** *No*

ONE MINUTE, he's introducing diners to one of the 40 or so beers he stocks from his homeland. The next, chef-owner Bernard Dehaene is showing guests how to eat mussels the Belgian way, using an empty shell to retrieve the "meat" from the others.

Steamed mussels, served by the kilo in double-decker pots, are the star attraction here, and the possibilities run from a simple partnership with wine and herbs to a more elaborate marriage with goat cheese, bacon and leeks.

If you thought a restaurant couldn't get any more Belgian than that, it can: There are cheese croquettes served with mustardy pickled vegetables, french fries (though Dehaene urges us not to call them "french"—he prefers "pommes frites") with mayonnaise, and a Flemish-style beef stew bolstered with dark beer.

> **Steamed mussels are the star attraction here, and the possibilities run from a simple partnership with wine and herbs to a more elaborate marriage with goat cheese, bacon and leeks.**

The snug room is pretty, with willow branches that decorate its windows and modern art on yellow walls. Near the tiny bar awaits the "chef's table"—six tall stools around three tall tables—and a great view of the scene. As for the title, Le Mannequin Pis takes its name from the famous fountain near the Grand Place in Brussels.

Les Halles   ★ ★

1201 Pennsylvania Ave. NW, Washington, DC (Downtown)

202-347-6848   www.leshalles.net

LUNCH: *Daily 11:30-4*   **ENTREES:** *$9.50-$26*
DINNER: *Daily 4-midnight*   **ENTREES:** *$10.50-$26*
PRE-THEATER: *M-Sat 5:30-7, 3-course prix fixe $17.89*
BRUNCH: *Sat-Sun 11:30-4*   **ENTREES:** *4-course prix fixe $17.89*
CREDIT CARDS: *All major*   **RESERVATIONS:** *Recommended*
DRESS: *Business casual*   **CROSS STREET:** *13th*
PARKING: *$5 valet Tu-Sat dinner*   **METRO:** *Metro Center*

THE WAITERS' FRENCH ACCENTS, the pressed-tin ceiling, the steaming choucroute that lands on your neighbor's table—everything about Les Halles suggests that you're sitting in a neighborhood dining room in Paris.

Some of the food is very good, particularly anything based on meat, such as the house-made pâté served with mustardy greens, and steak tartare, a cool mound of chopped raw beef seasoned just the way you ask for it and flanked by a pile of french fries. And I'm a fool for the warm salad of potatoes accented with goat cheese and black olives.

Salmon lapped with red wine sauce is best for its accessories — a bed of soft leeks and chopped shallots atop the fish — and much as I like the nest of frisee tossed with fried potatoes and browned garlic that cushions an entree of duck confit, the bird itself is tough and dry.

From the pastry chef come desserts both traditional (profiteroles, souffles, crepes) and more fashion forward (passion-fruit-and-raspberry flan, pineapple-coconut tart); there are about two dozen endings to consider, and they are available throughout the day, from 11:30 a.m. to midnight.

Underpinned by well-worn floors and pretty with half curtains in its picture windows, Les Halles's prime location near the Mall and several theaters means you'll find tourists in sweatshirts and tennis shoes alongside patrons dressed for a big night out—and dishes as simple as steamed mussels and macaroni and cheese or as serious as steak au poivre and tripe braised in cider.

I'm a fool for the warm salad of potatoes accented with goat cheese and black olives.

Le Tire Bouchon ★★

4009 Chain Bridge Rd., Fairfax, VA
703-691-4747   www.letirebouchon.com

LUNCH: *M-F 11:30-2:30* **ENTREES:** *$9-$17*
DINNER: *M-Th 5:30-9:30, F-Sat 5:30-10, Sun 5-9* **ENTREES:** *$16-$29*
CREDIT CARDS: *All major* **RESERVATIONS:** *Recommended* **DRESS:** *Casual*
CROSS STREET: *Main Street* **PARKING:** *Lot*
METRO: *No*

NOT A TRACE of the boisterous Italian restaurant that previously occupied this site, Il Lupo, remains. Red wainscoting segues into pale yellow walls, which serve as a canvas for a small collection of handsome French art posters and lovely gold-framed mirrors. The lighting is honeyed; the music leans toward Edith Piaf.

Here's the place to remember why lobster bisque became a classic. Seemingly half cream and half sea, the soup reverberates with the flavor of its namesake seafood. Rounded out with tarragon and brandy, plus a finger of choice lobster meat, this might be the single best recipe in the house. That's not to slight the other appetizers, several of which come very close to the bar set by the bisque. The rabbit pâté, made on the premises, is terrific, at once coarse and rich and pink, garnished with crunchy hazelnuts and sharp gherkins. Tender as they are, the snails are shy in the flavor department. The presentation couldn't be livelier, though: A waiter lifts the glass lid from a black iron dish to reveal an aromatic puff of steam and bubbling liquid surrounding the snails. It all but shouts, "Dig in!"

Here's the place to remember why lobster bisque became a classic.

There's more where that dramatic service comes from, every time someone orders a whole fish that needs to be filleted at a table, or a New York strip steak to be set aflame inches from where it will be eaten. But listen carefully to the recitation of specials, too, which tend to be among the standouts.

From the standing menu, I'm partial to the thin lamb steak and the duck breast. Pan-roasted pork is impressively thick but also dry, and its pared-apple accompaniment is harsh with calvados. In general, this is food that comforts rather than dazzles. But what's wrong with that?

Little Fountain Cafe

★★

2339 18th St. NW, Washington, DC (Adams Morgan)
202-462-8100   www.littlefountaincafe.com

DINNER: *Sun-Th 6-10, F-Sat 6-11* **ENTREES:** *$9.95- $23.95*
CREDIT CARDS: *MC, DC, V* **RESERVATIONS:** *Recommended*
DRESS: *Casual* **CROSS STREET:** *Belmont Road NW*
PARKING: *Street* **METRO:** *Woodley Park-Zoo/Adams Morgan*

TUESDAY NIGHT and you don't feel like cooking? The Little Fountain Cafe comes to the rescue with neighborly service and a nice roast chicken (and no one bats an eye if a book is your dining companion).

Saturday night with a date in tow? Low beamed ceilings, gentle lighting and some soft jazz provide just the right backdrop for getting better acquainted with the face across the table.

Thanks in part to its underground location, shoehorned between competitors in Adams Morgan, this intimate space has always felt like something of a secret. But there are plenty of explanations for its having been around 16 years now. While it roams the world for ideas, the menu aims to comfort rather than shock. There are fetching salads, steamed mussels and sometimes crab cakes dolled up with a sauce of thyme and crawfish to start a meal, and grilled veal chop, coriander-seared tuna and bow-tie pasta with shrimp to move on to.

In a city whose restaurants tend to pay scant attention to parting impressions, the Little Fountain Cafe bakes pretty and honest desserts.

The accessories—mushroom risotto with that veal, bites of tasso ham and fresh oregano in that pasta—always make nice statements. And in a city whose restaurants tend to pay scant attention to parting impressions, the Little Fountain Cafe bakes pretty and honest desserts. Hope to find a moist almond pound cake or a not-too-sweet chocolate tart lapped with butterscotch sauce and real whipped cream.

The gentle trickle you hear from the corner, meanwhile, reminds you that there really is a fountain in the place.

Local 16 ★

1602 U St. NW, Washington, DC (U Street Corridor)
202-265-2828   www.localsixteen.com

DINNER: *Sun-Th 5:30 pm-1:30 am, F-Sat 5:30 pm-2:30 am*   **ENTREES:** *$15-$22*
CREDIT CARDS: *All major*   **RESERVATIONS:** *Recommended*   **DRESS:** *Casual*
CROSS STREET: *16th*   **PARKING:** *Street*
METRO: *U Street-African Amer Civil War Memorial/Cardozo*

THE SCENE: a two-story restaurant on a dark city street. The time: after 8 on a Saturday night. In the two ground-floor dining rooms, large mirrors hung on crimson walls allow selected diners a view of the action even in remote corners. What looks like the cast of *Rent* weaves its way through the tightly spaced tables, carrying sweet-corn-and-parsnip risotto, curried coconut tofu and New York strip steaks to people who may or may not have ordered them. These patrons—some seated on benches hard enough to be church pews, others lucky to have landed at a cozy table (No. 30) near the big front picture window—must lean in to talk. The hardwood floor and pressed-tin ceiling, dressed up with handsome metal chandeliers, exaggerate every sound.

People go to restaurants for many reasons, some of which involve food. Other customers are content with drinks that show up in a timely fashion (best sipped on the rooftop bar), an atmosphere that stands out from the crowd of possibilities, and faces they find attractive. Local 16 was launched with a worthy goal—to buy ingredients from area farmers and to prepare them

Plump oysters in golden coats of batter show up with a creamy slaw and brassy remoulade for dipping.

in unfussy fashion—and some of the many meals I've had here have lived up to that mission statement. But not as many as I had hoped.

Focus on seafood. Good for sharing, sweet shrimp are tucked into won ton wrappers, fried to a gentle crackle and accompanied by a sesame dip. Plump oysters in golden coats of batter show up with a creamy slaw and brassy remoulade for dipping. But there seems to be a 50-50 chance of ordering a disappointment. Onion soup is a bust, a Cobb salad with ice-cold tomatoes gives a classic dish no r-e-s-p-e-c-t, and the New York strip steak is big—and bland.

Logan Tavern

(too new to assign stars)

1423 P St NW, Washington, DC (Logan Circle)
202-332-3710   www.logantavern.com

LUNCH: *M-F noon-5* **ENTREES:** *$6-$22*
DINNER: *Sun-Th 5-11, F-Sat 5-midnight* **ENTREES:** *$12-$22*
BRUNCH: *Sat-Sun 11-4* **ENTREES:** *$6-$22*
CREDIT CARDS: *AE, MC, V* **RESERVATIONS:** *Recommended for parties of 6 or more*
DRESS: *Casual* **CROSS STREET:** *14th* **PARKING:** *Street* **METRO:** *Dupont Circle*

DESPITE A CHORUS OF EARLY OBJECTIONS, Logan Tavern opened recently with the billing its owner always wanted. The problem? People feared that the word "tavern" might sully the neighborhood's image, says David Winer, who also owns Grillfish in Washington's West End. "I explained that some of the best places had tavern as part of their title," including Gramercy Tavern and Tavern on the Green, two popular New York destinations.

Besides, the restaurateur hopes that any negative connotation would be "dispelled by the decor and the food." Located in the new Hudson building across from Whole Foods market, the 100-seat dining room proves a welcoming retreat, dressed as it is with roomy booths, a communal wood table and outsized black-and-white photographs of the area from photographer Geoffrey Hodgdon; from the open

> **The 100-seat dining room proves a welcoming retreat, dressed as it is with roomy booths, a communal wood table and outsized black-and-white photographs of the area.**

kitchen in the rear comes an eclectic parade of homey meat loaf shored up with mashed potatoes, scallops atop red-sauced pasta and, my favorite, sliced roast pork edged in sweet Asian mustard.

Chef San Varith, born in Cambodia and late of Grillfish, brought eight or so of that restaurant's bestsellers with him, including ginger calamari and crab cakes. And, in keeping with the neighborhood theme, salads are included with entrees and no bottle of wine is priced over $39.

Love Cafe

(too new to assign stars)

1501 U St. NW, Washington DC (U Street Corridor)
202-265-9800   www.cakelove.com

OPEN: *M-Th 7:30 am-11 pm, F 7 am-midnight, Sat 9:30 am-midnight, Sun 9:30-10*
DESSERTS AND SANDWICHES: *$4-$7.50*
CREDIT CARDS: *MC, V* **RESERVATIONS:** *No*
DRESS: *Casual* **CROSS STREET:** *15th Street NW* **PARKING:** *Street*
METRO: *U Street-African Amer Civil War Memorial/Cardozo*

WARREN BROWN, the owner of Cakelove, the popular but tiny Washington bakery, finally figured out a way to let his customers have their cake and sit with it, too: He opened Love Cafe, just an eclair's toss across the street from Cakelove.

Patrons will find in his spinoff everything carried by the standup original—cupcakes, "crunchy feet" (small pound cakes), "buzz balls" (filled cream puffs)—as well as a half-dozen sandwiches, running from portobello and smoked salmon to grilled cheese and tuna salad. The savories are several notches above the usual: The BLT is slathered with a sunny lemon mayonnaise, for instance, and a tofu sandwich is offered two ways, with tofu flavored with balsamic vinegar or "tandoori" style. Breakfast waffles and French toast are on the horizon, promises the 33-year-old entrepreneur, who left a legal career for hotter fires when he opened Cakelove almost two years ago.

Long and narrow, the 50-seat Love Cafe makes a pleasant alternative to the ubiquitous chain coffeehouses. Its brick walls are punctuated by broad windows that pull in lots of light, and the color scheme proves cheerful in yellows and blues. Most of the furnishings—the mixed chairs and couches—were purchased from nearby stores on 14th Street or wrought from natural materials (the wood tile tables are particularly handsome). On a recent afternoon, baby strollers and laptops were evident in equal numbers.

> **Long and narrow, the 50-seat Love Cafe makes a pleasant alternative to the ubiquitous chain coffeehouses.**

There's no alcohol at Love Cafe, but there is a happy hour: Every Wednesday from 5 to 7:30 p.m., Brown offers his version of the popular chocolate cake with molten chocolate center—"lava cake," he calls it—for $3 each.

Lupo's Italian Chophouse ★★

416 Baltimore Ave., College Park, MD
301-277-6225   www.illupo.info

LUNCH: *M-Sat 11:30-4, Sun noon-4*   **ENTREES:** *$7-$22*
DINNER: *Sun-Th 4-10, F-Sat 4-11*   **ENTREES:** *$7-$22*
CREDIT CARDS: *All major*   **RESERVATIONS:** *Recommended*
DRESS: *Casual*   **CROSS STREET:** *Knox Road*   **PARKING:** *Lot*
METRO: *College Park*

L UPO'S ITALIAN CHOPHOUSE is that rare bird in Prince George's County: a serious restaurant. Even better, it's a place to eat that has no attachment to a chain. Opened in November 2002 by brothers Anthony and Peter Lupo, who also run Il Lupo in Fairfax, the Maryland off-shoot was designed with its neighbors in mind. This means there is $7 pizza to appease the University of Maryland set, and more elegant fish specials to draw the folks from nearby University Park. "We're trying to hit every base," says Anthony Lupo.

For the most part, the game plan works. A bowl of minestrone has me looking up to see if there is an Italian mother hovering over my shoulder. It's a generous serving of soup, with a clear broth supporting skin-on cubes of potato, soft noodles, carrots and celery. Fried calamari faces a lot of competition out there, and this kitchen's version is respectable. As for the pizza, its crust is pleasantly chewy and the toppings are fine.

Main courses yield a parade of tried-and-true Italian favorites, some executed better than others. If it's veal you're looking for, opt for the thick, smoky chop with velvety mushrooms over the veal piccata. Of the pasta dishes, I'm partial to squid scattered over a big bowl of linguine, simple and tasty. A bowl of spaghetti comes with a creamy meat sauce that sneaks some cumin into its seasoning. It's not very Italian, but the stuff sure is comforting. And if it's a straightforward piece of fish you want, grilled tuna fits the bill.

Of the pasta dishes, I'm partial to squid scattered over a big bowl of linguine, simple and tasty.

Lupo's should consider rewriting its endings. Tiramisu lacks both coffee or chocolate flavor, while zabaglione is too thick and without any suggestion of wine. The lone success turns out to carry an American accent: The warm apple crisp is rich with cinnamon, fruit and walnuts. Despite a few underachievers, some of us are happy to take Lupo's Chophouse as it is: a big fish in a tiny pond.

Maestro

Ritz-Carlton Hotel, Tysons Galleria, 1700 Tysons Blvd., McLean, VA
703-821-1515   www.maestrorestaurant.com

BREAKFAST: *M-F 6:30-11* **ENTREES:** *$12-$22*
DINNER: *Tu-Th 6-9, F-Sat 5:30-10, 3-to-7-course prix fixe, $72-$112*
BRUNCH BUFFET: *Sun 10:30-2* **PRICE:** *$61*
CLOSED: *Sat-Sun breakfast, Sun-M dinner* **CREDIT CARDS:** *All major*
RESERVATIONS: *Recommended* **DRESS:** *Jacket required*
PARKING: *Complimentary valet* **METRO:** *No*

RARE, NO-HOLDS-BARRED APPLAUSE is generally reserved for a passionate and dedicated chef with a long history of serving extraordinary food. There are exceptions, and one of them is Fabio Trabocchi. A mere 29 years old, he works with intensity and skill that belie his age, from a big stage set of a kitchen that practically spills into Maestro's elegant dining room. (When you call to book a table, you will be asked if you want a seat close to the action; grab the chance to see a first-rate performer.)

The chef's menu combines traditional and modern Italian recipes and changes with the seasons. Picture a little casserole of macaroni tossed with a crumble of sausage and ennobled with black truffles; crisp skate wing presented with sheets of green and yellow pasta and a gently foamy herb broth; and braised pork belly, its bands of fat wrapped around near-melting meat, its richness countered with sharp pink peppercorns. Each dish suggests a work of art. A glorious cheese cart and elegant desserts—I can still taste the warm and trembling chocolate-peppermint souffle—see patrons to dinner's end in high style.

> **When you call to book a table, you will be asked if you want a seat close to the action; grab the chance to see a first-rate performer.**

Trabocchi isn't the only maestro at Maestro. Watching over the dining room is a host who combines warmth with élan (forget your glasses? he has an elegant pair for you to borrow) and a sommelier who wants you to drink well no matter what your budget. Cesar Ritz would be proud.

Majestic Cafe

911 King St., Alexandria, VA

703-837-9117   www.majesticcafe.com

LUNCH: *Tu-Sat 11:30-2:30* **ENTREES:** *$8.50-$12*
DINNER: *Tu-Th 5:30-10, F-Sat 5:30-11, Sun 5:30-10* **ENTREES:** *$16.50-$22*
BRUNCH: *Sun 11-2:30* **ENTREES:** *$8-$13*
CLOSED: *M* **CREDIT CARDS:** *All major*
RESERVATIONS: *Recommended* **DRESS:** *Casual*
CROSS STREET: *N. Alfred Street* **PARKING:** *Street*
METRO: *King Street*

THE SWEETEST HOST STAND AROUND is found at this charming Old Town address, which often displays the handiwork of pastry chef Valerie Hill at the entrance to its small dining room. One day, a lemon-blueberry layer cake dares you to break your diet. Another time, the temptation is devil's food cake, as moist as can be, impossibly high and frosted with the kind of smooth white icing Fannie Farmer herself might have made way back when.

That skill and sense of generosity is a hallmark of everything that comes before the final course, too, be it a napoleon of fried won-ton skins and mushrooms, rich with sour cream and mustard, or juicy free-range chicken breast served with a nest of fettuccine; no ordinary noodles, these are flavored with ricotta cheese, country ham and wisps of arugula. And if Mom can't get you to eat your vegetables, this proudly American menu—with its side dishes of stewed tomatoes, garlicky broccoli and sweet potato with citrus-hazelnut butter—just might.

If Mom can't get you to eat your vegetables, this proudly American menu—with its side dishes of stewed tomatoes, garlicky broccoli and sweet potato with citrus-hazelnut butter—just might.

The meal comes in a lovely environment. Old black-and-white photos march across the walls, leading the eye to an open kitchen where chef Susan McCreight Lindeborg can be seen watching over each plate as if it were going out to a VIP—which, given the occasional drop-in by Mark Warner or Ted Leonsis, it sometimes is.

Makoto

4822 MacArthur Blvd. NW, Washington, DC (Palisades)
202-298-6866

LUNCH: *Tu-Th noon-2* **ENTREES:** *$8.95-$19.50*
DINNER: *Tu-Sun 6-10* **ENTREES:** *$10-$30*
CLOSED: *M* **CREDIT CARDS:** *MC, V*
RESERVATIONS: *Recommended* **DRESS:** *Business casual*
CROSS STREET: *Foxhall Road* **PARKING:** *Street*
METRO: *No*

WEAR CLEAN SOCKS. That's my advice to anyone interested in a meal at this most Japanese of Washington restaurants, whose patrons are asked to shed their shoes at the door before entering the spare, narrow, low-ceilinged dining room.

No one just drops by Makoto. With only 28 seats, including a small sushi bar, reservations are essential. Looking around, and eavesdropping, I often think half the diplomatic corps must come here to hoist chopsticks and drink sake (from a fragrant wooden box instead of a glass).

I imagine such diners feel at home perched on the wooden seats that double as coat holders, feasting on pristine sushi, flounder bound in cherry leaf, or soft-

> **I often think half the diplomatic corps must come here to hoist chopsticks and drink sake (from a fragrant wooden box instead of a glass).**

shell crab crunchy in a coat of rice-cracker crumbs and garnished with leek flower stems. This is all beautiful food, right down to the sparkling grape ice that signals the end of the $45 tasting menu.

A seat at the counter, overlooking the kitchen and three chefs, provides one of the most engaging cooking shows you're likely to tune in to.

Mandalay ★★

9091-A Baltimore Ave., College Park, MD
301-345-8540

LUNCH: *Tu-F 11-3, Sat 11-5, Sun noon-5* **ENTREES:** *$5.99-$8.99*
DINNER: *Tu-Th 5-9, F-Sat 5-10, Sun 5-9* **ENTREES:** *$5.99-$8.99*
CLOSED: *M* **CREDIT CARDS:** *MC, V* **RESERVATIONS:** *No*
DRESS: *Casual* **CROSS STREET:** *University Boulevard*
PARKING: *Lot* **METRO:** *College Park-U of MD*

THE SAMOSAS STUFFED with curried potato bring to mind an Indian kitchen, and the thick rice noodles stir-fried with chicken, cabbage and carrots would look at home on a Chinese menu. The presence of both these dishes in this spare, family-run dining room make perfect sense, though, since Burma has borrowed from its neighbors to come up with a cuisine that resembles an edible quilt.

Stock up on appetizers, particularly the salads, which include one that's a pleasantly musky shred of pickled tea leaves and another that's sharp with ginger and fried garlic and crunchy with cabbage and ground nuts. Ask the waiter for "spicy" and you get a searing response, perhaps sliced beef in tomato curry ignited with chilics.

Stock up on appetizers, particularly the salads, which include a pleasantly musky shred of pickled tea leaves.

Mohingar is a symbol of pride in Burma; taste what the fuss is about here, with a bowl of the beige soup, thick with rice noodles and flavorful with lemon grass and pureed catfish. Fine by itself, the liquid blossoms at the table with fresh lime and pungent cilantro.

The gentle prices—entrees average $7—keep the staff at Mandalay hopping and the 50 seats filled, much of the time by staff and students from the nearby university who flock here for an escape from books and cafeteria trays.

Mantis

1847 Columbia Rd. NW, Washington, DC (Adams Morgan)
202-667-2400

DINNER: *Daily 5:30-11* **TAPAS:** *$5-$8*
CREDIT CARDS: *AE, MC, V* **RESERVATIONS:** *No*
DRESS: *Casual* **CROSS STREET:** *Mintwood Place NW*
PARKING: *Street* **METRO:** *Woodley Park-Zoo/Adams Morgan*

"**V**ERY SOHO," a friend says as she surveys her surroundings. Drinking a pink martini, she is delighted to discover purse hooks beneath the bar. "This place reminds me of Montreal," another well-traveled pal says a few weeks later. Low aluminum chairs and sleek brown sofas hug the restaurant's glass walls, a minimalist statement that continues with bunches of pussy willows.

Mantis distinguishes itself with a menu of pan-Asian small plates, averaging $6 apiece; order two or three and you have a light meal. You might not be able to stop there, however. With few exceptions, these are vivid flavors and fetching arrangements that almost compel you to taste whatever you haven't already tried. Thus a tender and sweetly spiced beef satay seems inevitably to lead to a trio of zesty pork meatballs decorating a bowl of rice noodles tossed with a stinging house-made tomato-mango ketchup.

The calamari brings together lightly fried and gently grilled squid, both presented on a verdant sauce of cilantro and sake. Seared scallops, sweet as can be, are displayed on a brilliant backdrop of saffron cream. Fresh crab can be enjoyed two ways, as small cakes packed with bright herbs, or slipped into outsize steamed won tons

Seared scallops, sweet as can be, are displayed on a brilliant backdrop of saffron cream.

with cheese. Chopsticks are the utensils of choice here, but a fork and knife might work better for a nubby rockfish fillet, set on a smooth pool of red coconut curry.

Could we get some water? More napkins? Another round of drinks? The staff at Mantis is cordial but laid-back and inattentive, even when the place isn't crowded. And some dishes aren't on the same playing field. Still, I always leave Mantis with the sense that I've been well fed, well lubricated— and whisked away from buttoned-up Washington for not a lot of money.

Marcel's

2401 Pennsylvania Ave. NW, Washington, DC (Foggy Bottom/West End)
202-296-1666   www.marcelsdc.com

DINNER: *Sun 5:30-9:30, M-Th 5:30-10, F-Sat 5:30-11*   **ENTREES:** *$35-$42*
PRE-THEATER: *Three-course prix fixe nightly with round-trip limo service
to Kennedy Center, $42*
CREDIT CARDS: *All major*   **RESERVATIONS:** *Recommended*
DRESS: *Business casual*   **CROSS STREET:** *24th*
PARKING: *$5 valet*   **METRO:** *Foggy Bottom*

THERE'S ENOUGH SPARKLING STEMWARE on the tables to stock a
Tiffany showroom, and the golden lighting makes even tired faces
look as if they had just returned from a long holiday. A small fleet of
waiters in black jackets tends to customers' needs, while live piano music
floats into the dining room from the handsome bar. And those patrons who
have come here as a prelude to an evening of music or theater know that the
limousine parked out front, ready to whisk them to the Kennedy Center, is
part of the $42 three-course dinner.

Marcel's is nothing if not concerned about your pleasure. Working from a
raised open kitchen that looks onto his
audience, chef Robert Wiedmaier prepares a menu that's mostly rich and
primarily French. Plump mussels in a
shallow black casserole are enriched

**Chef Robert Wiedmaier
prepares a menu that's
mostly rich and
primarily French.**

with cream and scattered with thin fried garlic chips. A fist-size chunk of
sushi-grade tuna is sparked with fresh cracked pepper and poised on a fat
cake of shredded potatoes made more decadent with Gruyere. But there is
also a moist breast of pheasant, lamb loin served with turnip puree, or perfect
scallops sandwiching glistening caviar and lapped with buttery lemon sauce.

Forget your reading glasses? Ask the maitre d' for a pair to borrow from the
collection he keeps on hand. From start to finish, Marcel's thinks of everything.

Matchbox ★

713 H St. NW, Washington, DC (Chinatown)
202-289-4441

OPEN: *M-Th 11:30-10, F-Sat 11:30-11* **ENTREES:** *$10-$21*
CLOSED: *Sun* **CREDIT CARDS:** *AE, MC, V*
RESERVATIONS: *No* **DRESS:** *Casual*
CROSS STREET: *7th* **PARKING:** *Street*
METRO: *Gallery Place-Chinatown*

THE TRICK TO MAKING a New York–style pizza? "The secret is in the oven," claims Mark Neal. One of four partners behind this Chinatown destination, the restaurateur says he's using the revered John's Pizzeria in the Big Apple as the benchmark for the thin, crisp pies rolled out here.

In an attempt to duplicate the heat sources that Neal and company found on their extensive tour of New York's pizza joints, the quartet hired a mason from Portland, Maine, to build a brick oven that could get as hot as 900 degrees; a combination of hickory, cherry, oak and mahogany feeds the flames inside. Toppings run from house-made meatballs to vegetarian (my pick) and "fire and smoke," whose smoked Gouda and chipotle-spiked sauce unfortunately overwhelm the crust.

It doesn't take a CIA operative to figure out how Matchbox came by its name. The restaurant's theme is pounded home in the oak veneer tables, each of which is inlaid with matchboxes from around the world, and the skinny shape of the airy, 75-seat restaurant, spread over three floors.

It doesn't take a CIA operative to figure out how Matchbox came by its name.

Pizza isn't the only reason to drop by. Chef Graig Glufling, who previously cooked at Poste and Vidalia, broadens the menu with pasta, pecan-crusted chicken, and rockfish over a hash of juicy rock shrimp, potatoes and pancetta—the fish dish being the best. The sleeper? A plate of juicy miniburgers—choose three ($6), six ($9) or nine ($12)—served with a pile of lacy onion rings dusted with parsley, oregano and Romano cheese. And beer mavens should appreciate the draft choices from Germany, Belgium and Oregon.

Matsutake ★

Ronald Reagan Washington National Airport, Arlington, VA
703-417-0521

OPEN: *Daily 11:30-9* **ENTREES:** *$8.50-$34.95*
CREDIT CARDS: *All major* **RESERVATIONS:** *No (recommended at other locations)*
DRESS: *Casual* **PARKING:** *Garage*
METRO: *National Airport*

I ONCE TURNED a delayed flight into a delicious advantage when I discovered a fine place to eat at Ronald Reagan Washington National Airport: Matsutake, a small Japanese eatery in the B terminal near gate No. 23.

An offshoot of a restaurant of the same name in Herndon, the venue offers a welcome alternative to fast food. A blond wood sushi bar and walls the color of wasabi create a soothing pit stop, and a diner can count on helpful recommendations from the chefs: "Giant clams just came in today," one of them said, steering me to a firm, pleasantly chewy and sea-scented sushi option; just as satisfying were buttery toro (fatty tuna) and subtle raw sweet shrimp. Prices average about $4 for two pieces, all of good quality (though the rice might not be as vinegared as you'd prefer).

> A blond wood sushi bar and walls the color of wasabi create a soothing pit stop, and a diner can count on helpful recommendations from the chefs.

There's more than just raw fish to consider: Japanese dumplings, noodle soups, spider rolls crunchy with soft-shell crab, and deep-fried vanilla ice cream round out the menu. As an unexpected bonus, my waiter even volunteered to check the airline schedule posted out front so I wouldn't miss my next flight.

All in all, it sure beats a bag of pretzels at 30,000 feet.

OTHER LOCATIONS: *320 23rd St., Arlington, VA, 703-412-5301*
4121 Wilson Blvd., Arlington, VA, 703-351-8787
13049 Worldgate Dr., Herndon, VA, 703-787-3700

Meiwah ★

4457 Willard Ave., Chevy Chase, MD
301-652-9882   www.meiwahrestaurant.com

LUNCH: *M-F 11:30-3*   **ENTREES:** *$6.95-$23.95*
DINNER: *M-F 3-11, Sat-Sun 11:30-11*   **ENTREES:** *$8.95-$23.95*
CREDIT CARDS: *All major*   **RESERVATIONS:** *Recommended*   **DRESS:** *Casual*
CROSS STREET: *Hill Plaza*   **PARKING:** *Lot*
METRO: *Friendship Heights*

RESTAURATEUR LARRY LA has been a success in a basement (City Lights of China in Dupont Circle, which he sold six years ago) and on the ground level (with Meiwah in Washington's West End). Now he's branching out, and up, with a second Meiwah in Chevy Chase, ensconced on the second floor of a new office building.

With the exception of sushi (not offered in the District location), the menu in Maryland is identical to the one in Washington. Long and familiar, the list of possibilities runs to dumplings and soups, whole fish and Sichuan beef, Mongolian lamb and sweet-and-sour pork. Save your esoteric appetite for Chinatown. This is neighborhood Chinese restaurant cooking—more lemon chicken than birds' nest soup.

Steamed whole fish with its wash of gingery soy sauce proves delicate and moist.

Appetizers are generally crowd-pleasers. Spicy Chinese cabbage lives up to its billing, and scallops are deep-fried so that their outsides are lightly crisped but the centers remain soft and sweet. Spring rolls come piping hot.

"Tinkling bells pork" stops conversation as the ingredients are transferred from platter to hot skillet at the table. Once the vapor disappears and the noise dies down, we dig in to find thin folds of pork tossed with a bright garden of crisp vegetables. Another fine meat selection is orange beef, jazzed up with dried strips of orange peel. Steamed whole fish with its wash of gingery soy sauce proves delicate and moist, but Peking duck is a yawn.

It doesn't matter. Meiwah's neighbors are starved for places to eat that don't scream "chain," evidenced by a crowded foyer and a full house at every meal I've dropped into. All those people and all the hard surfaces add up to a low roar. It's a good thing the staff is quick and efficient, the tropical cocktails are big and potent, and the prices are so friendly.

SECOND LOCATION: *1200 New Hampshire Ave. NW, Washington, DC 202-833-2888*

Melrose ★★

1201 24th St. NW, Washington, DC (Foggy Bottom/West End)
202-419-6755

BREAKFAST: *M-F 6:30-11, Sat-Sun 7-11* **ENTREES:** *$8-$21*
LUNCH: *M-Sat 11-2:30* **ENTREES:** *$17-$33*
DINNER: *Daily 5:30-10:30* **ENTREES:** *$25-$36*
PRE-THEATER: *Daily 5:30-6:45, 3-course prix fixe $38*
BRUNCH: *Sun 11-2:30* **PRICE:** *$50*
CREDIT CARDS: *AE, DC, MC, V* **RESERVATIONS:** *Recommended*
DRESS: *Jacket preferred* **CROSS STREET:** *M Street NW*
PARKING: *Complimentary valet* **METRO:** *Foggy Bottom*

MELROSE IS MY READY ANSWER to a lot of restaurant questions. Dinner and dancing? A live band performs in the marble foyer on Friday (Latin) and Saturday (jazz) nights. Brunch? The lavish spread gives fresh meaning to the word buffet every Sunday. Peace and quiet? Well-spaced tables allow for discreet conversation. There's a lovely outdoor patio for al fresco dining, and there's no corkage fee for wine drinkers who bring in their own bottles on Sunday nights.

But what I like best about this hotel dining room, with its soaring windows and comfortable seating, is that it doesn't come across like your typical corporate affair. Brian McBride has quietly headed the kitchen for well over a dozen years now, but he and his international crew still cook as if they can't wait to please you. The biggest problem you'll have is eliminating things you want to try: Jumbo prawns on garlic polenta, Dover sole with chanterelle mushrooms, and rabbit served with apricots and sage all sound tempting.

A few of McBride's dishes have been around a long time, and you can taste why diners won't let them go: The chilled calamari salad is bright with lemon grass and mint, while the popular shrimp ravioli is balanced

The biggest problem you'll have is eliminating things you want to try.

by a sweet, summery corn sauce and the heat of cracked black pepper. With food like this, there's no chance of anyone falling asleep at the table.

Melrose also offers great crab cakes, a first-rate rack of lamb and a trio of dishes billed as healthful. That seared ahi tuna may be good for you, arranged with smoky peppers, hearts of palm and a garden of goodies, but guess what: It tastes good, too.

Melting Pot ★★

1220 19th St. NW, Washington, DC (Dupont Circle)
202-857-0777   www.meltingpot.com

DINNER: *Sun-Th 5-11, F-Sat 5-midnight*
ENTREES: *$16-$23, 3-course prix fixe for 2 $50-$52, 4-course prix fixe for 2 $70-$76*
CREDIT CARDS: *AE, MC, V* **RESERVATIONS:** *Recommended*
DRESS: *Business casual* **CROSS STREET:** *M Street NW*
PARKING: *Complimentary valet M-F* **METRO:** *Dupont Circle*

BRANCH 63 of this Florida-based fondue empire unfolds in a large underground dining room near Dupont Circle. An arty waterfall graces the entrance at the bottom of a flight of stairs; soft lighting and modern paintings add appealing touches to the sprawl beyond. As big as it is, the place feels intimate, with half walls that create zones of privacy throughout the expanse. Bunches of balloons here and there—and the occasional stretch limo parked outside—remind you that cooking your own food with the help of others is fun.

The drill begins with a tour of the menu led by an enthusiastic server. There's the Big Night Out ($76 for two), which features four courses that include fat lobster tails, morsels of marinated beef tenderloin, chicken-plumped ravioli and shrimp for dipping; and the Center Cut Combo ($70 for two), a carnivore's fantasy of filet mignon, sirloin, chicken and more. Less lofty but still worth your time are the vegetarian and themed fondues, including The French Quarter with andouille sausage.

Only a trip to Baskin-Robbins involves more decisions than a dinner at the Melting Pot: What kind of cooking liquid do you want? Which salad do you prefer? What sauces would you like to add to your cooked food? (There are many; the delicate curry and herbed green goddess both pair well with vegetables.) The genial waiters inevitably spend so much time explaining the menu, stir-cooking your appetizer, doling out sauces, suggesting proper cooking times for each ingredient and dispensing caution ("Don't put the hot fork directly in your mouth") that you might be tempted to invite them to take a seat. But with friends in tow and good ingredients on hand, the Melting Pot is a stirring way to spend a few hours.

OTHER LOCATIONS: *1110 N. Glebe Rd., Arlington, VA, 703-243-4490*
11400 Commerce Park Dr., Reston, VA, 703-264-0900
128 Rollins Ave., Rockville, MD, 301-231-8220
2348 Solomons Island Rd., Annapolis, MD, 410-266-8004

Meskerem ★★

2434 18th St. NW, Washington, DC (Adams Morgan)
202-462-4100   www.meskeremonline.com

LUNCH: *Daily noon-5*   **ENTREES:** *$7-$12.95*
DINNER: *Daily 5-midnight*   **ENTREES:** *$7.50-$13.95*
CREDIT CARDS: *AE, D, MC, V*   **RESERVATIONS:** *Recommended*
DRESS: *Casual*   **CROSS STREET:** *Columbia Road NW*   **PARKING:** *Street*
METRO: *Woodley Park-Zoo/Adams Morgan*

THE MORE I CHECK OUT the competition, the more I'm drawn to Meskerem. Among the capital's many Ethiopian restaurants, this one feels the most comfortable. The seating is spread across three levels; head for the low stools beneath the spoked ceiling of the top floor, or one of the window perches where you can peer out at a steady stream of passers-by (and they at you).

The menu is ambitious as well, starting with won-ton-like pastries stuffed with minced beef or collard greens; steamed shrimp with a zippy red dipping sauce; and a vivid salad of chopped beets, potatoes and chilies. From there, you can move on to a variety of mild or hot stewed meats, vegetables and seafood, presented on large trays lined with injera, the thick fermented pancakes that double as scoops for the food.

Dishes are meant to be eaten communally, over basketlike tables, and with the hands.

(The dishes are meant to be eaten communally, over basketlike tables, and with the hands.) I'm partial to the vegetarian sampler, which includes earth-toned dollops of pureed chickpeas, mashed lentils, potato salad with green chilies and soothing chopped greens—an artist's edible palette.

Michel Richard Citronelle ★★★★

3000 M St. NW, Washington, DC (Georgetown)
202-625-2150   www.citronelledc.com

BREAKFAST: *Daily 6:30-10:30*   **ENTREES:** *$9-$12.75*
LUNCH: *M-F noon-2*   **ENTREES:** *$16-$26; tasting menu, $45*
DINNER: *Sun-Th 6:30-9:30, F 6:30-10, Sat 6-10*
ENTREES: *4-to-8-course prix fixe, $75, $90, $100, $120*
CREDIT CARDS: *All major*   **RESERVATIONS:** *Recommended*
DRESS: *Jacket required at dinner*   **CROSS STREET:** *30th*
PARKING: *$5 valet*   **METRO:** *Foggy Bottom*

O NE OF THE FINEST displays of modern art in Washington isn't showcased at the Hirshhorn, but on a menu in Georgetown that blazes more trails than just about any other restaurant in the country. If that sounds like a stretch, you haven't dined at Michel Richard Citronelle, whose namesake chef never rests in his pursuit of excellence, and always hits the mark.

One dish, a riff on the ubiquitous carpaccio, neatly sums up Richard's breathtaking talent. An outsized white plate acts as a canvas for half a dozen perfect raw ingredients, each element—tuna, scallop, eel, jicama, octopus, pinwheels of bell peppers in three colors—sliced so thinly you can almost read through them. Light greens are strewn on top along with microscopic potato crisps and drizzles of basil oil and ginger cream. It all tastes as sublime as it looks. That appetizer is a high point among many dishes on the thoroughly modern menu.

The best paella in town is made by Richard—and it doesn't even use rice! (The clever chef substitutes finely chopped squid to form his mound, around which gather tiny mussels, rabbit and more.) Soups are stellar, and keep in mind that Richard was trained as a pastry chef. "Breakfast" for dessert translates into an eye-opening replica of toast with butter, a fried egg,

> **Everything is in perfect balance, and it all tastes as sublime as it looks.**

bacon and hash browns—except that nothing tastes the way you think it might.

The bright-eyed chef is the dining room's best ambassador, roving among the tables to joke and flirt with his audience, the favored of whom tend to be seated in view of the gleaming exhibition kitchen. Unknowns are also treated well, though some of the staff are definitely more solicitous than others.

Even so, such quibbles tend to be forgiven in light of what lands on your table: the most sophisticated food in the city—and some of the best, anywhere.

Minh's

2500 Wilson Blvd., Arlington, VA
703-525-2828

LUNCH: *M-F 11-3:30* **ENTREES:** *$5.95-$12.95*
DINNER: *Sun-Th 3:30-10, F-Sat 11-11* **ENTREES:** *$7.15-$12.95*
CREDIT CARDS: *All major* **RESERVATIONS:** *Recommended*
CROSS STREET: *Cleveland Street* **PARKING:** *Lot*
METRO: *Courthouse*

VISITORS HERE COULD USE A GUIDE to sort through the more than 100 choices on the menu, including the daily specials on a chalkboard, and there always is one, be it a waiter or an owner, at this quietly stylish Vietnamese restaurant.

The hard-working staff has led me on some mouthwatering expeditions, one night introducing me to shrimp-and-potato cakes, bundled in crisp lettuce and dipped in tangy fish sauce; another time pointing out "sizzling" catfish, which does just that as it comes to the table, cubed and buried beneath a mound of fresh herbs, peanuts, slivered red onions and rice noodles. A meal gets off to a good start with stir-fried squid—crisp outside, pleasantly chewy inside—with onions and bell peppers. Season the mix with a pinch of the accompanying salt-and-pepper blend and a spritz of lime.

Like Vietnamese cuisine in general, the repertoire here borrows from Chinese, French and even Indian kitchens. Since a lot of these dishes are variations on a theme, it's less of a stimulus overload than you might anticipate when you first see the list.

Like Vietnamese cuisine in general, the repertoire here borrows from Chinese, French and even Indian kitchens.

Even on my own, though, I've plucked winners from the lot, including crisp, sweet folds of beef with lemon grass, and a special of fried scallops with mint, onions and jalapenos served with a peppery dipping sauce.

Minh's wouldn't be my first choice for pho or a Vietnamese crepe. Still, as with so much of the cooking, a lot of thought has gone into the interior. Pretty with fancy pillows on the banquettes, aged-looking sideboards and walls in shades of olive and burgundy, it doesn't look like the kind of place where entrees average $8.

minibar at Cafe Atlantico ★★

405 Eighth St. NW, Washington, DC (Penn Quarter)
202-393-0812   www.cafeatlantico.com

DINNER: *Tu-Sat 5-10* **ENTREES:** *tasting menu $65*
CLOSED: *Sun-M* **CREDIT CARDS:** *All major*
RESERVATIONS: *Recommended* **DRESS:** *Business casual*
CROSS STREET: *D Street NW* **PARKING:** *$8 valet*
METRO: *Archives-Navy Memorial*

O NE OF THE WILDEST SHOWS in town unfolds at a six-stool counter on the second floor of Cafe Atlantico, where chefs Jose Andres and Katsuya Fukushima stage a $65 tasting menu that is as much an event as it is a meal. The 30 or so small plates remind patrons that Andres is a disciple of one of the world's most imaginative chefs, Ferran Adria of the fabled El Bulli in Spain. In Adria's world, soups race from hot to cold in the same sip, and unexpected but companionable combinations are the norm.

And so it follows at the laboratory known as minibar, where nothing is quite what you think it is. Your first taste might be a bust. "Chicken curry" popcorn gives me pause: *How many plates before this is over?* The disappointment lasts about 15 seconds, though, swept away by a silver dispenser the size of a breath freshener, which diners spray into their mouths, filling them with the bright flavors of lime, rum and mint—it's a mojito! Thrilling highs—and a few crashing lows— are around every corner of this roller coaster ride. Miniature cones of minced tomato and fresh basil might be followed by a savory mouthful of tuna seviche tucked into a "raviolo" of shaved jicama, then by "Maine lobster on the half shell": The presentation involves a plastic syringe filled with a rich and pure lobster emulsion, which diners shoot into their mouths. Altoids crushed over fish or Pop Rocks candy stirred into mango soup are gimmicks that wear thin fast, though.

To keep things lively, the chefs swap dishes—and surprises—in and out of their repertoire. My bill arrived not in a folder, but in an eggshell. Yours might hide in a fortune cookie. You just never know.

Mon Ami Gabi ★

7239 Woodmont Ave., Bethesda, MD
301-654-1234   www.monamigabi.com

LUNCH: *Tu-Sat 11:30-3* **ENTREES:** *$8.95-$28.95*
DINNER: *M-Th 5-10, F-Sat 5-11, Sun 4-9:30* **ENTREES:** *$14.95-$29.95*
BRUNCH: *Sun noon-3:30* **ENTREES:** *$8.95-$28.95*
CREDIT CARDS: *All major* **RESERVATIONS:** *Recommended* **DRESS:** *Casual*
CROSS STREET: *Elm Lane* **PARKING:** *$5 valet at dinner*
METRO: *Bethesda*

A NYONE WISHING to re-create a French bistro on foreign turf would be smart to pave the floor with tiny tiles and cover the banquettes in dark leather. There ought to be chalkboards touting daily specials, too, and waiters in long white aprons. Then maybe a little jazz to wash back a glass of Cotes du Rhone, just like in a Paris wine bar. And bonus points for a place whose walls look as if they'd been stained yellow not by a painter, but by years of diners puffing Gauloises.

Mon Ami Gabi is all of that and more. And sometimes less (seafood dishes and desserts need fine-tuning). An export from Chicago, the restaurant always plays to SRO crowds, and it's easy to see why. Defying Gallic stereotype, the waiters prove exceedingly gracious. The menu isn't a very long read, and it offers plenty that is

> **An export from Chicago, the restaurant always plays to SRO crowds, and it's easy to see why.**

familiar, from onion soup and frisee salad to steamed mussels and tarte Tatin. France's romance with the grape is underscored by a wine program that includes a cart of 10 or 60 bottles reflecting the different wine-growing regions, including Alsace, Bordeaux and the Loire; undecided diners are encouraged to try a splash of any wine they are curious about before making a commitment, even if it's just to a glass.

CAN YOU HEAR ME? Mon Ami Gabi is not for the hard of hearing or for anyone bothered by close encounters. It is, however, a reliable spot for a meat eater. Take your pick from steaks dolloped with herbed butter or punched up with brandy-peppercorn sauce or a bordelaise rich with wine and herbs. The best of the lot is the hanger steak. Ropy and tender, it becomes decadent with either mustard or anchovy butter, both assertive without overwhelming the beef.

Montmartre

327 Seventh St. SE, Washington, DC (Capitol Hill)

202-544-1244   www.montmartre.us

LUNCH: *Tu-Sun 11:30-2:30* **ENTREES:** *$11.95-$17.95*
DINNER: *Tu-Th 5:30-10, F-Sat 5:30-10:30, Sun 5:30-9*
ENTREES: *$15.95-$19.95* **CLOSED:** *M*
CREDIT CARDS: *AE, MC, V* **RESERVATIONS:** *Recommended*
DRESS: *Casual* **CROSS STREET:** *Pennsylvania Avenue SE*
PARKING: *Street* **METRO:** *Eastern Market*

THE LINE OUT THE DOOR on a Saturday night reminds me that while Capitol Hill doesn't have many memorable places to eat, this is part of the solution: a restaurant nearly as good as Georgetown's Bistrot Lepic, where the owners of this sunny dining room both previously worked.

The good-looking servers twist and turn like bumper cars as they navigate closely packed tables. Frisee salad scattered with gizzards and lardons, citrusy shrimp on risotto, and cauliflower soup dotted with saffron-tinged mussels all get dinner off to a fine start. You might move on to a nicely ropy hanger steak with crisped potatoes or sauteed tuna in a forest of chanterelles. I want to order the chicken, but the waiter shakes his head. "Try the rabbit," he says, and soon I'm

> I want to order the chicken, but the waiter shakes his head. "Try the rabbit," he says, and soon I'm fighting with my tablemates for the last of its succulent meat.

fighting with my tablemates for the last of its succulent meat, strewn with olives and served over a bed of creamy thin noodles that have soaked up the pan juices.

The intimate setting—beams overhead, a tiny bar looking into the kitchen—exudes the kind of charm you might expect in the country but are glad to find in the city.

Morrison-Clark Inn   *(0 stars)*

1015 L St. NW, Washington, DC (Mt. Vernon Square)
202-898-1200   www.morrisonclark.com

LUNCH: *M-F 11:30-2:30* **ENTREES:** *$14.50-$18*
DINNER: *M-Th 6-9:30, F-Sat 5:30-10* **ENTREES:** *$18-$32*
CHAMPAGNE BRUNCH: *Sun 11-2* **PRICE:** *3-course prix fixe $35*
CREDIT CARDS: *All major* **RESERVATIONS:** *Recommended*
DRESS: *Business casual* **CROSS STREET:** *11th* **PARKING:** *Complimentary valet*
METRO: *Mt. Vernon Sq/7th St-Convention Center*

HAD ENOUGH of flavored martinis or chicken wings after you've wrapped up a day at the office? You'll find a happy hour with a southern tilt on the broad veranda of the lovely old Morrison-Clark Inn, where early evenings on Wednesday and Thursday translate into restorative mint juleps and spiced pecans served by waiters in black vests. Come winter, the cocktail party moves indoors, and the drink choices switch to mulled cider and liqueur-laced coffees.

Stay on for dinner and you'll find yourself in a small room with a Victorian flavor. The windows, bordered in lace curtains, stretch skyward. Gold-framed mirrors and an antique sideboard rest against walls the color of rubies, while chandeliers drop from above.

The kitchen turns out fine soups. One day might yield a bowl of spicy carrot soup; another visit brings buttery clam chowder, full of tender clams, cubes of potato and a touch of sweetness from soft-cooked celery. The going gets bumpy early on, though, with mushy prawns paired with fruit salsa that doesn't mask the seafood's harsh seasoning. A skewer of duck, pineapple and papaya sheathed in rough-textured breading is served with what tastes like ketchup with a touch of heat.

Gold-framed mirrors and an antique sideboard rest against walls the color of rubies.

Dusted with kicky spices, the steak is decent, but it comes with a tower of sliced sweet potatoes, plus some baby carrots and broccoli rabe, all of which taste like reasons to jump on the Atkins bandwagon: They are bland. The best of the lot is probably the Cornish game hen, shiny from an Asian glaze and bedded on noodles.

It's a surprise, then, to find some charms among the desserts. Mango creme brulee tastes brightly of fruit and has just the right flame-singed glassy surface, and chocoholics get two pleasures in one with the chocolate tart topped with dense, midnight-colored chocolate sorbet.

Mr. K's ★

2121 K St. NW, Washington, DC (Downtown)
202-331-8868

LUNCH: *M-F 11:30-2:30* **ENTREES:** *$8-$18*
DINNER: *M-Th 2:30-11, F 2:30-11:30, Sat noon-11:30, Sun noon-11*
ENTREES: *$16-$38* **CREDIT CARDS:** *AE, DC, MC, V*
RESERVATIONS: *Recommended* **DRESS:** *Jacket preferred at dinner*
CROSS STREET: *21st* **PARKING:** *Complimentary valet after 5:45 pm*
METRO: *Foggy Bottom*

NO MATTER WHAT TIME your watch reads, Mr. K's makes it feel like 9 o'clock on a Saturday night—circa 1983. Its front drapes are always closed, its recessed lights are always low and the room, stocked with waiters in tuxedos and more gilt-edged touches than a nouveau-riche mansion, yields a style statement frozen in time. Think overstuffed chairs, dusty-rose-and-taupe color scheme and faux gold everywhere.

A lot of the cooking turns out to be a throwback, too. Shrimp toast is leathery and smacks of old age, while lamb with ginger and mushrooms is both gloppy and oily. Pork dumplings are pasty; sweet-and-sour ribs, while tender, emphasize sugar over tang. The seasoning is meant not to offend. Thus the scallops Marengo sauteed with scallions and peanuts in chili sauce only hints at heat —too bad, because the seafood is nice—and even the sorbet that bridges appetizer and entree is more about texture (rock-hard) than flavor (insipid).

> **Think overstuffed chairs, dusty-rose-and-taupe color scheme and faux gold everywhere.**

On a bright note, the spring rolls are crisp and piping hot, the Peking duck is decent (the waiters do all the bundling for you), and diners get a hot towel to refresh themselves with once they're settled in. Coffee is percolated at the table and chocolates come with the check. But I'll trade such frills for more polish on the plate, thanks.

Mykonos Grill

121 Congressional La., Rockville, MD
301-770-5999   www.mykonosgrill.com

LUNCH: *Tu-F 11:30-3:30, Sat-Sun noon-3:30* **ENTREES:** *$9.95-$19.75*
DINNER: *Tu-Th 3:30-10, F-Sat 3:30-10:30, Sun 3:30-9:30*
ENTREES: *$11.95-$22.95* **CLOSED:** *M* **CREDIT CARDS:** *All major*
RESERVATIONS: *Recommended* **DRESS:** *Business casual*
CROSS STREET: *Rockville Pike* **PARKING:** *Lot* **METRO:** *Twinbrook*

GREECE SPRINGS TO LIFE in this convivial suburban idyll. One cozy room suggests a faraway village courtyard in blue paint and white plaster; another looks onto an Aegean seascape (even if only by way of a mural). And in good weather, tables and pots of hanging flowers adorn an outdoor patio.

The menu plays along. Begin with stuffed grape leaves, whipped fish roe or eggplant split and filled with a blend of tomato, onion, white raisins and pine nuts. Venture further into the meal with tender pan-fried squid with garlicky potato dip, grilled rockfish accented with lemon and olive oil, or a trio of lamb chops accompanied by homey roast potatoes, carrots and soft-cooked green beans tossed with tomatoes.

There's nothing on the menu that you probably haven't encountered before, but even the standards are prepared with care. Rich green spinach and tangy feta cheese weave between sheets of crackling phyllo in an order of spanakopita, for instance, while moussaka translates into a surprisingly light sliced eggplant layered with meat and mashed potatoes so satiny that they resemble custard.

Periodically, a burst of flames interrupts conversation in the dining room, a spectacle that reminds us to try the pan-fried kasseri cheese, sprinkled with lemon juice and brandy and ignited at the table. Sure, the fireworks are fun, but even better is what happens as your tongue absorbs the crisp golden crust,

> **There's nothing on the menu that you probably haven't encountered before, but even the standards are prepared with care.**

gently sparked with citrus and alcohol, followed by a molten rivulet of cheese.

Given the setting and the cooking, it's small wonder that Sunday night looks like a party, nearly every seat filled. Is the host a bit gruff? Are the waiters too serious? At least their suggestions are helpful. Save space for dessert, which sidesteps Greek stereotypes. Ordering "desserts for two" brings very good baklava, walnut cake and phyllo-swaddled custard on a big plate. You can count calories tomorrow.

Natta Thai ★

153 Glyndon St. SE, Vienna, VA
703-242-4323

LUNCH: *M-Sat 11-3* **ENTREES:** *$5.95-$8.95*
DINNER: *Daily 5-10* **ENTREES:** *$6.95-$10.95*
CREDIT CARDS: *All major* **RESERVATIONS:** *No* **DRESS:** *Casual*
CROSS STREET: *Maple Avenue* **PARKING:** *Lot*
METRO: *Vienna/Fairfax-GMU/Dunn Loring-Merrifield*

DON'T EVERYBODY RUSH THE PLACE for a wicked plate of seafood stir-fried with chilies, garlic and basil. I've seen closets that are bigger than this fledgling Thai eatery, which probably accounts for its healthy carryout business.

Stick around to eat your food, though, and you'll experience sweet service in a pretty shoebox framed in peach-colored walls with pale blue trim. Ease in with bulbous chicken wings plumped with a mousselike filling of shrimp, crab and mushrooms or a slightly caramelized beef satay, juicy beneath its subtle curry seasoning. Then move on to pork and tender bamboo shoots draped in a creamy green curry, or whatever special your waitress encourages you to try. "The soft-shell crabs are fresh, not frozen," one of them shared on my midsummer visit.

> **Ease in with bulbous chicken wings plumped with a mousselike filling of shrimp, crab and mushrooms.**

Not every dish makes my hit parade. The shrimp in a bowl of nicely tangy hot-and-sour soup could be fresher, and the steamed vegetable dumplings are pasty and less appealing for their cloying soy sauce (note to kitchen: Turn down the sugar dial). Natta Thai is good to know about if you find yourself nearby, hungry and in search of a bit of pampering with your garden roll or duck salad.

Nectar

824 New Hampshire Ave. NW, Washington, DC (Foggy Bottom/West End)
202-298-8085   www.nectardc.com

LUNCH: *M-F 11:30-2:30*   **ENTREES:** *$14-$18*
DINNER: *Sun-Th 5-10, F-Sat 5-11*   **ENTREES:** *$25-$28*
CREDIT CARDS: *AE, V, MC*   **RESERVATIONS:** *Recommended*
DRESS: *Business casual*   **CROSS STREET:** *I Street NW*
PARKING: *$6 valet*   **METRO:** *Foggy Bottom*

WHO CARES IF THE DINING ROOM is small, cramped and dressed on a shoestring? That Nectar sits within walking distance of the Kennedy Center is reason enough to put this restaurant in your little black book of places to eat.

Location isn't its sole asset: There's plenty on chef Jamison Blankenship's modern American menu to engage you, too. Duck on a perfect puddle of pureed parsnips, and pumpkin soup floating crisp sweetbreads hint at a sophisticated hand in the kitchen. So does the (lunch-only) tuna burger, presented between sweet-potato brioche and accompanied by gorgeous, light-as-air potato chips: In the world of fish sandwiches, it comes in second only to Michel Richard's first-class model. Indeed, seafood is a strength here—and delicious details are the rule—be it the signature scallops crowned with matchsticks of chorizo for a sweet-racy marriage, or loup de mar, a beautiful piece of crisp-skinned bass poised on sweet peas and lapped with a lightly frothy kaffir leaf sauce.

The desserts, created by restaurant director Jarad Slipp (as suave a host as they come), manage to be both elegant and

Seafood is a strength here, and delicious details are the rule.

playful: A late-summer fruit crisp comes in a miniature Dutch oven, flanked by—aha!—a flute filled with a warm and frothy White Russian "milkshake."

Did I mention the small and exciting wine list, each choice offered by the glass as well as the bottle? Not all the staff live up to the example set by their masters, but eating at Nectar is like good theater. You don't want dinner to end.

New Fortune ★★

16515 S. Frederick Ave., Gaithersburg, MD
301-926-8828

OPEN: *Sun-Th 11 am-1 am, F-Sat 11 am-2 am* **ENTREES**: *$5.95-$14.50*
CREDIT CARDS: *All major* **RESERVATIONS**: *Recommended*
DRESS: *Casual* **CROSS STREET**: *S. Westland Drive*
PARKING: *Lot* **METRO**: *Shady Grove*

AWASH IN RED CARPET and illuminated with chandeliers, this Chinese feeding hall is about as intimate as Tiananmen Square. With 450 seats and a stage for banquets, it's built on the scale of a country with more than a billion citizens.

A diner could visit every day for half a year and still not sample every dish on the epic menu. Seafood dishes, including "salt and pepper" squid and scallops, tend to be the kitchen's strong suit. At lunch, when dim sum is served, New Fortune feels like a trip to Canton. A flotilla of food carts crisscross the expanse, their bow-tied attendants hawking everything from appetizer-size plates of roast duck to rice gruel, from spidery deep-fried taro cakes to spareribs draped in black bean sauce.

> **At lunch, when dim sum is served, New Fortune feels like a trip to Canton.**

Kids love the show, and parents appreciate the speedy service. Late dinner hours (until 1 a.m. weekdays, 2 a.m. weekends) and modest tabs make up for the occasional clinker from the kitchen.

New Heights   ★★

2317 Calvert St. NW, Washington, DC (Woodley Park)
202-234-4110   www.newheightsrestaurant.com

DINNER: *Sun-Th 5:30-10, F-Sat 5:30-11* **ENTREES:** *$18.50-$36*
BRUNCH: *Sun 11-2:30* **ENTREES:** *$9.50-$14*
CREDIT CARDS: *All major* **RESERVATIONS:** *Recommended*
DRESS: *Casual* **CROSS STREET:** *Connecticut Avenue NW*
PARKING: *Complimentary valet* **METRO:** *Woodley Park-Zoo/Adams Morgan*

GUIDED BY OWNER UMBI SINGH, this veteran contemporary-American restaurant has played host to a long line of innovative cooks, among them Alison Swope (now at Andale), Melissa Ballinger (Pizzeria Paradiso), Greggory Hill (David Greggory) and John Wabeck (Firefly). While there have been plenty of constants over the years—the black bean pâté has remained on the menu seemingly forever—each chef has also brought his or her personal touch.

A graduate of New York's French Culinary Institute, Arthur Rivaldo is the kitchen's current occupant, and much of what he does is very appealing. Garlicky langoustines ride to the table with an ultramoist

Once a trouble spot, desserts now give patrons reasons to linger.

corn tamale and a zesty dollop of salsa, while barbecued quail shows up with a fine avocado salad and crisp yuca fries. Blackened tuna with baby bok choy and a wasabi mayonnaise reminds diners that the chef feels free to traverse the world for inspiration. The restaurant considerately offers half and full portions of several dishes, including a lusty bison hanger steak and palak paneer, a nod to the owner's Indian background. Once a trouble spot, desserts now give patrons reasons to linger; fall tempted them with a ginger-redolent spice cake and bite-size apple turnovers dusted with sugar. And the wine list is a small treasure of boutique finds.

New Heights starts with a cozy bar on the ground floor (perfect for a quiet after-work drink) and continues up a flight of stairs to a long dining room, part of which is raised. My preference is for one of the tables hugging the broad windows, with their treetop views. Modern art dresses up the walls in shades of tangerine and blue-gray, and the place is made more interesting with a few triangular tables. New Heights may be nearly 18 years old, but it's aging gracefully.

Nick & Stef's ★★

601 F St. NW, Washington, DC (Penn Quarter)
202-661-5040

LUNCH: *M-Sat 11:30-3* **ENTREES:** *$14-$32*
DINNER: *M-Sat 5-11* **ENTREES:** *$18-$32*
CLOSED: *Sun (except MCI event nights)* **CREDIT CARDS:** *All major*
RESERVATIONS: *Recommended* **DRESS:** *Casual*
CROSS STREET: *6th* **PARKING:** *$10 valet on event nights*
METRO: *Gallery Place-Chinatown*

WHO SAYS A STEAKHOUSE has to be dark and macho? Nick & Stef's charts a modern path, dressing its dining room in pale wood and silky gold fabric and doling out sleek French knives along with its fine, dry-aged meat. An import from California with a tony bar on the side, it's the kind of place where women are made to feel as comfortable as men.

My ideal game plan starts with shrimp cocktail or a tangy Caesar salad and continues with a rib-eye or porterhouse, cooked the way I ask and best rounded out with luscious creamed spinach sprinkled with toasted bread crumbles for delicate crunch. Alas, the menu has been scaled back considerably since the restaurant's glamorous launch, when diners could choose from a dozen types of

My ideal game plan starts with shrimp cocktail or a tangy Caesar salad and continues with a rib-eye or porterhouse.

potato accompaniments alone and that Caesar salad was expertly tossed at the table and seasoned to your liking.

Once a trailblazer, Nick & Stef's is now just another good steakhouse in a city that is full of them. Its location in the MCI Center puts it within a couple of blocks of the Shakespeare Theatre, too, which means the restaurant can be hushed or hyper depending on whether there's anything going on in the area.

Nizam's

523 Maple Ave. W, Vienna, VA
703-938-8948   www.nizamsrestaurant.com

LUNCH: *Tu-F 11- 2:30* **ENTREES:** *$8.50-$17.50*
DINNER: *Tu-Th 5-10, F-Sat 5-11, Sun 4-9* **ENTREES:** *$13.95-$21.95*
PRE-THEATER: *Tu-Sat 5:30-8:30, 3-course prix fixe $49.95*
CLOSED: *M* **CREDIT CARDS:** *AE, D, MC, V*
RESERVATIONS: *Recommended* **DRESS:** *Casual*
CROSS STREET: *Nutley Street* **PARKING:** *Lot*
METRO: *Vienna/Fairfax-GMU*

DONER KEBAB IS TYPICALLY a weekend special in most Turkish restaurants, but Nizam Ozgur, whose guests come from far and wide for a taste of that classic lamb dish, has begun serving it every night that his kitchen is open. On any given day, Ozgur says, more than half of his audience orders doner kebab; one taste of the meat, carved into thin slices from a verticle spit and arranged on a plate with sauteed tomatoes and tangy yogurt, reveals why: It is a lusty feast.

Another excuse to check out the 26-year-old restaurant is manti, sheer house-made pasta plumped with spiced beef. But you don't have to be a dedicated carnivore to appreciate this kitchen, whose appetizers include slender "cigars" stuffed with dill-flecked feta cheese; grape leaves filled with rice, pine nuts and currants; and several ways to splurge on eggplant: fried,

You don't have to be a dedicated carnivore to appreciate this kitchen.

broiled and pureed into a smooth dip, and stuffed with a sweet-tangy mix of onions, tomatoes and garlic.

The service is personable (Ozgur's son just might be your waiter), and the dining room, with its pleasant music and red booths, is as good for romance as it is for a family night out.

Nora

★

2132 Florida Ave. NW, Washington, DC (Dupont Circle)

202-462-5143   www.noras.com

DINNER: *M-Th 5:30-10, F-Sat 5:30-10:30*
ENTREES: *$26-$31, tasting menus $58-$64*
CLOSED: *Sun*   **CREDIT CARDS:** *AE, D, MC, V*   **RESERVATIONS:** *Recommended*
DRESS: *Casual*   **CROSS STREET:** *R Street NW*   **PARKING:** *$5 valet*
METRO: *Dupont Circle*

BACK WHEN THIS RESTAURANT opened in 1979, and many American chefs were just beginning to take their inspiration from gardens rather than cans, Nora Pouillon was enlightening diners with additive-free beef raised on a diet of alfalfa and seaweed. Zoom ahead to today. Free-range chicken and organic mixed greens are as much a part of the dining scene as cell phones and online restaurant reservations.

Now recognized as "America's First Certified Organic Restaurant," Nora can pride itself on many things, from its loyal clientele of famous names to its fascinating, albeit pricey, wine list, featuring an all-star cast of pinot noirs from Burgundy and the United States. Watched over by a conscientious staff, this is an expense-account dining room that dresses as if every day were Casual Friday: Charming quilts adorn the whitewashed brick walls, and a wooden model airplane drops from the center of the beamed ceiling.

For all the history and all the accolades, though, Nora requires some digging to find a meal to remember. Duck confit partnered with lentils and caramelized pears is best for its fruit, while fish steamed in paper with baby turnips, bok choy and red wine sauce tastes like spa food, more penance than pleasure. An appetizer of beef short ribs tucked into a crisp quesadilla and ignited with a wicked salsa is fine, but the dish looks out of place on a menu of this caliber.

What's simple on the ever-changing menu is what tends to be best: crisp-skinned mackerel anointed with lemon-caper butter and treated to roasted artichokes, for instance, and a tart, flaky and not too sweet, incorporating whatever fruit is in season. Consistency might not be a hallmark of Nora, but commitment is: Try to name another restaurant that bothers to triple-filter the water in your glass.

Obelisk

2029 P St. NW, Washington, DC (Dupont Circle)
202-872-1180

DINNER: *Tu-Sat 6-10* **PRICE:** *5-course prix fixe $58*
CLOSED: *Sun-M* **CREDIT CARDS:** *DC, MC, V*
RESERVATIONS: *Recommended* **DRESS:** *Casual*
CROSS STREET: *21st* **PARKING:** *Street*
METRO: *Dupont Circle*

O BELISK IS SUCH A REASSURING RESTAURANT. Small, spare and softly lit, the 36-seat dining room gives the illusion of someone's home. Its staff doesn't change much; the servers, helpful and gracious, are so knowledgeable about the food that you'd swear they knew the recipes by heart. And season after season, the kitchen offers some of the finest Italian cooking outside that country.

Chef Peter Pastan may be an American, but his spirit is across the ocean, which means he cooks to the tune of the season and knows that good ingredients don't need much embellishment on their way to the table. Obelisk's set-price menu spans five courses, with no more than

Fine breads welcome you, and dessert sends you home on a sweet high.

three or four choices per course. Still, it's tough deciding between supple fish ravioli, glossed with butter sauce, and feathery wide noodles tossed with chanterelles and fresh thyme. A knob of anchovy paste makes for a macho beef filet, while a green sauce that tastes of an herb garden enhances a plate of sweet grilled shrimp.

Fine breads welcome you, and dessert sends you home on a sweet high; the ethereal Amarone-infused custard tastes like silk crossed with wine. From the handwritten menu to the band of mirrors positioned at eye level, a design detail that allows everyone a view, Obelisk is a restaurant of quiet distinction.

Oceanaire Seafood Room ★★

1201 F St. NW, Washington, DC (Downtown)
202-347-2277   www.theoceanaire.com

LUNCH: *M-F 11:30-5* **ENTREES:** *$8.95-$29.95*
DINNER: *M-Th 5-10, F-Sat 5-11, Sun 5-9* **ENTREES:** *$15.95-$39.95*
CREDIT CARDS: *All major* **RESERVATIONS:** *Recommended*
DRESS: *Business casual* **CROSS STREET:** *12th* **PARKING:** *$7 valet at dinner*
METRO: *Metro Center*

DINERS STEP BACK IN TIME at this dashing ode to fish, where meals begin with a complimentary relish tray, big band music plays in the background, and the bathroom doors indicate "Gents" or "Powder Room." Sleek as an ocean liner—say, the *Queen Mary*—the vast dining room is a looker, decorated as it is with outsized red leather booths and more curves than at Hugh Hefner's manse.

Consider some oysters on the half shell to start: There are typically a dozen varieties from which to choose, and they come to the table nicely shucked and glistening. "Try not to use these," a waiter instructs, pointing to the cocktail sauce and mignonette that accompany the bivalves, which are so fresh and sweet they shouldn't be slurped with anything but a sip of white wine.

The menu is epic and changes daily, but there are a few constants: lovely crab cakes, fine grilled squid, and shrimp de jonge, an old-fashioned recipe featuring baked butterflied shrimp, lightly breaded and spiked with cayenne and

A seafood restaurant with the sensibility (and prices) of a steakhouse, Oceanaire is not for the faint-hearted.

paprika. Pay attention to anything your waiter recommends, like the Panamanian "bigeye" tuna, which looks like steak, cuts like silk and gets an Asian accent with pickled ginger and seaweed salad. Crisp-seared coho salmon might sit on a pool of mustard cream, while sturgeon can be had "dirty"—lightly blackened in the Cajun fashion—yet balanced with mango relish.

A seafood restaurant with the sensibility (and prices) of a steakhouse, Oceanaire is not for the faint-hearted. A side dish of creamed corn brims with almost a bushel's worth of that sweet vegetable; the hash browns are the size of a hub cap; and a request for fruit crisp yields enough dessert for a quartet of eaters. Look elsewhere if you prefer to dine in peace. During the lunch and dinner rushes, Oceanaire rocks and roars.

Olazzo ★

7921 Norfolk Ave., Bethesda, MD
301-654-9496

LUNCH: *M-F 11:30-2:30* **ENTREES:** *$5.50-$10*
DINNER: *Sun-Th 5-9:30, F-Sat 5-10:30* **ENTREES:** *$10.50-$15*
CREDIT CARDS: *All major* **RESERVATIONS:** *No*
DRESS: *Casual* **CROSS STREET:** *Cordell Avenue*
PARKING: *Street* **METRO:** *Bethesda*

IF YOU'RE LOOKING for stuffed zucchini blossoms or tagliatelle with sea urchin, this is not the Italian restaurant for you. But if it's simple, homey flavors with a Middle American bent you're after, come on in.

Big, fresh-tasting clams adorn a turban of linguine, hot and garlicky, while meatballs nearly the size of tennis balls show up on penne washed with a light tomato sauce. Pasta cardinale teams bites of chicken with sun-dried tomatoes that lend color and zip to its cream sauce.

Pay attention to the recitation of specials, for these dishes tend to show the kitchen at its best: One day it was the trout, simply grilled and accented with citrus, that snared a winner. Good on its own, the fish was paired with nice skin-on mashed potatoes and bright asparagus. Plump and plentiful, steamed mussels bathe in a lemony white wine broth.

Olazzo can be quirky. From across the street, diners are drawn like moths to what they think is a dining room with a flickering hearth; once inside the dark cave of a restaurant, they discover that the flames framed in brick are faux, just a nonstop DVD of burning logs. The young staff aims to please but is short on finesse, which means dishes tend to be auctioned off ("Who gets the primavera?")

> **Pay attention to the recitation of specials, for these dishes tend to show the kitchen at its best.**

rather than placed in front of the people who ordered them. Even so, it's hard not to have fun with Dean Martin singing "That's Amore" in the background and fried calamari served in what looks like a martini glass designed for the Hulk.

Old Ebbitt Grill ★

675 15th St. NW, Washington, DC (Downtown)
202-347-4801 www.ebbitt.com

BREAKFAST: *M-F 7:30-11* **ENTREES:** *$5.95-$9.95*
LUNCH: *M-F 11-5* **ENTREES:** *$7.95-$20.95*
DINNER: *M-F 5-midnight, Sat-Sun 4-midnight (light fare until 1 am)*
ENTREES: *$12.95-$20.95*
BRUNCH: *Sat-Sun 8:30-4* **ENTREES:** *$8.95-$20.95*
CREDIT CARDS: *All major* **RESERVATIONS:** *Recommended*
DRESS: *Casual* **CROSS STREET:** *F Street NW*
PARKING: *Complimentary valet after 6, all day Sun* **METRO:** *Metro Center*

SECRET SERVICE AGENTS, tourists, business types—everyone seems to end up in downtown Washington's grand Victorian-style saloon, conveniently located near the White House and dressed in dark wood, gleaming brass, antique gas chandeliers and enough green velvet to suggest a forest.

A member of the Clyde's restaurant empire, Old Ebbitt Grill is a great convenience: usually open for at least two meals a day, big enough to accommodate any size group, and offering an American menu that takes into account plain and fancy tastes. And the service is as friendly as it gets.

But I'd be willing to sacrifice some of the variety and smiles for food that had more charm. The once-great hamburgers aren't so great anymore, and they come with fries that smack of a factory. At the height of summer, crumbled feta and fresh basil do their best to revive a salad dominated by large, pink, cottony slices of tomato. Breakfast finds decent beef hash and stiff pancakes; lunch yields good fish and chips with creamy coleslaw—and thin, overcooked liver with onions.

Old Ebbitt Grill is a great convenience: usually open for at least two meals a day, big enough to accommodate any size group, and offering an American menu that takes into account plain and fancy tastes.

So why bother? Because no restaurant in the city has a better raw bar than this one. Oyster lovers can always count on lots of choices of pristine bivalves and something crisp and refreshing to knock them back with.

Old Europe   ★★

2434 Wisconsin Ave. NW, Washington, DC (Glover Park)
202-333-7600   www.old-europe.com

LUNCH: *Tu-Sat 11:30-2:30, Sun 12:30-4* **ENTREES:** *$4.75-$13.25*
DINNER: *M-Sat 5-10, Sun 4-9* **ENTREES:** *$14.35-$22.85*
CREDIT CARDS: *AE, DC, MC, V* **RESERVATIONS:** *Recommended*
DRESS: *Casual* **CROSS STREET:** *Calvert Street NW*
PARKING: *Street* **METRO:** *Tenleytown-AU*

OLD EUROPE on a Friday night feels like Oktoberfest even in spring-time, what with the tables pushed together to seat groups of beer-drinking friends and a pianist pounding out cheerful tunes.

Even at a quiet weekday lunch, there's no mistaking this room for anything but Teutonic. The air smells sweetly of pork and sauerkraut, and the walls are crammed with enough wooden crests, antique steins and idyllic landscapes to outfit a small castle. It borders on a Disney-esque stereotype, except that it's just what you might find abroad.

The kitchen is determined that you won't leave hungry. Most of the appetizers are the size of light entrees, while the main courses appear to be built for two. Sauerbraten is flanked with light potato dumplings sauced with a subtle brown gravy and a nest of soft, shredded cabbage whose flavor dances from sweet to sour. Sausages of snap and savor ride to the table with crisp herbed potato pancakes and lush, caraway-scented sauerkraut. Veal is pounded thin,

> **The air smells sweetly of pork and sauerkraut, and the walls are crammed with enough wooden crests, antique steins and idyllic landscapes to outfit a small castle.**

swabbed in egg and dusted with bread crumbs, then pan-fried to a crackling gold. Spritzed with lemon, it's a Wiener schnitzel of distinction. Acting like bookends to these hearty meals are seasonal beers and fine desserts (splurge on the decadent Sacher torte, chocolate cake punctuated with apricot filling).

In a field that doesn't encourage longevity, Old Europe is a grand dame with more than half a century of gemütlichkeit to its credit.

Old Glory

★

3139 M St. NW, Washington, DC (Georgetown)
202-337-3406   www.oldglorybbq.com

LUNCH: *M-Sat 11:30-3* **ENTREES:** *$9.95-$20.95*
DINNER: *Daily 3-midnight (bar menu until 1 am)* **ENTREES:** *$9.95-$20.95*
BUFFET BRUNCH: *Sun 11-3* **PRICE:** *$11.95*
CREDIT CARDS: *All major* **RESERVATIONS:** *No*
DRESS: *Casual* **CROSS STREET:** *Wisconsin Avenue NW*
PARKING: *Street* **METRO:** *Foggy Bottom*

BAM! A MEAL IS OFF TO AN ENTERTAINING START when your server bids you welcome, noisily branding a paper-topped table with an inky blue stamp of the restaurant's eagle insignia.

The brick-and-wood Old Glory ignores its Georgetown address to play the part of a roadside barbecue joint. The air smells of woodsy smoke; the cooking whisks you to the South. As in fried green tomatoes, chopped beef brisket and half a dozen different sauces—some tangy, some hot, others mustardy or sweetly spicy—that acknowledge the heavy competition for supremacy among the country's many barbecue capitals.

You won't leave hungry. The meaty, oak-grilled chicken wings are as pumped up as anything you've spotted at Gold's Gym, and a combination platter of pulled pork shoulder and beef brisket (both satisfying, but better with sauce) could carry even a trencherman through tonight and

The air smells of woodsy smoke; the cooking whisks you to the South.

tomorrow. Although the beans bake up too sweet, both the potato salad and collard greens bring to mind a good home kitchen. And there are smiles all around when a giant brownie, buried in ice cream, nuts and whipped cream, shows up, followed by free Tootsie Roll Pops with the check.

O'Learys

310 Third St., Annapolis, MD
410-263-0884

DINNER: *M-Th 5-10, F-Sat 5-11, Sun 5-9* **ENTREES:** *$23-$49*
CREDIT CARDS: *AE, DC, MC, V* **RESERVATIONS:** *Recommended*
DRESS: *Business casual* **CROSS STREET:** *Severn Avenue*
PARKING: *Lot* **METRO:** *No*

SOME RESTAURANTS LEAVE YOU guessing as to where you are. Not this place. Sea grass waves around the façade, photographs of Annapolis grace the walls inside, and the windows in the handsome main dining room capture a slice of the waterfront in the distance. (Locals might remember the location as the former residence of Capt. Herb Sadler, a fisherman who sold his catch in front of his home way back when.)

Come hungry. The portions are substantial, and every dish is accessorized with gusto. Order grilled mahi-mahi and the fish turns up with an Asian-flavored glaze, fragrant Basmati rice and a tropical salsa that goes down like a trip to Hawaii—pretty swell. It doesn't need the nut-crusted shrimp that accompany it, but I have to admit: Those crunchy shrimp are as addictive as potato chips.

It would be hard to find better soft-shell crabs than the ones here, so plump and juicy beneath their golden coats, spiked with cayenne and brightened with lemon zest. Just as memorable: sweetly fresh shrimp curled on

> **It would be hard to find better soft-shell crabs than the ones here.**

top of a warm cornmeal cake veined with smoky bits of bacon. When a waitress informs you that the crab cakes at O'Learys are "held together by sheer willpower," it's nice to find out she's almost right. Abundant with jumbo lump crabmeat, the cakes are also rich with mayonnaise, softly crunchy with Japanese bread crumbs and subtly seasoned with Old Bay spice and (believe it or not) vanilla. Veer from the seafood dishes, though, and you might be disappointed.

Many of the good-looking people who frequent O'Learys look as if they just dropped by for a bite after a day on the boat. They seem pleased to be docked in a place where the service is as agreeable as the cooking and the wine list is taken seriously.

Olives ★★

1600 K St. NW, Washington, DC (Downtown)
202-452-1866   www.toddenglish.com

LUNCH: *M-F 11:30-2:30* **ENTREES:** *$13-$19*
DINNER: *M-Sat 5:30-10:30* **ENTREES:** *$18.50-$32*
PRE-THEATER: *M-Th 5:30-6:45, 3-course prix fixe $35*
CLOSED: *Sun* **CREDIT CARDS:** *All major*
RESERVATIONS: *Recommended* **DRESS:** *Business casual*
CROSS STREET: *16th* **PARKING:** *$6 valet at dinner*
METRO: *Farragut North/West*

NEW ENGLAND MEETS ITALY in this offshoot of the original Olives, the Boston restaurant made famous by chef Todd English, who now counts similarly named kitchens around the country.

Herbed ricotta, mussels and diced potatoes might decorate a pizza, its thin crust perfumed with smoke from Olive's impressive wood-fired oven. Pastas include floppy tortelli stuffed with butternut squash and sauced with brown butter, and the more original black olive pasta, tangy from its goat cheese filling and zingy with a ring of tomato sauce. From the ocean comes rockfish, grilled to a fine crisp and bedded on a clam-flecked risotto; from the field there are lamb loin chops that could be more tender and flavorful but get a boost from a chunky wreath of chopped eggplant and lamb sausage.

> From the ocean comes rockfish, grilled to a fine crisp and bedded on a clam-flecked risotto.

Bringing up the rear of the long menu, meanwhile, are a fluffy lemon meringue tart and a crème brulee tingling with passion fruit. These are large portions of food that don't shy away from brassy flavors and multiple accessories (that rockfish comes with both steamed and fried clams, plus an herbed broth).

Come to think of it, everything's big at Olives: the servers' smiles, the background music, the multileveled dining room in shades of green that could pass for the backdrop to an opera. Solo diners make a beeline for the counter overlooking the busy open kitchen; consider a seat in front of the action a free cooking class.

Ortanique ★

730 11th St. NW, Washington, DC (Downtown)
202-393-0975   www.ortaniqueontheweb.com

LUNCH: *M-F noon-2:30*   **ENTREES:** *$11-$16*
DINNER: *M-Th, Sat 5:30-10, F 5:30-11*   **ENTREES:** *$20-$35*
CHEF'S TABLE: *M 7:30, 5-course prix fixe $50*
CLOSED: *Sun*   **CREDIT CARDS:** *AE, DC, MC, V*
RESERVATIONS: *Recommended*   **DRESS:** *Casual*
CROSS STREET: *G Street NW*   **PARKING:** *$8 valet at dinner*
METRO: *Metro Center*

ELLOW CURTAINS PLUNGE from a ceiling two stories high, and Technicolor fish cavort in a 350-gallon aquarium that provides almost as much fuel for conversation as the minty mojitos half the drinkers at the bar appear to be nursing. The soundtrack brings to mind an island getaway, and so does much of the menu. Anyone for some conch fritters?

"Cuisine of the sun" trumpets the menu, and it's true; this kitchen gives a tropical lilt to several commonplace restaurant dishes, like crab cakes, which here are shaped from jumbo lump crab, the Japanese bread crumbs called panko, a touch of curry and little else, then draped with fruit salsa, to nice effect. Calamari shows off flawless frying and tiny shocks of heat in its seasoning. The Caesar salad is also unorthodox, and delicious, scattered with crisp won ton threads and colorful with halved cherry tomatoes. Seviche is a given in a restaurant like this, but all the versions I've tried here are out of balance, unpleasantly tart (though the accompanying tostone sandwiched with guacamole is scrumptious). Baby back ribs fried in a wisp of batter are meaty and tender but lack spunk. If meat is what you're after, try the fist-sized jerked pork chop. It tingles with spices and gets a pleasing raisin sauce.

> **Calamari shows off flawless frying and tiny shocks of heat in its seasoning.**

If the food is mixed, the entertainment keeps me coming back. The seductive bar, illuminated with lamps in pineapple shapes, is a fun place to meet for drinks (beer and wine are half price on Monday and Wednesday), and live music sweetens the scene on Tuesday night and Thursday through Saturday.

Oval Room ★★

800 Connecticut Ave. NW, Washington, DC (Downtown)
202-463-8700   www.ovalroom.com

LUNCH: *M-F 11:30-3*   **ENTREES:** *$12.95-$22.95*
DINNER: *M-Th 5:30-10, F-Sat 5:30-10:30*   **ENTREES:** *$16-$25*
CLOSED: *Sun*   **CREDIT CARDS:** *All major*
RESERVATIONS: *Recommended*   **DRESS:** *Casual*
CROSS STREET: *H Street NW*   **PARKING:** *Complimentary valet at dinner*
METRO: *Farragut West*

THE NAME REMINDS DINERS that the White House is nearby, while the people who flock here, at lunch in particular, tend to be those who either shape or make headlines. Hello, Mr. Stephanopoulos. Nice to see you, Senator Feinstein. ("It's pundit day!" a server jokes as she surveys the roomful of competing talking heads one busy afternoon.) A small row of tables near the front window offers occupants that great Washington asset: both privacy and a view of the room.

The Oval Room isn't just a place to see and be seen but also a fine modern-American restaurant—enough of the time. Bite-size cheese puffs add pizzazz to the bread basket. Salads and soups all taste as good as they look. A rich lobster bisque, nice grilled shrimp, and moist trout on a

Heed your waiter's suggestions; mine pushed veal medallions, and I was happy to have made their acquaintance.

bed of lentils and bacon-laced collard greens reveal a kitchen that knows its way around ingredients from the water.

Heed your waiter's suggestions; mine pushed veal medallions, and I was happy to have made their acquaintance after tasting the extraordinarily succulent meat, poised on a puree of fava beans and ringed with sauteed chanterelles. But a pork chop proves lackluster, a braised lamb shank is tender but just adequate. Pastas run from lovely gnocchi with fall mushrooms and truffle cream to fusilli smothered with a muddle of white beans, bitter greens and shrimp. And desserts are mixed.

A cosseting staff helps make any meal more enjoyable, though, and the rooms, dressed up with contemporary art on walls in a soothing shade of celery, weave style with comfort. A bit more consistency from the kitchen is all that is missing from this otherwise pleasing picture.

Palena

3529 Connecticut Ave. NW, Washington, DC (Cleveland Park)

202-537-9250   www.palenarestaurant.com

DINNER: *Cafe M-Sat 5:30-10, Dining Room Tu-Sat 5:30-10* **CAFE ENTREES:** *$9*
DINING ROOM: *3-course prix fixe $50; 4-course $57; 5-course $64*
CLOSED: *Sun* **CREDIT CARDS:** *AE, D, MC, V*
RESERVATIONS: *Recommended* **DRESS:** *Business casual*
CROSS STREET: *Porter Street NW* **PARKING:** *Street* **METRO:** *Cleveland Park*

FRANK RUTA MAY BE THE LEAST KNOWN of Washington's top chefs. Year after year, the former White House chef quietly goes about his business, eschewing the limelight in his small basement kitchen. Though he has them, there are no raves framed on the restaurant's walls; the chef's appearances in the dining room are so infrequent, they make sightings of Halley's comet seem like a regular gig.

He's probably too busy turning out delicate raviolini filled with pureed sweet corn and arranged on a plate with buttery chanterelles, tender cockles and sorrel. Or maybe he's grilling one of the city's most succulent beef rib steaks, which arrives with a posse of sauteed fingerling potatoes, bright parsley puree and roasted pepper stuffed with sweet onion relish. Wherever he can, he personalizes his food, making his own noodles and curing his own bacon for a lovely pork tenderloin.

> **The former White House chef quietly goes about his business, eschewing the limelight in his small basement kitchen.**

Desserts don't surprise like they used to; the cookies and caramels are as good as ever, but the pastry chef might want to come up with some fresh finishes.

Christened for Ruta's mother's birthplace in Italy, Palena has been made more accessible with the introduction of a bar menu in the front cafe. There, perched at a barstool or tucked in a booth, patrons dig into hamburgers, roasted half chicken, Caesar salads, maybe a simple pasta or precisely cooked fish—everything a comfort and everything a role model for the competition.

P.S. At the cafe, everything is also priced at $9 each.

Palm ★ ★

1225 19th St. NW, Washington, DC (Dupont Circle)
202-293-9091   www.thepalm.com

LUNCH: *M-F 11:45-3* **ENTREES:** *$11-$19*
DINNER: *M-F 3-10, Sat 6-10, Sun 5:30-9:30* **ENTREES:** *$15-$38*
CREDIT CARDS: *All major* **RESERVATIONS:** *Recommended*
DRESS: *Casual* **CROSS STREET:** *N Street NW*
PARKING: *Complimentary valet at dinner* **METRO:** *Dupont Circle*

WHEN IT COMES TO FRESH GOSSIP and newsworthy names, no steakhouse in town can compete with the Palm. Day and night, the place swells with movers and shakers, some of whose likenesses are caricatured on the walls. Women are welcome, but the Palm is really a guy's place, back-slappingly boisterous and watched over by hosts who look as if they've seen it all and servers who play the roles of confidants.

After a chopped salad perked up with anchovies or a bowl of lobster bisque with enough cream to sink a ship, meat is the way to go, naturally: The rib-eye is thick and succulent, lamb chops come three plump models per order, and the New York strip tastes prime and aged because it is. Further, all the meat is cooked just the way you want it (not so the cottage fries, which might show up with an unfortunate bronze, rather than gold, tan).

> **The rib-eye is thick and succulent, lamb chops come three plump models per order, and the New York strip tastes prime and aged because it is.**

Shrimp cocktail is standard issue, creamed spinach actually tastes of its vegetable, and the Key lime pie is too big and too sweet to finish.

The Palm isn't a wise choice for a romantic rendezvous: Its hardwood floors and pressed-tin ceiling trap the noise and make conversation difficult, particularly at prime time. But you'll feel like an insider when you look up from a great piece of meat to catch James Carville or Wolf Blitzer strolling in.

SECOND LOCATION: *1750 Tysons Blvd., McLean, VA, 703-917-0200*

Perry's ★

1811 Columbia Rd. NW, Washington, DC (Adams Morgan)
202-234-6218   www.perrysadamsmorgan.com

DINNER: *Daily 5:30-11*   **ENTREES:** *$14-$19*
BUFFET BRUNCH: *Sun 10:30-2:30*   **PRICE:** *$22.95*
CREDIT CARDS: *All major*   **RESERVATIONS:** *Recommended*
DRESS: *Casual*   **CROSS STREET:** *Biltmore Street NW*
PARKING: *$10 valet after 6:30*
METRO: *Woodley Park-Zoo/Adams Morgan*

NOT SO LONG AGO, this long-lived second-story restaurant in Adams Morgan was best known for its rooftop tables in good weather and its drag brunches on Sunday, period. Save for sushi, much of the menu tasted as if it were on life support.

Enter Sidra Forman, whose minimalist philosophy at the late Ruppperts was based on small portions of dishes that spoke to the season. At Perry's, she serves as more of a teacher than a cook, preaching the joys of careful shopping and simple handling. "It's all about ingredients and love and care," she tells the kitchen staff, which has done an admirable job of following her lead. So pumpkin soup, scattered with a few pumpkin seeds, relies almost exclusively on the richness of the roasted vegetable for its flavor, and veal sweetbreads get their spark from a slight char and some vinegary lentils. In another quietly delicious dish, the sweetness of seared scallops plays off roasted fresh corn.

You may not notice the absence of butter with your bread basket, which arrives instead with ramekins of minced olives and caramelized onions for spreading on the slices. Roast chicken proves

> **Veal sweetbreads get their spark from a slight char and some vinegary lentils.**

meaty and juicy, and it's simply but winningly arranged with fingerling potatoes and snap peas. Lamb chops might be cooked a moment too long, but they are flattered by a garnish of fresh figs.

Reached by a steep flight of stairs, Perry's loftlike dining room is an inviting place to find yourself. Its red curtains and dark wood are balanced by low orange couches and a light fixture that resembles an octopus—a mix of serious and whimsical design details that continue with a small fireplace to one side and a bright sushi counter up front. The clientele, meanwhile, looks as if it just stepped from an MTV audience: It runs young and current.

Persimmon ★

7003 Wisconsin Ave., Bethesda, MD
301-654-9860

LUNCH: *M-F 11:30-2* **ENTREES:** *$11-$14*
DINNER: *Daily 5-10* **ENTREES:** *$19-$27*
PRE-THEATER: *Daily 5-6, 3-course prix fixe $30*
CREDIT CARDS: *All major* **RESERVATIONS:** *Recommended*
DRESS: *Casual* **CROSS STREET:** *Leland Street* **PARKING:** *Street*
METRO: *Bethesda*

MUCH LIKE THE BRILLIANT FRUIT that gives this storefront dining room its name, Persimmon is tangy, sweet and not at all shy. There's nothing subtle about ringlets of sauteed squid and diced tomato on a creamy puddle of rosemary-veined polenta, or a trio of big ravioli with a punchy blue cheese and mushroom filling and a dash of white truffle oil. Fried oysters are a house signature; their nubby coats are fired by wasabi, and the Asian theme is extended by a dipping sauce on the side.

Nice as the golden crab cakes are, with their roasted-corn salad, stuff from the turf tends to outshine stuff from the surf. The sage-scented grilled pork chop is very good, the barbecued rack of lamb showy and delicious, with a pecan crust and a mustard-tinged potato gratin alongside.

> **Nice as the golden crab cakes are, with their roasted-corn salad, stuff from the turf tends to outshine stuff from the surf.**

The small space is loud at rush hour and in need of some design rethinking; at these prices, should we really have to look at bunches of fake flowers on the wall? Persimmon the fruit makes a cameo appearance only at dessert, in a lovely cheesecake.

Pesce

★★

2016 P St. NW, Washington, DC (Dupont Circle)
202-466-3474

LUNCH: *M-F 11:30-2:30* **ENTREES:** *$13.95-$17.95*
DINNER: *M-Th 5:30-10, F-Sat 5:30-10:30, Sun 5-9:30*
ENTREES: *$13.95-$23.95*
CREDIT CARDS: *All major*
RESERVATIONS: *Recommended (dinner reservations for parties of 6 or more only)*
DRESS: *Casual* **CROSS STREET:** *20th* **PARKING:** *$5 valet at dinner*
METRO: *Dupont Circle*

T HE ROSTER OF COOKS who have worked at Pesce during its decade-long run in Dupont Circle reads like a directory of Washington chefs: David Craig, now at Black's Bar and Kitchen in Bethesda; Jamie Stachowski, currently running eCiti Cafe & Bar in McLean; Justin Nielsen, who came to Pesce from the Danish Embassy. Their strengths vary, but each has put his stamp on what began as a partnership between superstar chefs Roberto Donna and Jean-Louis Palladin. Neither founder is involved anymore (Donna sold his interest several years ago, Palladin died in 2001), but their original idea of a casual place for people to find a good piece of fish survives.

Simplicity and freshness rule. Too bad the choices, scribbled on a roving chalkboard, change every day; you can never count on finding a favorite dish. That was my thought as I cleaned a plate of rockfish, moist beneath a nubby polenta crust and supported by colorful diced beets and lentils. I'd be happy to try the whole baby flounder again, too, if it ever comes back. Dotted with garlic and herbs, the fish had a hot, snowy-white interior and was simply

The kitchen's pastas are like little black dresses: always in good taste.

but beautifully served with grilled red and yellow peppers, onions and eggplant. The kitchen's pastas, meanwhile, are like little black dresses: always in good taste.

Pesce doesn't look like the sort of place where you'd expect to shell out $70 a head for dinner, though I like its loose style. Whimsical wooden fish and sunny table covers lend a splash of color to the small dining area, which includes a cozy bar. I'm always glad to find myself there, eating seafood that tastes as if it had been caught that same morning and prepared by cooks who know what they're doing, no matter which one is running the kitchen at any given meal.

Pizzeria Paradiso ★★

3282 M St. NW, Washington, DC (Georgetown)
202-337-1245

OPEN: *M-Th 11:30-11, F-Sat 11:30-midnight, Sun noon-10*
ENTREES: *$7.95-$17.95* **CREDIT CARDS:** *D, DC, MC, V*
RESERVATIONS: *No* **DRESS:** *Casual*
CROSS STREET: *Potomac Street NW* **PARKING:** *Street*
METRO: *Foggy Bottom*

I T LOOKS STRANGE: no lines trailing from the entrance of a Pizzeria Paradiso? Yet that's the case at the Georgetown offshoot of the popular Dupont Circle eatery, thanks to double the number of seats in this newer location.

As with the original Paradiso, there's a big oven painted with a sunburst, and the Neopolitan-style pies that share the same toppings—salami, pesto, spinach, mussels—and oak-wood-perfumed crusts. A current favorite is a pillowy round scattered with tomato chunks, garlic, Parmesan and botargo (dried gray mullet roe); a soft-cooked egg hidden beneath the cheese yields a pleasant surprise.

Pizza is the main attraction but not the only lure. Both locations serve a fine antipasto of cured Italian meats and cheese; panini ranging from roasted vegetables to pork sharpened with hot pepper and garlic; and simple, satisfying endings: Hope for pistachio gelato or sliced pears splashed with Marsala and baked to a pleasant sweet softness. Details matter. The lemonade is fresh, the sangria packs a punch.

Pizza is the main attraction but not the only lure.

Small and snug, the Dupont Circle restaurant is set off with a barrel-shaped ceiling painted to suggest stone ruins and a soft blue sky. Its sibling feels airier, with big front windows overlooking the street. And it's warm, too, with brick walls and beams overhead. Looking for a place to celebrate for less than a king's ransom? Just inside the front door there's a cozy bar; downstairs, a private party room with its own fireplace.

SECOND LOCATION: *2029 P St. NW, Washington, DC, 202-223-1245*

Prime Rib ★★

2020 K St. NW, Washington, DC (Downtown)
202-466-8811   www.theprimerib.com

LUNCH: *M-F 11:30-3* **ENTREES:** *$10-$25*
DINNER: *M-Th 5-11, F-Sat 5-11:30* **ENTREES:** *$19.95-$36.95*
CREDIT CARDS: *AE, DC, MC, V* **RESERVATIONS:** *Recommended*
DRESS: *Jacket & tie* **PARKING:** *Complimentary valet at dinner*
CROSS STREET: *20th* **METRO:** *Farragut West/North*

ITS LOYAL CLIENTELE knows the Prime Rib as more than just a restaurant. Set off with Louis Icart lithographs of scantily clad women on gilt-edged black walls, the Prime Rib is a ritual, an event, a celebration of a time when real men didn't know what quiche was, let alone eat it. There are no female servers in evidence, but there is a dress code: "Jackets and ties are requested for gentlemen," callers are informed when they make reservations.

Take the place at its word and indulge in its signature attraction. The prime rib is as thick as the White Pages and as rosy as you request. Bursting with juices, the meat is served with a heap of horseradish for a bit of electricity. No other protein on the menu—not the veal chop, not the rack of lamb or the New York strip steak—can match the prime rib for savor. Of the fish dishes, rockfish is simply broiled and served with lemon.

The best of the beginnings are also the richest: creamy crab cakes and velvety lobster bisque.

The appetizers embrace the usual steakhouse staples. Fat shrimp drape over the rim of a cocktail glass, poised to take a dip in a sinus-clearing cocktail sauce. Oysters on the half shell tend to be fresh but thin, even in colder months. Caesar salad comes out punching with a tangy dressing. The best of the beginnings are also the richest: creamy crab cakes and velvety lobster bisque. As for side dishes, crisp potato skins and green beans tossed with tomato and onion outshine the gluey creamed spinach.

The Prime Rib refers to itself as "the civilized steak house," a promise it frequently delivers. But not always. Unless you are a known commodity, the greeting at the door can be gruff and the waiters tend to go through the motions of serving. The last time I was in, no one ever bothered to pour my wine or check back after the food was delivered. For $100 a head one expects more pampering.

Even at its off moments, though, the Prime Rib has the competition beat as far as comfort is concerned, from the leather chairs to the live piano, even at lunch. There are more delicious places to go for a classic steak experience, but none are as handsome or as steeped in tradition as this address.

Rafagino ★

9570 Old Keene Mill Rd., Burke, VA
703-451-1570

DINNER: *Tu-Th 5-9, F-Sat 5-10, Sun 5-9* **ENTREES:** *$12.95-$24.95*
CLOSED: *M* **CREDIT CARDS:** *All major* **RESERVATIONS:** *Recommended*
DRESS: *Business casual* **CROSS STREET:** *Lee Chapel Road*
PARKING: *Lot* **METRO:** *No*

NEVER MIND THE RESTAURANT'S shopping center location or its generic facade. Rafagino is full of little surprises, and one of them is the understated elegance of its dining room. This is the domain of the dashing Paulo Carvalho, as debonair as any maitre d' in Washington, who greets newcomers as if they were regulars and regulars as if they were intimates. Even before you take your first bite of food, he and his staff make you glad you're there.

Several appetizers keep you in that buoyant frame of mind, and they come from a kitchen headed by Carvalho's wife, Rosa Buono. Mussels show up in a hinged copper pot, which opens at the table to reveal a puff of steam aromatic with cilantro and jalapeno. Cool folds of raw beef tenderloin sprinkled with capers, olive oil and a bright pesto make for a carpaccio to remember. Salads change with the day; one of my recent favorites brought together orange slices arranged with sharp red onions and tangy crumbles of goat cheese.

Unlike most upscale Italian restaurants, pasta isn't just a course unto itself at Rafagino but also accompanies the meat and fish entrees. The best of the main attractions have been veal sheathed in cheese and onions and a special of sea bass combined with bow-tie pasta.

Mussels show up in a hinged copper pot, which opens at the table to reveal a puff of steam aromatic with cilantro and jalapeno.

Not all memories are glowing. Thin slices of roast pork are draped in a mustard cream sauce that does a great imitation of melted Velveeta, and leg of lamb with a light wash of red wine sauce is a stodgy performer. Both dishes tasted as if they came from another kitchen—much like the showy bakery-bought cakes on Rafagino's enormous dessert tray. That's your cue to stick to something simple, like the delicate creme caramel, tiramisu or refreshing mango sorbet—all made here and all satisfying.

Rail Stop ★★

6478 Main St., The Plains, VA
540-253-5644   www.railstoprestaurant.com

LUNCH: *W-Sat 11-3* **ENTREES:** *$6.50-$12.50*
DINNER: *Tu-Th 5-9, F-Sat 5-9:30, Sun 5-8:30* **ENTREES:** *$14.25-$24*
BRUNCH: *Sun 10-3* **ENTREES:** *$6-$12.50*
CLOSED: *M, Tu lunch* **CREDIT CARDS:** *All major*
RESERVATIONS: *Recommended* **DRESS:** *Casual*
CROSS STREET: *Route 55/Fauquier Avenue*
PARKING: *Street* **METRO:** *No*

AN HOUR'S DRIVE from downtown Washington, the Rail Stop feels a world away, with its small porch out front and a miniature train inside that occasionally chugs around the ceiling of the front dining room. Time your visit right, and you might even run into actor Robert Duvall, a local resident and one-time co-owner of the place who continues to take his meals here when he's not off playing another character.

Chef Tom Kee's small menu is as up-to-date as anything you would expect to see in the Nation's Capital. At lunch there might be a bowl of chili—but also a sandwich of grilled shrimp, basil oil and sun-dried tomatoes.

The best of the homemade desserts tends to be whatever sounds homiest.

Evenings are even more ambitious. Duck roll sweetened with hoisin and plum sauces and roesti framed in sautéed mushrooms and capped with goat cheese butter can be followed by a fine pork chop ringed in an apple-cider sauce zipped up with cloves and star anise, or roast salmon slathered with a creamy horseradish sauce. The best of the homemade desserts tends to be whatever sounds homiest.

Aim for a seat in the front room (there are several). Small and cozy, the space ends with a tiny counter that gives anyone lucky enough to grab one of its four stools a view of the open kitchen—and an entertaining cooking show.

Raku

7240 Woodmont Ave., Bethesda, MD
301-718-8680

LUNCH: *M-F 11:30-2:30, Sat-Sun 11:30-3* **ENTREES:** *$7.25-$18*
DINNER: *Sun-Th 5-10, F-Sat 5-10:30* **ENTREES:** *$8.25-$22*
CREDIT CARDS: *AE, MC, V* **RESERVATIONS:** *Recommended*
DRESS: *Casual* **CROSS STREET:** *Bethesda Avenue*
PARKING: *$5 valet at dinner* **METRO:** *Bethesda*

I DON'T EVEN NEED FOOD in front of me to get excited about Raku in Bethesda. The setting alone makes you feel better, even on the grayest of days. Suspended from on high, outsize parasols in gumdrop colors compete for my attention with an inviting sushi bar and more bamboo than Tian Tian and Mei Xiang probably enjoy at the zoo in a week. Then the East-meets-West dishes start showing up. Fried dumplings filled with chicken and pork and ringed with pineapple star anise sauce. Pumpkin soup jump-started with cilantro and ginger chips. One of the best spring rolls you'll ever crunch into, its thin wrapper yielding to a pure, steamy filling of hot scallop, sea bass and shrimp. Sichuan-style strip steak, dull and vaguely seasoned, brings me down to earth, but smoky glazed pork ribs and miso-marinated cod keep me coming back for more.

Outsize parasols in gumdrop colors compete for my attention with an inviting sushi bar and more bamboo than Tian Tian and Mei Xiang probably enjoy at the zoo in a week.

No wonder the restaurant, one of many on its block, is always crowded.

The deft hand behind this fresh and clever food? Masaru Homma, who once worked his magic at Sushi-Ko in Washington and whose presence, unfortunately, is missing at the Raku in Dupont Circle.

SECOND LOCATION: *1900 Q St. NW, Washington, DC, 202-265-7258*

Ray's the Steaks

★★

1725 Wilson Blvd., Arlington, VA
703-841-7297

DINNER: *M-Th 6-10, F-Sat 5:30-11, Sun 5:30-8:30* **ENTREES:** *$12.95-$25.95*
CREDIT CARDS: *All major* **RESERVATIONS:** *Recommended*
DRESS: *Casual* **CROSS STREET:** *Rhodes Street*
PARKING: *Lot* **METRO:** *Courthouse*

MOST STEAKHOUSES AROUND TOWN feel as if they could have been ordered up from a central warehouse. At one after another, the drill goes like this: Big hunks of meat are brought to the table by big guys in ties, who encourage you to order a big red wine. The rooms all tend to look formal and masculine, and everything but the sprig of parsley that garnishes your protein of choice is à la carte.

Ray's the Steaks takes more of a mom-and-pop approach. The owner, who is also the cook, might answer the phone himself. Between turning meat on the grill, he also makes occasional forays into the Spartan dining room to chat up customers or carve their Chateaubriand. And the young waitresses elicit smiles when they use their bodies as diagrams to tell you where the different cuts of meat—aged and butchered on the premises—come from.

Name your favorite steak, and it's likely to be found here. Robustly flavored New York strip can be had simply with sautéed garlic or gussied up with brandy mushroom cream, port wine or a crust of black peppercorns. There is very good rib-eye, too, lapped with cool horseradish cream or ignited with Cajun seasonings. And, depending on the day, the kitchen might have on hand those less tender but still tasty cuts of beef, such as hanger steak and culotte, from the boneless bottom portion of the sirloin. The cost of the entrees includes mashed potatoes and creamed spinach served family-style in small black skillets. Both make good companions to the main attractions. The wine list, meanwhile, is as focused as the menu, its choices few but solid.

Name your favorite steak, and it's likely to be found here.

Ray, incidentally, is a nickname given to chef Michael Landrum by a former girlfriend. She's history, but "the play on words was too good to resist," he says. Much like his affordable tribute to meat.

Roof Terrace

(too new to assign stars)

John F. Kennedy Center for the Performing Arts,
2700 F St. NW, Washington, DC (Foggy Bottom/West End)
202-416-8555   www.kennedy-center.org/visitor/restaurant_terrace.cfm

DINNER: *Sun-Th 5-8 on performance evenings, F-Sat 5-9 (condensed menu available Th-Sat half-hour after last curtain)* **ENTREES:** *$20-$32*
BUFFET BRUNCH: *Sun 11:30-2:30* **PRICE:** *$33.95*
CREDIT CARDS: *AE, DC, MC, V* **RESERVATIONS:** *Recommended*
DRESS: *Business casual* **CROSS STREET:** *New Hampshire Avenue NW*
PARKING: *Garage/Street* **METRO:** *Foggy Bottom*

GONE IS THE DATED INTERIOR with its imposing chandeliers. Caramel-colored suede wall coverings and illuminated chrome-and-glass columns now make for a warmer setting in this recently renovated restaurant atop the Kennedy Center, where the views have traditionally topped the performances on the plate.

Director of restaurant operations Geoffrey Fisher admits that before the $4 million redo, the 300-seat Roof Terrace "was never a restaurant I'd go to if I wasn't going" to a performance in the same building. With a new look and a new menu, he says, he's aiming to create "a fantastic restaurant that just happens to be at the Kennedy Center."

It's still too soon to see if that will happen—or if the $26-an-entree average will be justified—

The modern American fare includes main dishes of pistachio-crusted rack of lamb, braised beef short ribs with chive dumplings, and duck breast with braised cabbage.

but helping him toward that lofty aim is former Ardeo chef Frederic Przyborowski, whose modern American fare includes crab cakes, duck spring rolls and corn-laced seafood chowder to start, and main dishes of pistachio-crusted rack of lamb, braised beef short ribs with chive dumplings, and duck breast with braised cabbage.

As an alternative to the inevitable postshow traffic jams, the new Roof Terrace has extended its schedule: Patrons can be seated up to 30 minutes after the last curtain call. Why fight the crowd when you could be eating chocolate velvet cake with brandied cherries?

Sakoontra ★ ★

12300-C Price Club Plaza, Fairfax, VA

703-818-8886   www.sakoontra.com

LUNCH: *M-Sat 11:30-3* **ENTREES:** *$5.95-$9.95*
DINNER: *Daily 3-10* **ENTREES:** *$6.95-$14.95*
CREDIT CARDS: *AE, DC, MC, V* **RESERVATIONS:** *Recommended*
DRESS: *Casual* **CROSS STREET:** *West Ox Road*
PARKING: *Lot* **METRO:** *No*

A GLANCE AT THE MENU finds all the dishes you'd expect of a Thai kitchen, from crisp-fried spring rolls to pad thai to curries reverberating with various degrees of heat (all better with a beer that keeps its cool in a frosted glass, or a tangy lemonade).

As in so many such restaurants, I'm tempted to hang around the appetizers, at the risk of ignoring the main dishes. Green-lipped mussels are moistened by a broth with red chili, lemon grass and purple basil—a SWAT team of sharpshooting enhancers. Single-bite dumplings show up sweet with ground shrimp and pork and crunchy with water chestnuts; dunk one into the accompanying dish of soy sauce, vinegar and sugar and what was mild goes a little wild. Shrimp cakes are fine; chicken wings come fat with a filling of bean thread, pork and crab; and tom yum (soup) gets a nice blast of lemon grass in its seasoning.

Repeat after me: Order dish No. 21, a salad. The aptly named "yum watercress" proves a colorful jumble of chicken and shrimp, red onion slivers and cashews, cilantro and scallions, all singing backup for the headliner of deep-fried watercress. A few bites in, people are scanning their PalmPilots to figure out how soon they can return. Among entrees, recent lures have been shrimp stir-fried with ginger and garlic and sweetened with honey, and a special of catfish ignited with red curry and pepper seeds.

Single-bite dumplings show up sweet with ground shrimp and pork and crunchy with water chestnuts.

Splashy in blues and purples, and accessorized with a tuk-tuk (Thai taxi) up front, the welcoming Sakoontra borrows its name from a character in a Thai fairy tale and is kid-friendly in other ways, too: The food comes out faster than at the drive through at that place with the golden arches.

Samantha's

631 E. University Blvd., Silver Spring, MD
301-445-7300

OPEN: *Sun-Th 11-11, F-Sat 11 am-midnight* **ENTREES**: *$8.95-$14.95*
CREDIT CARDS: *AE, D, MC, V* **RESERVATIONS**: *No*
DRESS: *Casual* **CROSS STREET**: *Piney Branch Road*
PARKING: *Lot* **METRO**: *Silver Spring*

IT MIGHT BE EARLY on a Sunday evening, but at Samantha's the mood is like a Saturday fiesta. In flow eager-looking customers, hoping to find a vacant seat in this plain but cheerful pink dining room; out from the kitchen comes a steady parade of sparkling seviche, fried pork heaped with fingers of yuca, and pupusas filled with seafood—generous portions of food that also taste like a Salvadoran grandmother had a hand in their making.

> **It's not just the pitchers of margaritas that put smiles on all the faces.**

It's not just the pitchers of margaritas that put smiles on all the faces. The tamales are as soothing as ever, the oniony steak is robust and well seasoned, and the fish is fresh and delicious; a special of garlicky whole red snapper with carefully cooked vegetables deserves permanent status on the bill of fare.

Oh, there are some Mexican dishes, too, but tacos and enchiladas should not be the reason you're here. There really is a Samantha, by the way: She's seven years old, the youngest member of the Jorge Garcia family and a frequent presence in her father's restaurant.

SBC Cafe

✔ *Critic's Pick*

★ ★

2501 McNair Farms Dr., Herndon, VA
703-793-7388

LUNCH: *M-F 11:30-2:30* **ENTREES:** *$7.95-$10.95*
DINNER: *Tu-W 5-9, Th-Sat 5-10* **ENTREES:** *$10.95-$18.95*
CLOSED: *Sun* **CREDIT CARDS:** *All major*
RESERVATIONS: *Recommended* **DRESS:** *Casual*
CROSS STREET: *Centerville Road* **PARKING:** *Lot* **METRO:** *No*

"**W**HERE IS EVERYBODY?" my pal wonders aloud as she contemplates a soup that's so vivid, it could pass for a desert sunset. The puree of grilled peppers is half gold and half orange, two bold swirls enlivened by creamy green thunderbolts of cilantro sauce spiked with garlic and jalapeno.

She must have read my mind. SBC Cafe brims with fetching ideas, but as far as I can tell, too few people know about them, at least when it comes to dinner. SBC Cafe is squeezed between a car wash and a dry cleaner on one side of a nondescript shopping mall. If you blink driving by, you could easily miss it.

The menu roams around, doing justice to many ports of call, from the Deep South to Thailand to South America. While one of you might be easing into a meal with a tangy Caesar salad, another might be spooning up a bowl of conch

Here is the uncommon menu where you can point just about anywhere on the page and call up a winner.

chowder, a memento the chef picked up from a few years spent in St. Augustine, Fla.

Here is the uncommon menu where you can point just about anywhere on the page and call up a winner. Fish? Meat? Both categories produce hits. Rockfish, a mainstay, remains moist beneath its coat of crushed tortilla chips and gets a spirited assist from some tomato salsa and a squeeze of lime. And it took a trip to Herndon to discover one of the best Cuban sandwiches I've had in recent memory. SBC Cafe operates on a modest budget, which means your coffee is poured into a paper cup and the bread arrives in a flimsy plastic basket. Yet there are plenty of thoughtful touches—good wines, soft music —throughout the meal. Pass the word. Food of this caliber should be shared with others.

Sea Catch ★★

1054 31st St. NW, Washington, DC (Georgetown)
202-337-8855   www.seacatchrestaurant.com

LUNCH: *M-Sat noon-3* **ENTREES:** *$7.25-$18*
DINNER: *M-Sat 5:30-10* **ENTREES:** *$15-$32*
CLOSED: *Sun* **CREDIT CARDS:** *All major* **RESERVATIONS:** *Recommended*
DRESS: *Casual* **CROSS STREET:** *M Street NW* **PARKING:** *Complimentary valet*
METRO: *Foggy Bottom/Rosslyn*

SMACK IN THE HEART OF GEORGETOWN, yet tucked away like a good secret, the setting alone whets my appetite. In fall and winter, I gravitate to either the front room, with its marble seafood bar, fireplace and low beamed ceiling, or the more formal rear, awash in wood, mirrors and peachy lighting that takes years off everyone's face. Spring and summer, I ask to be seated outside on the deck hugging the C&O Canal—if there's a more relaxing spot in the neighborhood to knock back some fresh oysters or tuck into lobster, it's not on my radar.

Wherever I land, the kitchen often enough makes me glad I'm there. The crab cakes are rich and good, set off with a julienne of bright vegetables and a brassy remoulade. Salads go beyond the expected to include creamy avocado, crushed hazelnuts and pink grapefruit tossed with dewy greens.

From the grill comes a dozen or so finny options, from sesame-crusted tuna served with a hash of saffron-sauced leeks to whole grilled fish.

From the grill comes a dozen or so finny options, from sesame-crusted tuna served with a hash of saffron-sauced leeks to whole grilled fish, maybe silver snapper laced with herbs that perfume its flesh (and better with a side dish like the nutmeg-fragrant gratin potatoes, in a portion fit for a family). Service can be pleasant and efficient at one meal, indifferent the next: If my waiter had bothered to check in with me after my linguine and clams showed up, I would have told him the seafood was gritty.

The cooking isn't always as careful or as consistent as you might wish, but sure bets exist. Chef Jeff Shively's sweetly spiced pumpkin pie with pecans tastes like the family treasure it is.

Seasons ★★

Four Seasons Hotel
2800 Pennsylvania Ave. NW, Washington, DC (Georgetown)
202-944-2000

BREAKFAST: *M-F 6:30-11, Sat 7-noon, Sun 7-9* **ENTREES:** *$6.25-$28*
LUNCH: *M-F noon-2:30, Sat noon-2* **ENTREES:** *$14-$28*
DINNER: *Daily 6-10:30* **ENTREES:** *$25-$40, 3-course prix fixe $40*
BUFFET BRUNCH: *Sun 10:30-2:30* **PRICE:** *$58*
CREDIT CARDS: *All major* **RESERVATIONS:** *Recommended*
DRESS: *Business casual* **CROSS STREET:** *28th*
PARKING: *Complimentary valet* **METRO:** *Foggy Bottom*

IF THERE'S A BETTER power breakfast in town, I have yet to taste it. Custardy scrambled eggs, perfect French toast, fresh carrot juice and regular celebrity sightings—Look! Andre Agassi!—make for a heady weekday eye-opener. Even better, the Four Seasons Hotel setting, with its broad windows and soothing green and yellow palette, resembles a lush garden patio. A sea of space between tables ensures that what the Hollywood director says to the famous journalist stays just between them. "Everything to your liking?" a debonair host wants to know. At moments like this, the only response is "yes!" Soft-shell crab in a light curry-scented batter and roseate duck breast served with delicate gnocchi lure me back for lunch and dinner.

Alas, other dishes can be far less memorable. Rack of lamb is boring. Seafood stew sports bites of fish that have seen better days. Even the bread basket and a Caesar salad smack of standard-issue fare. And as much as I enjoy the California ease of the dining room, stylish but never stuffy, I also wish the waiters would ask how I want my meat cooked and get the right

> **Soft-shell crab in a light curry-scented batter and roseate duck breast served with delicate gnocchi lure me back for lunch and dinner.**

plates to the right people. Considering the tab, a diner shouldn't have to ask for a glass of water, either.

Yet just when I find myself dismissing Seasons as Another Hotel Restaurant, I tuck into a sandwich that teams buttery swordfish with slices of lemony brioche, or an elegant (and scrumptious) apple pie. The maitre d' wants to know if, as a solo diner, I might enjoy a newspaper, or a laptop, both of which he's happy to bring to my table. Meanwhile, famous faces all around me enliven the scene. *The West Wing* wasn't filmed here, but it could have been.

1789

★ ★

1226 36th St. NW, Washington, DC (Georgetown)
202-965-1789   www.1789restaurant.com

DINNER: *M-F 6-10, Sat 5:30-11, Sun 5:30-10*   **ENTREES:** *$18-$38*
PRE-THEATER: *Nightly until 6:45, 3-course prix fixe, $30*
CREDIT CARDS: *All major*   **RESERVATIONS:** *Recommended*
DRESS: *Jacket required*   **CROSS STREET:** *Prospect Street NW*
PARKING: *Complimentary valet*   **METRO:** *Foggy Bottom/Rosslyn*

I T'S BEEN AROUND only since 1962, yet 1789 is as steeped in tradition as any Washington monument. Here's where generations of Georgetown University students have been given a respite from cafeteria fare by their visiting parents, and countless men have proposed to their girlfriends (and later returned to celebrate them having said yes). It's a handsome backdrop to these life moments, five nicely aged dining rooms spread over three floors.

For all its Federal charm and decorum—guys, be sure to wear a jacket—it's no dinosaur. The American menu is just about as modern as any in town. Thus, roasted red pepper soup is freshened with basil and orange; grouper adopts an Asian accent with its gingery coconut broth; and the vegetarian sampler is a true celebration of the season rather than some kind of penance. That

The American menu is just about as modern as any in town.

said, the more tradition-bound diner knows he or she can count on good crab cakes, an even better veal chop and roast rack of lamb lapped with red wine sauce, a 1789 mainstay. Desserts run to fruit crisps, chocolate cake and lemon chess pie—classics all.

Signatures ★★

801 Pennsylvania Ave. NW, Washington, DC (Penn Quarter)
202-628-5900   www.signatures-dc.com

LUNCH: *M-F 11:30-3* **ENTREES:** *$14-$22, 3-course prix fixe $23.33*
DINNER: *M-Th 5:30-10, F-Sat 5:30-10:30* **ENTREES:** *$22-$35*
PRE- AND POST-THEATER *M-Sat 5:30-6:30, 9 pm 3-course prix fixe $30.03*
CLOSED: *Sun* **CREDIT CARDS:** *All major*
RESERVATIONS: *Recommended* **DRESS:** *Business casual*
CROSS STREET: *9th* **PARKING:** *Complimentary valet at dinner*
METRO: *Archives-Navy Memorial*

"**I**'M HALFWAY THROUGH THE MENU and I don't see anything I recognize yet," I overhear an out-of-town business type joke to his equally baffled tablemates as he reads aloud from the dinner menu at Signatures. "What's Nigerian paprika coating? … and Forbidden Radicchio Risotto?" The waiters here earn their pay, going into epic explanations of what the restaurant's chef, the Ivory Coast–born Morou Ouattara, has been cooking since he left Red Sage and took over the kitchen of this civilized restaurant overlooking the Navy Memorial.

One thing is certain: The menu is not a predictable rehash of contemporary American restaurant cooking. Sea bass carpaccio is tricked out with "pisco sour" foam; the humble-sounding grilled cheese sandwich comes with seared foie gras and rhubarb pickles; and a filet of ostrich shares its plate with corn fritters, grilled peaches and an ancho-orange glaze. But behind some of the many adjectives and techniques, there's plenty of good taste to hold a diner's attention. The menu woos fish fanciers with sushi and big spenders with the likes of

The humble-sounding grilled cheese sandwich comes with seared foie gras and rhubarb pickles.

Kobe beef, a domestic version of the prized Japanese beef revered for its buttery texture and rich marbling. Desserts, however, taste like afterthoughts.

The space is grand without being stuffy. Guests settle into wide yellow leather chairs and eat with gleaming Christofle silverware, surrounded by curtains the shade of champagne and wood buffed to a fine glow. The autographed photos and other documents that decorate the soft blue walls and give the restaurant its name are available for purchase—something to keep in mind for that Picasso buff or Lenny Bruce fan the next time a big birthday rolls around.

Singh Thai

2311 Wilson Blvd., Arlington, VA
703-312-7118

LUNCH: *Daily 11:30-3* **ENTREES:** *$5.95-$10.95*
DINNER: *Sun-Th 5-10, F-Sat 5-11* **ENTREES:** *$7.95-$12.95*
CREDIT CARDS: *AE, D, MC, V* **RESERVATIONS:** *Recommended*
DRESS: *Casual* **CROSS STREET:** *N. Adams Street* **PARKING:** *Lot*
METRO: *Courthouse*

THIS FAMILY-RUN PURVEYOR of angel wings, pad thai and mango with sticky rice manages to pack in a lot of flair despite having fewer than 40 seats. Fresh flowers grace the tabletops. Shards of blue tile turn the bar into a pretty mosaic. And the walls soothe tired eyes with soft shades of orange and green.

From the small kitchen, hidden behind a curtain, comes a long list of hits: spicy ground chicken salad, sliced grilled beef set off by a zippy lime and fish sauce, deep-fried frog's legs scattered with fried basil, and terrific catfish and duck preparations. This is one Thai chef who hasn't toned down his cooking to appeal to an

Shards of blue tile turn the bar into a pretty mosaic.

American palate. And the tabs are gentle. Entrees average less than the price of most movies—and encourage repeat viewings.

Smith Point ★★

1338 Wisconsin Ave. NW, Washington, DC (Georgetown)
202-333-9003

DINNER: *W-Sat 6:30-11* **ENTREES:** *$19-$23*
CLOSED: *Sun-Tu* **CREDIT CARDS:** *AE, MC, V* **RESERVATIONS:** *Recommended*
DRESS: *Casual* **CROSS STREET:** *O Street NW* **PARKING:** *Street*
METRO: *Foggy Bottom*

NAMED FOR A SLICE OF NANTUCKET, Smith Point doesn't make itself easy to get to know. It's underground and hasn't done much to promote itself even in its own neighborhood. It also keeps unusual hours: Dinner is served after 6:30 p.m. and only three nights a week. But chef David Scribner's food, with its emphasis on freshness and simplicity, is worth the inconvenience.

The fire-engine-red tomatoes riding alongside his very good crab cakes are as full-flavored as they are colorful, and the mainstays in his salads—say, baby arugula tossed with fennel, blue cheese and apple, or pink and gold roasted beets teamed with goat cheese and crostini—are prime. With few exceptions, meat and fish are both accorded respect. A crusty lamb kebab alternates meat with charred red onion and sits on rice pilaf threaded with fresh herbs and punched up with bits of feta cheese; it's billed as an appetizer but portioned like a light main course. An entree of seared scallops on sage-scented grits plays sweet off salty, contrasting an apple-cider reduction with shavings of cured Virginia ham.

> **A crusty lamb kebab alternates meat with charred red onion and sits on rice pilaf threaded with fresh herbs and punched up with bits of feta cheese.**

The sleeper on the menu? Chicken pot pie. Its chicken pieces are big and moist, the carrots are cooked just right, the thyme and bay leaf are pronounced, and the white sauce is delicate. The crowning glory, though, is the crust, a light and buttery disk that floats above the assembly like an edible Frisbee.

Once you're settled in, Smith Point comes across as warm and inviting. The entrance is lined with votive candles; tented glass skylights and numerous plants conjure a greenhouse; slate floors, exposed brick walls and photographs of Nantucket bring to mind a New England tavern.

My only gripe is that I might want that pot pie earlier in the week but can't have it.

Sorak Garden ★★

4308 Backlick Rd., Annandale, VA
703-916-7600

OPEN: *M-Sat 11-11, Sun 11-10* **ENTREES:** *$13.95-$45.95*
CREDIT CARDS: *All major* **RESERVATIONS:** *Recommended*
DRESS: *Casual* **CROSS STREET:** *Little River Turnpike*
PARKING: *Lot/complimentary valet* **METRO:** *Dunn Loring-Merrifield*

NAMED FOR A MOUNTAIN in Korea famed for its beauty, Sorak Garden lives up to the designation with an artful interior. Rich wood, lush plants and Korean artifacts are everywhere; strings of tiny white lights hang in the main dining room.

Busy as it can get, it's a lovely environment in which to sample the hearty and boldly flavored cooking of Korea. Crisp dumplings in the shape of half-moons are stuffed with juicy crumbled beef, and squid and sweet peppers are scattered over a pleasantly gelatinous "pancake." Grills built into the table-tops are used to stir-cook the barbecue for which Korea is famous, and entrees are preceded by a colorful parade of snacks, or panchan.

The menu is big, ranging from noodles to casseroles to sushi, although raw fish is not the best reason to come here. The various hot pots are. A little black

The menu is big, ranging from noodles to casseroles to sushi.

cauldron of brick-red broth, thick with cabbage, pork slices and custardy tofu, steams and bubbles as it is set before you; this kimchi soup takes its color from potent red chilies.

Good news: Where once I complained about indifferent service, lately I'm pleased to report smiling welcomes and help with grilling your shrimp, beef, squid or vegetables at the table.

Southside 815 ★

815 S. Washington St., Alexandria, VA

703-836-6222 www.southside815.com

LUNCH: *Daily 11:30-4* **ENTREES:** *$9.95-$18.95*
DINNER: *Sun-Th 5-10:30, F-Sat 5-11* **ENTREES:** *$9.95-$18.95*
BRUNCH: *Sun 11-2:30* **ENTREES:** *$6.95-$8.95*
CREDIT CARDS: *All major* **RESERVATIONS:** *Recommended for parties of 6 or more*
DRESS: *Casual* **CROSS STREET:** *Green Street*
PARKING: *Lot* **METRO:** *King Street*

Y'ALL BETTER COME HUNGRY. The appetizers are apportioned like entrees and the main dishes would leave even a linebacker groaning at this southern-inspired restaurant, where an ocean of cream gravy blankets a first course of sweet-potato biscuits strewn with folds of Virginia ham, and fritters the size of golf balls are shaped from crab and corn (and better after a dip in their peppery jelly).

An ocean of cream gravy blankets a first course of sweet-potato biscuits strewn with folds of Virginia ham.

Entrees, on the other hand, don't always hold up their end of the meal. Blackened catfish is shy on the promised heat, the brick-size meatloaf is too compact, and a pork chop sandwich, crunchy beneath its cracker breading and zipped up with hot pepper relish, is more notable for what it comes with: fresh coleslaw and sweet pickles.

It's all presented by young and pleasing servers in a warm-with-wood dining room painted in shades of green peas and purple eggplant. If there's a centimeter of space left for dessert, make it peach pound cake sweetened with caramel sauce and ice cream between its several moist layers.

Spices ★★

3333-A Connecticut Ave. NW, Washington, DC (Cleveland Park)
202-686-3833

LUNCH: *M-F 11:30-3* **ENTREES:** *$8-$12*
DINNER: *M-F 5-11, Sat noon-11, Sun 5-10:30* **ENTREES:** *$9-$19*
CREDIT CARDS: *AE, DC, MC, V* **RESERVATIONS:** *Recommended*
DRESS: *Casual* **CROSS STREET:** *Macomb Street NW*
PARKING: *Street* **METRO:** *Cleveland Park*

S PICES GIVES US PLENTY OF REASONS to seek it out, one of them being its location across the street from the Uptown, one of the last great movie houses around.

Another is the restaurant's moderately priced menu of Japanese, Thai, Chinese and other Asian dishes: It's no problem if you want sashimi and your mate wants pad thai or Peking chicken, because the gang's all there, and delicious to boot—as are scallion pancakes invigorated with sweet-and-sour sauce, and curry puffs filled with gently spiced potatoes and ground chicken.

Did I mention how stylish the place looks? The long blond sushi bar is backed by soothing yellow-green walls, and a small alcove across from it assures privacy for anyone sitting there. The stir-fried pork is enlivened with basil and fiery

> **It's no problem if you want sashimi and your mate wants pad thai or Peking chicken, because the gang's all there, and delicious to boot.**

with chilies, and I always make time for a refreshing house signature, the ginger salad. The lilting music, the warm service, the fresh and appealing food served on lovely plates with twiglike chopsticks might seem familiar: Spices is owned by its Cleveland Park blockmate, the distinguished Yanyu.

Stardust ★

608 Montgomery St., Alexandria, VA
703-548-9864   www.stardustrestaurant.com

LUNCH: *M-F 11:30-5* **ENTREES:** *$8-$15*
DINNER: *M-Th 5-10:30, F-Sat 5-11, Sun 4:30-9:30* **ENTREES:** *$15-$24*
CREDIT CARDS: *All major* **RESERVATIONS:** *Recommended* **DRESS:** *Casual*
CROSS STREET: *N. Washington Street/GW Parkway* **PARKING:** *Street*
METRO: *Braddock Road*

O NE ROOM IS PAINTED PALE GREEN, has a half-roof and sports a faux aquarium in its fireplace. Another is moody in soft purple, comfy with booths and offers pretend windows through which diners can see stars. There's a mannequin wearing sunglasses near the host stand and leopard-print couches in the bar, all of which makes this neighborhood restaurant look as if it had been dressed with random orders from eBay. So don't expect the menu to be mainstream.

Stardust's chef, Pat Phatiphong, is Thai, and that accent finds its way into a number of dishes (skewered pork gets backup from jasmine rice and peanut dipping sauce), though the food isn't easily classified. (Which part of the globe gets credit for

> **Stardust's chef, Pat Phatiphong, is Thai, and that accent finds its way into a number of dishes.**

spinach salad tossed with bacon but also "Siberian" dressing and a garnish of smoked mussels?) There's not a single dessert worth sticking around for—the pecan pie tastes like a candy bar, hazelnut creme brulee reveals no sign of its featured flavor—but there are enough satisfying performances to keep you in your seat until the third act. One of them is an appetizer of shrimp tempura, hot, light, juicy and invigorated with a drizzle of wasabi mayonnaise. Another is whole fried fish, maybe sweetly fresh flounder dressed up with ribbons of carrot and beet and a frame of bok choy.

But oysters are baked under too much Parmesan, chicken wings show up dry beneath their red wine glaze, and fettuccine with Gorgonzola sauce, sweet corn, spinach and pine nuts is pleasant—nothing more. Not so the staff, which is invariably energetic and efficient.

Sunflower

2531 Chain Bridge Rd., Vienna, VA
703-319-3888   www.crystalsunflower.com

LUNCH: *M-Sat 11:30-4* **ENTREES:** *$5.75-$11*
DINNER: *M-Sat 4-9:30, Sun noon-9:30* **ENTREES:** *$7.50-$11*
CREDIT CARDS: *All major* **RESERVATIONS:** *No* **DRESS:** *Casual*
CROSS STREET: *Nutley Street* **PARKING:** *Lot* **METRO:** *Vienna/Fairfax-GMU*

A S ITS NAME MIGHT SUGGEST—and a roomful of lacy curtains, toy bees suspended from the ceiling and sunflower-shaped table lamps support—this vegetarian restaurant adds up to an oasis of quiet good cheer. Servers with beatific smiles circulate through the small, pale-green dining room, attending to the needs of their appreciative audience with the calm of yoga instructors.

If you don't eat meat, Sunflower is a refreshing alternative to all those restaurants that think having a green salad and a plate of cheese pasta on the menu is enough to keep you happy. The cooking here is both varied and delicious, with an Asian sensibility and an emphasis on what's good for you.

If you do eat meat, chances are you won't miss it here. Spring rolls plumped with organic cabbage, carrots and nutty mushrooms crackle between the teeth. Grilled asparagus arrives with a scattering of red pepper batons and chili-spiked toasted almonds; it could easily pass for a first course from a stylish restaurant in downtown Washington. There are "sushi" wrought from bean curd and brown rice and General Tso's

The cooking here is both varied and delicious, with an Asian sensibility and an emphasis on what's good for you.

Surprise, the surprise being that what your tongue thinks is fried morsels of chicken draped in spicy kung-pao sauce is actually tasty chunks of soy protein. And Popeye's Favorite combines pureed spinach and potatoes in a pleasing shepherd's pie seasoned with black pepper sauce.

Alcohol has no home here; in keeping with the restaurant's holistic theme, fresh squeezed juices and organic teas (try lotus root with a hit of ginger) are offered instead. A person could eat here every day for a month and not sample everything on the bill of fare—or tire of the cooking, except perhaps for the desserts, which use no eggs, dairy or sugar (and taste like it).

Sushi Aoi ★

1100 New York Ave. NW, Washington, DC (Mt. Vernon Square)
202-408-7770

LUNCH: *M-F 11:30-2:30* **ENTREES:** *$8.50-$14.50*
DINNER: *M-Sat 5-10:30* **ENTREES:** *$9.50-$19.50*
CLOSED: *Sun* **CREDIT CARDS:** *AE, DC, MC, V*
RESERVATIONS: *Recommended* **DRESS:** *Casual*
CROSS STREET: *11th* **PARKING:** *Street*
METRO: *Metro Center*

WEIGHING IN at a mere 55 seats, Sushi Aoi packs abundant style into its small space. Shiny bamboo poles grace the little tangerine-colored foyer, while the walls of the dining room segue from soothing yellow-green to blue-gray. Singles gravitate to the welcoming sushi bar; groups have the option of two big tables near the front window, where a rice-paper screen can be pulled around for privacy.

More than good looks draw crowds, particularly at lunch, to this restaurant across from the old convention center in downtown Washington. The chef has a sure way with raw fish and vinegared rice. Connoisseurs on a budget know to time their visits to Sushi Aoi; between 5 and 7 p.m., Monday through Saturday, a lot of the sushi—including salmon, tuna, flounder and eel—is available at $1 apiece (and can be washed back with sake or beer for $2.50 a drink).

A gentle way to ease into a meal is with a bowl of clear broth rounded out with bites of chicken and soft dark greens, or osuimono. If it's something more forceful you're after, seek out the pork-filled dumplings, served with fruity ponzu sauce and bound in wrappers ignited with wasabi (here come the tears!). Of the fried dishes, tempura and gyoza are upstaged by lightly breaded and simply seasoned squid. Green tea noodles show up on a small bamboo plate with chopped scallions and dark brown dunking sauce. Light and satisfying, the entree is just the ticket before that meeting back at the office.

> **A gentle way to ease into a meal is with a bowl of clear broth rounded out with bites of chicken and soft dark greens, or osuimono.**

Sushi-Ko

2309 Wisconsin Ave. NW, Washington, DC (Glover Park)
202-333-4187   www.sushiko.us

LUNCH: *Tu-F noon-2:30*   **ENTREES:** *$9.50-$17*
DINNER: *M-Th 6-10:30, F 6-11, Sat 5:30-11, Sun 5:30-10*   **ENTREES:** *$16-$23*
CREDIT CARDS: *AE, MC, V*   **RESERVATIONS:** *Recommended*   **DRESS:** *Casual*
CROSS STREET: *Calvert Street NW*   **PARKING:** *$4 valet at dinner*
METRO: *Woodley Park-Zoo/Adams Morgan*

OPENED IN 1976, Sushi-Ko is not just one of Washington's longest-lived Japanese restaurants but also one of the city's most influential kitchens. While some of its many chefs have gone on to glory elsewhere (think Kaz Sushi Bistro in downtown Washington, Raku in Bethesda), Sushi-Ko continues to be a leader of the pack. Its sushi has been made available to the masses, at Whole Foods stores, and its French-accented wine list has evolved into an inventory for Burgundy lovers to swoon over.

These days, Koji Terano leads the charge. His influence can be tasted in sushi that remains first-rate and in quiet refinements on what came before: Miso soup is more complex with the addition of enoki mushrooms, smoked mussels and crisp-edged diced eggplant. Meanwhile, tuna is displayed "five ways" on a long plate. One bite, marinated in soy sauce and sake, nods to an old Japanese custom; another is served as a refreshing tartare, banded in seaweed and accented with fish roe; a third morsel, of toro (fatty tuna), is rich and smoky from its brief encounter with a grill. Another of Sushi-Ko's many "small dishes" is eel, sweet beneath its glaze of soy sauce and sugar, bedded on mache and adorned with a delicate fan of avocado.

For $3 extra, you can order your sushi with grated fresh wasabi (Japanese horseradish). This detail is telling, for even in Japan, many restaurants use the less expensive powdered wasabi, which is reconstituted with water.

Lesser dishes occasionally sneak in. "Spicy" tuna roll is beautiful, with a flowerlike crown of raw tuna, but the filling itself is disappointingly flat. Such disappointments turn out to be rare lapses during otherwise fine performances—meals eaten in spare, smart surroundings and watched over by an intelligent staff.

Sushi Taro ★★

1503 17th St. NW, Washington, DC (Dupont Circle)
202-462-8999   www.sushitaro.com

LUNCH: *M-F 11:30-2* **ENTREES:** *$6.95-$18*
DINNER: *M-Th 5:30-10, F-Sat 5:30-10:30* **ENTREES:** *$13-$40*
CLOSED: *Sun* **CREDIT CARDS:** *All major* **RESERVATIONS:** *Recommended*
DRESS: *Casual* **CROSS STREET:** *P Street* **PARKING:** *Street* **METRO:** *Dupont Circle*

I'VE NEVER BEEN TO TOKYO, but I imagine Sushi Taro would look right at home there. On any given night at this second-story restaurant, a throng of Japanese suits are pampered by waitresses in beautiful kimonos and by chefs in blue caps positioned behind a long stretch of a sushi counter. Handsome rice paper screens and a few low tables surrounded by shoeless diners complete the scene.

The sushi bar's prominence is my cue to go fish. Salmon, yellowtail, sweet shrimp—all the usual suspects show up on the sushi menu, and they taste as if they'd been caught that morning. But here's the place to venture beyond your comfort zone and try ingredients that you won't always find at your neighborhood sushi parlor. The display cases are lined with amberjack, three kinds of mackerel and even more varieties of clam, from arctic surf to orange. If you think all tuna tastes the same, conduct an experiment and request the three grades of tuna available at Sushi Taro. You'll discover why the fattiest of the three (toro) costs almost twice as much as the regular (maguro, priced at $4.50 for two pieces) and a couple of dollars more than medium-fatty (chu-toro, $6.25). The toro is simply exquisite, like butter crossed with the sea. Sushi maestros will tell you that the little pillow of rice that supports the featured ingredient is just as important as the fish itself. At Sushi Taro, the grains are firm, plump and moist, their flavor a

The toro is simply exquisite, like butter crossed with the sea.

gentle balance of rice wine vinegar, salt, sugar and dried seaweed.

There's more than just raw fish to be savored here. I'm particularly fond of the appetizers, including the delicate steamed dumplings (shumai), and it pays to ask if such seasonal treats as smelts or soft-shell crabs are available. The former, rich and meaty, are deep-fried and invigorated with a clear sauce that's at once subtly sweet and tangy; the latter are treated to a lightly crackling tempura batter that allows the clean, sweet flavor of the crab to rule. A parade of fried, broiled and simmered meats is also offered, but with fish as good as this, why stray beyond the raw deal?

Taberna del Alabardero ★★

1776 I St. NW, Washington, DC (Downtown)
202-429-2200   www.alabardero.com

LUNCH: *M-F 11:30-2:30* **ENTREES:** *$17-$24*
DINNER: *M-Th 5:30-10:30, F-Sat 5:30-11*
ENTREES: *$23-$37, 9-course tasting menu $85*
CLOSED: *Sun* **CREDIT CARDS:** *All major* **RESERVATIONS:** *Recommended*
DRESS: *Casual* **CROSS STREET:** *18th* **PARKING:** *Validated garage at dinner*
METRO: *Farragut West*

THERE IS NO MORE dignified restaurant in Washington than Taberna del Alabardero. In a series of Old World dining rooms, waiters in tuxedoes attend to the wishes of what appears to be half of Washington's social register. And even in a city that lives to work, it is not unusual to see guests at Taberna del Alabardero lingering over two-hour-plus lunches.

One of the best appetizers I've sampled in recent memory is chef Enrique Sanchez's preparation of pig's feet. Lightly smoked meat is cooked with a ragout of vegetables, then chopped, rolled, lightly breaded and sauteed to a crisp golden edge; the earthy flavors get a nice lift from the garlic sauce and tender clams that ring the pork. On a lighter note, risotto veined with asparagus

Red mullet demonstrates the kitchen's comfort level with fish

and garnished with artichoke chips speaks to the season. Entrees are no less appealing. Chicken scattered with soft cloves of garlic and lapped with herb-flecked gravy tastes like something a skilled Spanish grandmother might make; and red mullet, dappled with a verdant spinach sauce and arranged in a little stack on spinach sweetened with raisins and figs, demonstrates the kitchen's comfort level with fish.

Despite a note on the menu limiting paella to a minimum of two diners, the classic rice dish is offered for one if you bother to ask, and in multiple styles. I opted for arroz negro, the version tinted black with squid ink. Unfortunately, it tasted warmed over. A casserole of braised partridge was terrific, though.

Come dessert, you can go the traditional route and order crema catalana, that Spanish cousin to creme brulee. More unexpected is mango "ravioli," shaved mango pretending to be pasta and wrapped around a mousselike filling of manchego, cream cheese and whipped cream. A dab of Granny Smith apple granita adds welcome punctuation to this refreshing experiment.

Taste of Morocco ★★

3211 N. Washington Blvd., Arlington, VA
703-527-7468

LUNCH: *Tu-F 11:30-2:30* **ENTREES**: *$7.95-$13.95*
DINNER: *Daily 5-11* **ENTREES**: *$10.95-$19.95*
BRUNCH: *Sun 11:30-3* **ENTREES**: *4-course prix fixe $9.95*
CREDIT CARDS: *AE, D, MC, V* **RESERVATIONS**: *Recommended*
DRESS: *Casual* **CROSS STREET**: *Wilson Boulevard* **PARKING**: *Lot*
METRO: *Clarendon*

THE WARM WELCOME BEGINS ON THE PHONE. "We look forward to seeing you," a host says after I reserve a table. Inside the restaurant, Moroccan music spirits guests far away as they sink deep into pillowed banquettes. Glistening olives and cubes of bread show up to ward off any hunger pangs as the menus are doled out. Instead of a pitch to order the most expensive items, a waiter volunteers that the multicourse "feasts," averaging $40 a couple at dinner, are the most economical way to enjoy the place.

The kitchen makes two kinds of bisteeya. One encases ground chicken, almonds and eggs—the classic filling—in onionskin-thin, flaky and buttery phyllo; as is customary, the surface is lightly dusted with sugar and cinnamon. Less common but

> **Less common but even more delicious is bisteeya stuffed with squid, fish and fresh coriander.**

even more delicious is bisteeya stuffed with squid, fish and fresh coriander along with glassy vermicelli that picks up the tint of the seasonings, including cumin and saffron.

If bisteeya sounds like too heavy a way to begin a meal, there are salads of cucumber and tomato, coriander-spiked carrot, and cumin-scented eggplant to mull over. They are all good and fresh tasting.

Much of the rest of the menu is devoted to tagines, a word that refers both to Moroccan stews and to the glazed earthenware dishes, capped with conical lids, in which they're cooked. My preference is for the lamb tagines, offered with soft-cooked vegetables in a saffron sauce, stewed with prunes and sprinkled with sesame seeds, or blended with almonds and raisins.

Weekend belly dancing turns dinner into dinner-and-a-show. If you've opted for one of the feasts, you're probably not going to have room for much more dessert than some minted tea, poured with dramatic flair into tiny glass cups.

Taverna Cretekou

(0 stars)

818 King St., Alexandria, VA

703-548-8688   www.tavernacretekou.com

LUNCH: *Tu-F 11:30-2:30, Sat noon-3:30*   **ENTREES:** *$8.95-$17.95*
DINNER: *Tu-F 5-10, Sat 3:30-10:30, Sun 5-9*   **ENTREES:** *$12.95-$24.95*
BRUNCH BUFFET: *Sun 11-3* **PRICE:** *$16.95*   **CLOSED:** *M*
CREDIT CARDS: *AE, MC, V* **RESERVATIONS:** *Recommended* **DRESS:** *Casual*
CROSS STREET: *S. Alfred Street* **PARKING:** *Street* **METRO:** *King Street*

DINING AT THIS LONG-TIME Greek restaurant in Old Town after an absence of a couple of years was a shock, like going to a high school reunion to find that the dashing captain of the football team had lost all his hair and packed on a paunch. *What happened?*

Just about everything on the once-proud menu tastes like a carbon copy of a carbon copy of the original, from the leaden kasseri cheese, which the waiter doesn't bother to ignite at the table, to grilled whole red snapper that smacked of last week's catch. Baby eggplant is burdened with a dessert-sweet stuffing of chopped tomatoes, raisins, onions and pine nuts. Lamb chops yield an unpleasant aftertaste, and baklava requires a steak knife to cut through its rubbery layers.

If you only sampled the whipped fish roe and moussaka, you might think nothing was amiss; both dishes are as good as I remember them from years past. Launched in 1974, the restaurant retains its good bones, with white-washed walls, a vaulted ceiling up front and a brick-lined courtyard with a grape arbor in the rear.

Launched in 1974, the restaurant retains its good bones, with white-washed walls, a vaulted ceiling up front and a brick-lined courtyard with a grape arbor in the rear.

The waiters are cordial, but you go to a restaurant to eat, not to bond with the staff.

Tavira

8401 Connecticut Ave., Chevy Chase, MD
301-652-8684   www.tavirarestaurant.com

LUNCH: *M-F 11:30-2:30*   **ENTREES:** *$6.95-$13.95*
DINNER: *M-Th 5:30-10, F-Sat 5:30-11, Sun 5-9*   **ENTREES:** *$16.95-$24.95*
CREDIT CARDS: *All major*   **RESERVATIONS:** *Recommended*
DRESS: *Casual*   **CROSS STREET:** *Chevy Chase Lake Drive*
PARKING: *Lot*   **METRO:** *No*

GET PAST THE UNDERGROUND LOCATION in a remote Chevy Chase bank building, because the payoff is delicious, and even rare around here: the sensual cooking of Portugal, a subtle but distinctive cuisine that weaves together a lot of garlic, whole fish, salt cod in different guises and such enhancers as piri-piri, a hot chili seasoning.

You could almost close your eyes, point anywhere on the menu and snare a winning plate. Will it be garlicky shrimp, fried cod fritters or a potato puree with sausage and kale—the classic caldo verde? All are very appealing introductions.

You could almost close your eyes, point anywhere on the menu and snare a winning plate.

The entrees make decisions difficult, too. Seafood, sausage and roasted peppers get a backdrop of saffron-perfumed rice in a Portuguese take on paella, while grilled chicken gets a kick from some of that piri-piri and a side of airy homemade potato chips.

Duarte Rebolo, the passionate host, is eager to please. With its low ceilings and yellow walls, Tavira offers an intimate atmosphere in which to pretend you're on vacation, if only for a few hours.

Teasim ★

2009 R St. NW, Washington, DC (Dupont Circle)
202-667-3827   www.teaism.com

OPEN: *M-Th 8 am-10 pm, F 8 am-11 pm, Sat 9:30 am-11 pm, Sun 9:30-10*
ENTREES: *$7-$9.50*
CREDIT CARDS: *AE, D, MC, V* **RESERVATIONS**: *Recommended*
DRESS: *Casual* **CROSS STREET**: *Connecticut Avenue NW*
PARKING: *Street* **METRO**: *Dupont Circle*

GREEN, BLACK, WHITE—you can choose from dozens of teas at these stylish settings scattered across the city. But Teaism is much more than a place just to sip.

In the morning, I show up at one of the (self-service) counters for cilantro scrambled eggs with tea-smoked salmon and a refreshing yogurt-based lassi. Later in the day, there are an attractive vegetable bento box, a nice Thai chicken curry with sticky rice, and a juicy, first-rate burger, made not with beef but with organic ostrich and perched on a toasted bun with a pinch of grated ginger and a side of chunky coleslaw. Oh, the beef bento comes out a little dry and chewy, and the bland veggie burger smacks too much of Haight-Ashbury, circa 1968.

Teaism is much more than a place just to sip.

Still, these sleek little dining rooms, wrought from warm wood and stone floors, offer a serene and health-conscious alternative to golden arches and corporate coffeehouses. Small wonder that on any given day, young families may find themselves next to business types seated next to first-daters ("So, you're from California . . .").

OTHER LOCATIONS: *400 Eighth St. NW, Washington, DC, 202-638-6010*
800 Connecticut Ave. NW, Washington, DC, 202-835-2233

TenPenh

1001 Pennsylvania Ave. NW, Washington, DC (Downtown)
202-393-4500   www.tenpenh.com

LUNCH: *M-F 11:30-2:30* **ENTREES:** *$13-$18*
DINNER: *M-Th 5:30-10:30, F-Sat 5:30-11* **ENTREES:** *$13-$28*
CLOSED: *Sun* **CREDIT CARDS:** *All major*
RESERVATIONS: *Recommended* **DRESS:** *Casual*
CROSS STREET: *10th* **PARKING:** *$5 valet at dinner*
METRO: *Archives-Navy Memorial*

WHEN PEOPLE COMPLAIN about how dull Washington is, I feel compelled to ask if they've been to TenPenh. Always busy and always exciting, this stylish downtown restaurant serves the kind of food that makes you sit up and take notice. And the setting is its equal. Picture brilliant silk fabrics, details in teak and an exhibition kitchen.

I never tire of the menu, be it a lunch of mussels swimming in a fragrant yellow curry or a dinner of whole fried catfish with an herby and electric dipping sauce. Spice-rubbed folds of beef give an Asian twist to steak salad, while a fistful of tender shrimp adorns a refined red curry rounded out with juicy fresh pineapple and basil. ("It's our most popular dish," a waitress says, and one bite reveals why.) Endings—lovely ice creams, a small pyramid of chocolate mousse—are sweet and elegant.

Spice-rubbed folds of beef give an Asian twist to steak salad, while a fistful of tender shrimp adorns a refined red curry rounded out with juicy fresh pineapple and basil.

Reservations for this fashion show are a must, though there are first-come, first-served alternatives if you haven't planned ahead: The big marble bar is a fine spot to dine, as are the sidewalk tables facing Pennsylvania Avenue. No matter where you sit, though, you'll find the service gracious and informed. Even better, TenPenh is within easy walking distance of several of Washington's most popular theaters.

Thaiphoon ★★

2011 S St. NW, Washington, DC (Dupont Circle)
202-667-3505   www.thaiphoon.com

LUNCH: *M-F 11:30-3:30*   **ENTREES:** *$5.95-$12.95*
DINNER: *Sun-Th 3:30-10:30, F-Sat 11:30-11*   **ENTREES:** *$7.95-$12.95*
CREDIT CARDS: *All major*   **RESERVATIONS:** *Recommended*
DRESS: *Casual*   **CROSS STREET:** *Connecticut Avenue NW*
PARKING: *Street*   **METRO:** *Dupont Circle*

ONCE YOU'VE MADE its acquaintance, Thaiphoon doesn't let you forget it. The interior catches the eye with a window-wrapped dining room up front and cozy booths in the rear painted the colors of asparagus, burnt orange and lemon. Stylish amber lights illuminate a menu whose moderate prices encourage frequent visits. Thaiphoon is one of those rare restaurants where, no matter what seat you land in, you've got a view of something interesting (my companion might be savoring the sidewalk scene today, but I've spotted a late-lunching Betty Friedan).

The noodle dishes run oily and the desserts leave me cold. It took some exploration, but eventually I tasted why there's often a wait for one of Thaiphoon's 80 or so seats. For the most part, this is food that wakes up your mouth, brought to you by servers who manage to slip some graciousness your way every time they stop by your table.

No one in the neighborhood serves a soup brassier than the demure-looking chicken and mushrooms floating in a broth of coconut milk. A bowlful of beige, the soup nevertheless roars with

Fried won ton skins in crisp triangles hide pinches of curry-tinged chicken, onions and potatoes.

the peppery heat of galangal and a bracing jolt of lime. Fried won ton skins in crisp triangles hide pinches of curry-tinged chicken, onions and potatoes; the sweet-sharp cucumber dipping sauce makes a nice complement. Peanut-sprinkled, citrus-splashed papaya salad is good, but even better is shredded, honey-roasted duck tossed with ginger, chili paste, greens and more. And among the entrees, you'll do just fine with seafood, be it steamed rockfish perfumed by lemon grass or a special of shrimp with pineapple and a tingling tomato sauce. The best of the vegetables: bright, crisp string beans, delicately batter-fried and enlivened by garlic sauce. It's the stuff of late-night, home-alone junk-food fantasies.

SECOND LOCATION: *1301 S. Joyce St., Arlington, VA, 703-413-8200*

Tosca

★★★

1112 F St. NW, Washington, DC (Downtown)
202-367-1990   www.toscadc.com

LUNCH: *M-F 11:30-2:30*   **ENTREES:** *$13-$18*
DINNER: *Sun-Th 5:30-10:30, F-Sat 5:30-11*
ENTREES: *$16-$34, 4-course tasting menu $45*
CHEF'S TABLE: *Eight-to-10-course for 4 to 10 guests, $85 per person*
CREDIT CARDS: *AE, DC, MC, V*   **RESERVATIONS:** *Recommended*
DRESS: *Business casual*   **CROSS STREET:** *11th*
PARKING: *$5 valet at dinner*   **METRO:** *Metro Center*

NAMED NOT FOR PUCCINI'S OPERA but for the daughter of chef Cesare Lanfranconi, Tosca is my ready response to many dining queries. Where to go for a formal business lunch? A fancy dinner before a show? A special occasion? This northern Italian restaurant comes to the rescue with a spare but stylish interior and equally inviting food.

Not everyone appreciates the cool elegance of the space—a snapshot in beige with splashes of teal—but I find it a soothing environment even when three-quarters of the crowd is rushing through dinner to catch a concert. Zucchini blossoms stuffed with sweet crab are fried in a tempura-like batter; crisp and hot, they rest on a shallow pool of garlic sauce. Octopus is shaved as thin as paper and spread out into a pink-and-white mosaic with fennel, sliced artichokes and a jolt of lemon. Lanfranconi's starches are superb—he previously cooked at Galileo, after all. He slips local tomatoes inside tiny ravioli and invigorates them with summery basil sauce, and perfumes a rustic pork sausage risotto with truffles.

> **Not everyone appreciates the cool elegance of the space, but I find it a soothing environment even when three-quarters of the crowd is rushing through dinner to catch a concert.**

Desserts are better than ever these days, and they play by the calendar: In late summer, diners can find a fine polenta cake garnished with juicy cherries and a flaky tart of tomato marmalade presented with a scoop of basil ice cream. (Trust me, it works.)

2941

2941 Fairview Park Dr., Falls Church, VA
703-270-1500   www.2941restaurant.com

LUNCH: *M-F 11:30-2:30* **ENTREES:** *$11-$20*
DINNER: *M-Sat 5:30-10, Sun 5-9* **ENTREES:** *$22-$38*
BRUNCH BUFFET: *Sun 11-2:30* **PRICE:** *$39*
TASTING MENUS: *Available at lunch ($25, $35) and dinner ($55-$100)*
CREDIT CARDS: *All major* **RESERVATIONS:** *Recommended*
DRESS: *Business casual* **CROSS STREET:** *Route 50*
PARKING: *Complimentary valet* **METRO:** *Dunn Loring-Merrifield*

T HE WALK FROM CAR TO ENTRANCE alone is captivating. Shaped from glass and steel, 2941 rises elegantly from its wooded office setting, fronted with a pond stocked with colorful fish and capturing a lake view with a fountain in the near distance. Inside, honeyed lighting and strategically placed hearths give warmth to the cavernous main dining room; chairs covered in tangerine- and periwinkle-colored fabric add a playful touch.

It's the perfect backdrop for chef Jonathan Krinn's lovely cooking: saffron-tinged risotto wreathed with perfect seasonal vegetables, wild salmon tickled with a sauce of lemon and sorrel, maybe lamb presented two ways, as loin and tenderloin, both straightforward but luscious (appetizers are more cleverly presented than entrees here). Desserts continue the pleasures. I'm fond of anything revolving around fruit, be it the glamorous pineapple tart gilded with spicy black pepper ice cream or a trio of fruit soups paired with a refreshing scoop of a flattering sorbet (green apple tastes plucked from its tree).

Desserts continue the pleasures. I'm fond of anything revolving around fruit.

The evening isn't over until a cloud of cotton candy, house-made marshmallows and chocolate-covered almonds lands on your table. If you're lucky, the affable chef might even bid you farewell himself, sending you out into the night with a loaf or two of 2941's fine bread—baked, you should know, twice a day by the chef's father.

2 Amys

3715 Macomb St. NW, Washington, DC (Upper NW)

202-885-5700

OPEN: *Tu-Sun 11-11* **ENTREES:** *$7.95-$12.95*
CLOSED: *M* **CREDIT CARDS:** *MC, V*
RESERVATIONS: *No* **DRESS:** *Casual*
CROSS STREET: *Wisconsin Avenue NW* **PARKING:** *Street*
METRO: *Tenleytown-AU*

P EOPLE WHO EXPECT a lot of razzle-dazzle with their pizza might not care for this Neapolitan-flavored outpost near Washington National Cathedral. The crusts at 2 Amys are minimally dressed, its staff doesn't sing "Happy Birthday" and the dining rooms are simple and spare.

All of which is why I love the place—it has the spirit of a real Italian pizzeria. Who needs a whole brick of melted cheese on a pizza when the crust, blistered from time in an oven fueled by oak, is good enough to eat by itself? (Not that you should try it that way: Topping choices such as rapini, anchovies and hot pepper, or capers, cockles and grana should not be missed.) The young staff is casual yet smart; you know they've tasted the Italian wines, which are delicious and moderately priced, poured in a back bar illuminated with bare bulbs dangling from on high. The broad

> **Who needs a whole brick of melted cheese on a pizza when the crust, blistered from time in an oven fueled by oak, is good enough to eat by itself?**

wood tables and cheerful yellow walls, meanwhile, add to rather than detract from the pleasure of eating a pie here (though I can see how the white tiles up front remind some people of restrooms).

First, ease in with an appetizer: The deviled eggs with green sauce are wonderful, as are salt cod fritters and any of the simple salads; the one made from orange slices decked out with olives, red onions and a fruity drizzle of olive oil is my current pick. The straightforward desserts, on the other end of the meal, follow suit. Frankly, it's tough to choose between a hunk of Gorgonzola paired with chestnut honey and a Marsala custard so seductive it really ought to carry an R rating.

Two Quail

(0 stars)

320 Massachusetts Ave. NE, Washington, DC (Capitol Hill)
202-543-8030   www.twoquail.com

LUNCH: *M-F 11:30-2:30*   **ENTREES:** *$8-$12*
DINNER: *Sun-Th 5-10, F-Sat 5-11* **ENTREES:** *$19-$25*
PRE- AND POST-THEATER: *Daily 3-course prix fixe, $25*
CREDIT CARDS: *All major* **RESERVATIONS:** *Recommended*
DRESS: *Business casual* **CROSS STREET:** *Third Street NE* **PARKING:** *Street*
METRO: *Union Station*

I N ONE OVERDRESSED ROOM ALONE, there is a stuffed deer head sporting pearls, a Sunset Boulevard sign and enough swags, fringes and fabric to pad the Orient Express 10 times over. If Auntie Mame and Morticia Addams got together to decorate a townhouse, Two Quail is what their effort might look like.

Softly lighted and carved into cozy nooks, some of which have curtains that can be pulled together for more privacy, the restaurant has long spelled romance for some diners. Unfortunately, they also have to order food to sit there. Much of the menu is depressing, starting with the big public bread basket that patrons must reach into to retrieve a dry slice and ending with a tray of

> **Softly lighted and carved into cozy nooks, the restaurant has long spelled romance for some diners.**

cliched desserts. Bridging those posts from season to season might be past-their-prime fried oysters, "Heavenly Shrimp Pillows" whose tiny bland shrimp don't merit the billing, dry pork with fruit chutney and equally arid chicken with corn bread stuffing.

To accompany the entrees, diners get rice that smacks of Uncle Ben's and crinkle-cut vegetables that taste as if they had been raised not in a garden but in a freezer. Lights at the end of the tunnel come in the form of the occasional interesting salad or spinach-and-crab-stuffed rainbow trout. The jazzy music is a welcome touch, too— but even the pluses are negated by servers who sometimes act as if they'd rather be anywhere but here.

Vidalia

1990 M St. NW, Washington, DC (Downtown)
202-659-1990   www.vidaliadc.com

LUNCH: *M-F 11:30-2:30* **ENTREES:** *$12.50-$18.75*
DINNER: *M-Th 5:30-10, F-Sat 5:30-10:30, Sun 5-9:30* **ENTREES:** *$23-$29.50*
CREDIT CARDS: *All major* **RESERVATIONS:** *Recommended* **DRESS:** *Casual*
CROSS STREET: *20th* **PARKING:** *$5 valet at dinner*
METRO: *Dupont Circle/Foggy Bottom*

VIDALIA RECENTLY TURNED 10—the equivalent of middle age in the restaurant world—and its owners had to decide what to do with their southern-themed dining room in the city's West End: Relocate or renovate? People weren't exactly clamoring to eat in an underground restaurant, Jeff and Sallie Buben realized, yet the neighborhood was emerging as one of Washington's more colorful places to eat.

They ended up staying put, signing a 15-year lease and shuttering Vidalia for a month-long, million-dollar makeover. A wall of silk magnolias now accompanies diners from entrance to host stand, and the cream-colored dining room has been spruced up with fabric in elegant shades of gold, green and blue. A communal table makes for a friendlier bar. Clean and modern, the revised restaurant does just fine without windows.

> **Seafood is a strong draw, but meats, including a thick pork chop, are no less compelling.**

The kitchen appears to have been reenergized by the transformation. (Even the bread basket, filled with warm popovers, corn bread and onion focaccia, tastes better than in seasons past.) Seafood is a strong draw—think tuna tartare, she-crab soup, shrimp and grits—but meats, including a thick pork chop, are no less compelling. Save space for a side dish, an honor roll of southern staples such as hush puppies, oniony turnip greens and macaroni and cheese updated with goat cheese and elegant with truffle shavings. The wine list, composed by sommelier Doug Mohr, is a joy to read and a pleasure to choose from.

Endings keep pace with what comes before them: They run large and showy. A constant on the menu is lemon chess pie. One taste and you'll understand why the South is revered for its sweets—and why it's so nice to see Vidalia back.

Wazuri

1836 18th St. NW, Washington, DC (Dupont Circle)
202-797-4930   www.wazuri.com

LUNCH: *W-Sun noon-5* **ENTREES:** *$10.50-$15.50*
DINNER: *Sun-Th 5-10, F-Sat 5-midnight* **ENTREES:** *$12-$19.95*
CREDIT CARDS: *All major* **RESERVATIONS:** *Recommended*
DRESS: *Casual* **CROSS STREET:** *T Street NW* **PARKING:** *Street*
METRO: *Dupont Circle*

IT TOOK KOJO DAVIS to give Washington something it really needed: an African restaurant of distinction. That's not to take away from, among others, the dozens of area Ethiopian places that season the landscape. But in his cheery, orange-and-yellow dining room, the former manager of the nearby Bukom Cafe is offering a much broader geography lesson, with food that he says represents the places Africans came from, sailed to or eventually called home. Hints of Brazil and Louisiana, among other points on the map, pop up on the menu.

So there are treats such as mafe, braised lamb draped in a kicky peanut sauce and bedded on couscous, and dorko dorko, a sweetly spiced duck tagine partnered with a sweet-potato gratin. Wazuri's callaloo isn't the grassy soup of greens you might have

Hints of Brazil and Louisiana, among other points on the map, pop up on the menu.

tasted in the Caribbean, but it is delicious nevertheless, a pale orange liquid that tastes of cream, bell peppers, leeks, potatoes and bay leaf. A salad billed as Sandaga combines earthy green lentils with bits of red pepper on a plate that is ringed by warm mussels and creamy slices of banana, a combination that sounds offbeat but goes over well on the palate.

The cocktails here are eye-openers—even the rum punch, a blend of fruit juices, grenadine and the obvious liquor, is nothing like the bubble-gum-flavored cocktail we've come to expect; Davis, a frequent presence at the entrance, specialized in drinks at his former watering hole.

Wazuri promises "A Taste of Africa," and it offers just that, plus good music, a diverse clientele and rooftop tables when the weather says yes.

Woodlands ★★

8046 New Hampshire Ave., Langley Park, MD
301-434-4202

LUNCH: *Daily 11:30-3* **ENTREES:** *$6.95 buffet ($8.95 Sat-Sun)*
DINNER: *Sun-Th 3-9:30, F-Sat 3-10* **ENTREES:** *$6.95-$14.75*
CREDIT CARDS: *AE, MC, V* **RESERVATIONS:** *No* **DRESS:** *Casual*
CROSS STREET: *University Boulevard/Route 193* **PARKING:** *Lot*
METRO: *College Park-U of MD*

LOCATED IN A MODEST SHOPPING STRIP, the dining room is big, clean and barely decorated, with Indian art on the walls, while the service runs matter-of-fact. Woodlands isn't much to look at or to linger in. No one seems to care, though, because the kitchen more than compensates for such minimalism with vegetarian cooking that packs 'em in—notice all the Indian families here?—with its care and consistency.

Dosa, the pleasantly sour crepe made with rice and lentils, can be sampled more than a dozen different ways.

To start, there are snacks of lentil doughnuts and unfortunately heavy pakora. Dosa, the pleasantly sour crepe made with rice and lentils, can be sampled more than a dozen different ways; one of my standbys involves a filling of buttery, cumin-fragrant potatoes and onions. Like all the dosas, this one is accompanied by coconut chutney and sambhar, a sort of vegetable soup. Together, they bring a lot of pleasure for $6.

Of the rice dishes, I'm partial to the pilaf accented with sweet-tart tamarind and mixed with nuts and raisins. Brassy pickles and tangy yogurt sauce transform the entree into a minifeast of flavors and textures. There's more to explore: curries, including soft-crisp okra in a brick-red tomato-and-onion sauce, and uthappam, aptly described by a companion as "Indian pizza." Its blistered surface (more rice flour and lentils) acts as a savory canvas for peas, carrots and onions.

If you have a hard time deciding, consider lunch and the buffet, an ever-changing bargain at $6.95 weekdays, $2 more on the weekend. Woodlands doesn't serve alcohol, but it does pour a fine mango lassi and a milky tea perfumed with cardamom, cloves and ginger.

OTHER LOCATIONS: *4078 Jermantown Rd., Fairfax, VA, 703-385-1996*
18216 Contour Rd., Gaithersburg, MD, 301-963-4466

Wurzburg Haus ★

7236 Muncaster Mill Rd., Rockville, MD
301-330-0402 www.wurzburghaus.com

LUNCH: *M-Sat 11:30-4* **ENTREES:** *$8.75-$13.95*
DINNER: *M-Th 4-9, F-Sat 4-10, Sun noon-9* **ENTREES:** *$9.75-$18.95*
CREDIT CARDS: *All major* **RESERVATIONS:** *Recommended*
DRESS: *Casual* **CROSS STREET:** *Redland Road* **PARKING:** *Lot*
METRO: *Shady Grove*

IT'S THE LITTLE THINGS that draw me to the Wurzburg Haus. The grandfatherly accordion player who amuses diners on the weekend. Full-flavored beer, served in a cool gray mug. A warm welcome: When the navigator in my group pulled an Amelia Earhart and we showed up an hour late for a dinner reservation on a busy night, the host couldn't have been more accommodating. And when was the last time you stopped talking because you were busy exploring a bread basket?

Set in a shopping center, this dining room is more congenial than attractive. The framed posters look straight out of a German tourism office, and the green carpet bears witness to heavy traffic. Nevertheless, the many filled seats attest to the restaurant's charm. It wants you to want to be there. So "Our Vegetarian Friends" have options of omelets, vegetable plates and Parmesan-breaded zucchini, and "Our Little Friends" can choose from a sausage with home fries, a half-sandwich with potato salad, even a pancake with ice cream (though the kid in me would go for the very good spaeztle, squiggly little dumplings served with gravy). There are even a few plates for light appetites. If you're expecting a fine German wine, you're out of luck, though; a gewurztraminer from Fetzer goes down like liquid bubble gum.

A cheat sheet for the place would go something like this: Ease in with the spinach salad, refreshing with oranges and showered with warm bacon bits. Move on to the fine, crisp-crusted Wiener schnitzel or the thick, pink, smoked pork loin, flanked with boiled potatoes and sauerkraut. Steer clear of the salty potato pancakes, along with the listless trout and the apple strudel, which begs for a hit of whipped cream to relieve its dryness. But be sure to fit in some cheesecake. Dense and creamy and not too sweet, it's one more reason to rescue German cooking from the endangered species list.

Yanyu ★★★

3435 Connecticut Ave. NW, Washington, DC (Cleveland Park)
202-686-6968

LUNCH: *W-Sat noon-2:30* **ENTREES:** *$12-$20*
DINNER: *Tu-Th 5:30-10:30, F-Sat 5:30-11, Sun 5:30-10:30* **ENTREES:** *$15-$38*
CHEF'S TABLE: *Four multiple-course tasting menus $30-$55*
CLOSED: *M* **CREDIT CARDS:** *AE, DC, MC, V*
RESERVATIONS: *Recommended* **DRESS:** *Business casual*
CROSS STREET: *Ordway Street NW* **PARKING:** *$5 valet at dinner*
METRO: *Cleveland Park*

THE MORE I EXPLORE Asian restaurants around the area, the more I appreciate Yanyu. Its service is solicitous. The space, graced with handsome murals of long-ago rulers, is very appealing: Will it be a booth upstairs or a table near the floor-to-ceiling windows on the ground floor? The menu dances from Hong Kong to Malaysia to Vietnam, from calamari ignited with hot green peppers, to lily bulb dumplings hiding a goodie bag of chicken and water chestnuts beneath a topknot of caviar, to silken sea bass. No Asian restaurant within 100 miles carves a finer Peking duck or pours from a better wine list, including such finds as Turley zinfandel and Caymus "Conundrum."

Can't decide what to eat? There are four different tasting menus, requiring 90 minutes of your time, you're told, and it is time well spent. Not content to serve just what it always has, the kitchen dishes out rich surprises: Duck liver on a finger of gently vinegared rice, anyone? Called "foie gras sushi," it's nothing short of an inspiration.

> **No Asian restaurant within 100 miles carves a finer Peking duck or pours from a better wine list.**

Yechon ★★

4121 Hummer Rd., Annandale, VA
703-914-4646

OPEN: *Daily 24 hours* **ENTREES:** *$8.95-$24.95*
CREDIT CARDS: *AE, D, MC, V* **RESERVATIONS:** *No*
DRESS: *Casual* **CROSS STREET:** *Little River Turnpike/Route 236*
PARKING: *Lot* **METRO:** *Franconia-Springfield*

L OOKS CAN BE MISLEADING. With its low-slung roof, brown wood siding and splash of neon, from the outside this restaurant could pass for a cowboy bar. Open the doors, though, and you'll discover another world: a room bustling with costumed waitresses who are pouring beer and ladling soup, and an SRO crowd of animated diners, many of them hip, young and Korean American.

Their tables are crowded with little dishes of snacks, salads and condiments, the typical lead-ins to a Korean repast: pickled cucumber, silvery dried fish, sweet shredded radish, bean sprouts, potato salad, fish cake and several kinds of kimchi—as much a staple in Korea as ketchup is in the United States. Everyone around you is ordering soup or barbecue, and you should follow that lead. Out might come a little cauldron of dae gu mae woon tang: a simmering broth, fiery with chilies and brimming with chunks of cod and tofu, enoki mushrooms and vegetables. Heady stuff. Or a platter of tender, sweet-edged slices of beef (bulgogi) with sesame seeds and scallions, destined to be rolled up with rice and soybean paste in the crisp lettuce leaves that accompany them. The sushi is ordinary in comparison.

> **Everyone around you is ordering soup or barbecue, and you should follow that lead.**

Service is rushed but helpful, and the hours couldn't be more convenient: Yechon is open 24/7.

Yee Hwa ★

1009 21st St. NW, Washington, DC (Downtown)
202-833-1244

LUNCH: *Daily 11:30-3* **ENTREES:** *$8.95-$16.95*
DINNER: *Daily 3-10* **ENTREES:** *$10.95-$32.95*
CREDIT CARDS: *All major* **RESERVATIONS:** *Recommended*
DRESS: *Casual* **CROSS STREET:** *K Street NW* **PARKING:** *Street*
METRO: *Foggy Bottom*

AS A WORLD CAPITAL, Washington dishes up plenty of global cooking, be it the stews of Ethiopia, the curries of India or the potato dishes made famous by Peru. One cuisine that is abundant in the suburbs of Northern Virginia but pretty much missing from the city is Korean—until earlier this year. That's when Yee Hwa opened downtown and began offering spicy codfish soup, marinated short ribs, the signature kimchi (pungent pickled vegetables) and even Korean wine, or soju, on its menu.

A weave of hearty and bold flavors, the cooking at Yee Hwa unfolds in a dining room of warm wood, sea-blue carpet and pale-rose booths; glass partitions between the tables are etched with the name of the restaurant in Korean characters. Part of the menu is Japanese, but Japanese food is not the reason to come here. Bibim bap—that lusty marriage of rice, shredded beef and vegetables, served with hot chili paste in a heavy stone bowl—definitely is. At night, the table grills come out, allowing diners the chance to stir-cook their way to a meal of barbecue, Korean-style.

> **A weave of hearty and bold flavors, the cooking at Yee Hwa unfolds in a dining room of warm wood, sea-blue carpet and pale-rose booths.**

Yoko ★

332 Elden St., Herndon, VA
703-464-7000 www.yokorestaurant.com

LUNCH: *M-Sat 11:30-2:30* **ENTREES:** *$7.95-$14.50*
DINNER: *M-Th 5:30-10, F-Sat 5:30-10:30, Sun 5:30-9:30*
ENTREES: *$7.50-$23.50* **CREDIT CARDS:** *All major*
RESERVATIONS: *Recommended* **DRESS:** *Casual*
CROSS STREET: *Herndon Parkway* **PARKING:** *Lot* **METRO:** *No*

HALF A DOZEN MEALS at Yoko have taught me this: To find the restaurant's best assets, all you need to do is use your eyes. Notice how busy all three sushi chefs always seem to be? The long, narrow dining room with its display of Japanese masks and its well-trafficked wood floor is pretty in a spare fashion, but it's the dozen or so seats at the sushi bar that connoisseurs seem most interested in (unless they also want to keep up with whatever game is playing on the TV set, mounted in the rear).

A complimentary fillip of custardy tofu slices, animated with red chili and sesame oil, starts a meal off on a hospitable note, and you're wise to continue with something uncooked. All the usual suspects—salmon, flounder, mackerel and sea urchin—can be found on the sushi and sashimi menu, as can baby octopus, pleasantly chewy and subtly sweet from its soy sauce glaze, and raw, sweet shrimp sushi, trailed by an escort of spiky, deep-fried shrimp heads. "Try it, it's very good," one of the helpful waitresses coached my tablemates as she set the plate down. She was right: The heat of the crunchy delicacy is foiled by its cool daikon garnish.

Frying isn't the restaurant's strong suit, though. The pale batter that clings to the tempura dishes, and the mouthful of oil

> **My detours from sushi have been most successful when they've included udon and hamachi kama.**

one encounters with every bite of vegetable, shrimp or chicken tempura, indicates fat that's not hot enough to cook them properly; the exceptions are the pan-fried dumplings of beef and vegetables (gyoza) and delicate shrimp (shumai). My detours from sushi have been most successful when they've included udon, its thick wheat noodles filling a big bowl of broth along with wisps of greens, mushrooms and pink-edged fish cake slices, and hamachi kama. The wafer-crisp skin of this broiled, salt-sprinkled yellowtail jaw yields to a delicate interior and a meaty treat. A relaxing jazz soundtrack and a staff that easily juggles soloists, dates and small families add to the dining charms.

Yuan Fu ★★

798 Rockville Pike, Rockville, MD
301-762-5937

LUNCH: *Daily 11-4:30* **ENTREES:** *$5.95-$13.95*
DINNER: *Sun-Th 4:30-10, F-Sat 4:30-10:30* **ENTREES:** *$7.95-$13.95*
CREDIT CARDS: *D, MC, V* **RESERVATIONS:** *Recommended*
DRESS: *Casual* **CROSS STREET:** *Mount Vernon Place*
PARKING: *Lot* **METRO:** *Rockville*

A N ADMISSION: I'm not generally an advocate of food manipulated to look like something other than what it is. But this vegetarian Chinese kitchen convinces me that there can be delicious exceptions.

The color photographs on the menu look much like crab and duck, for instance, and the smells that follow those dishes are truly fragrant. But the orange-flavored "beef," seemingly caramelized morsels in a citrusy dark sauce, turns out to be soybean protein, while the kung pao "shrimp," tossed with bright green peppers and peanuts, is actually white yams having some fun with your taste buds. That nicely crisped skin on the "fish?" It's seaweed.

As you might expect, actual vegetables are paid great respect; don't miss the sliced, battered eggplant or the crackling spinach pancake, accented with sesame seeds and electrified by some hot mustard sauce. Tucked into a small shopping strip, this dining room is pretty in green and nice enough for toasting a special occasion—although since there's no alcohol, it'll have to be with a soda or tea.

> **The orange-flavored "beef," seemingly caramelized morsels in a citrusy dark sauce, turns out to be soybean protein.**

Zaytinya

★ ★ ★

701 Ninth St. NW, Washington, DC (Penn Quarter)
202-638-0800   www.zaytinya.com

LUNCH: *Daily 11:30-2:30*   **ENTREES:** *$12.95-$25.95 (mezze $3.50-$7.95)*
DINNER: *Sun-M 5-10, Tu-Sat 5-11:30*   **ENTREES:** *$12.95-$25.95*
BRUNCH: *Sun 11:30-3*   **ENTREES:** *$3.50-$17.95*
CREDIT CARDS: *All major*   **RESERVATIONS:** *Only before 6:30 pm*
DRESS: *Casual*   **CROSS STREET:** *G Street NW*   **PARKING:** *$10 valet at dinner*
METRO: *Gallery Place-Chinatown*

JOSE ANDRES BROUGHT US A TASTE of his native Spain with the tapas bar Jaleo and delivered the flavors of Latin America with the spirited Cafe Atlantico. Entertaining as both those restaurants are, these days my favorite destination involves the soulful cooking of Greece, Lebanon and Turkey at the busy chef's latest restaurant.

Zaytinya is a big and happy place, awash in white and blue to reflect the sun-drenched Aegean and perfect for many occasions: a solo snack at the welcoming bar; a date near the downstairs fireplace or up high, overlooking the party below from 20 feet; maybe a group outing at the long communal table.

Wherever you land, the drill is mezze, small plates of mostly luscious appetizers meant to be served as they are ready and best shared with others. And whatever your taste,

Zaytinya is a big and happy place, awash in white and blue to reflect the sun-drenched Aegean and perfect for many occasions.

there will be something to make you swoon. It might be soft fritters shaped from apricot, carrot and pine nuts and paired with a light pistachio sauce. Or a bowl of tender squid, tossed with tendrils of spinach, bronzed garlic and fresh dill, everything moistened with a bright lemon sauce. Raw beef is mixed with cracked wheat for a kind of Lebanese steak tartare, spread in a thin layer on its plate and jazzed up with fresh mint and sharp radish. The daily specials—squash blossoms stuffed with feta cheese, anyone?—make decisions even more difficult, and if you don't save room for dessert, you'll be missing out on some of Washington's finest.

There is warm, football-shaped pita bread to start and worthy Greek wines to fuel a meal. Yes, it's loud. And Zaytinya doesn't take reservations after 6:30 p.m. But the price is right, the crowd is fun, and who else in town can feed 750 diners a day and do it so memorably?

✅ *Critic's Pick*

Zest

★★

11791 Fingerboard Rd. (Route 80), Monrovia, MD
301-865-0868   www.eatatzest.com

LUNCH: *Tu-Sat 11:30-2:30* **ENTREES:** *$7.50-$10.50*
DINNER: *Tu-Th 5-9:30, Fri-Sat 5-10* **ENTREES:** *$16-$25*
CHEF'S TABLE: *Tu-Th, 5-course tasting menu at dinner, $45*
CLOSED: *Sun-M* **CREDIT CARDS:** *AE, D, MC, V*
RESERVATIONS: *Recommended* **DRESS:** *Casual*
CROSS STREET: *Green Valley Road/Route 75* **PARKING:** *Lot*

ZEST IS AN APT NAME for the spirited restaurant created by buddies David Jones and Keith Sleppy. Both men cook, but either is likely to greet you at the door or personally deliver your food. "Try this," Jones might say, dropping a savory flan garnished with country ham on the table. "Our intern made it the other night." The complimentary treat proves pretty and seductive, like much of the cooking here.

With a focus on Maryland ingredients, the modern American menu is broken into tastings, appetizers and entrees, the first category composed of a half-dozen or so hors d'oeuvres, maybe grilled squid with oregano and lemon or fried green tomatoes topped with a sparkling tomato-basil relish. Nearly an hour northwest of Washington, Zest offers

Nearly an hour northwest of Washington, Zest offers cooking every bit as fashionable as what you might get in the big city.

cooking every bit as fashionable as what you might get in the big city but are pleased to find in this cheerful yellow dining room. A delicate seviche of scallops, shrimp and buttery lobster is arranged on a pillow of fluffy rice. Grilled swordfish shows up with a roasted pepper hiding tasty julienned vegetables. A gutsy fist of succulent beef tenderloin (from Mount Airy, the menu shares) gets some nice company in a flossy green salad and fine potato gratin.

Always enthusiastic, the service tends to be young and hesitant, and desserts don't live up to the promise of what precedes them. But the wine list is a winner, and there's as much passion packed on most plates as an episode of *Sex and the City*.

Zola

800 F St. NW, Washington, DC (Penn Quarter)
202-654-0999 www.zoladc.com

LUNCH: *M-F 11:30-3* **ENTREES:** *$10-$23*
DINNER: *M-Th 5-10, F-Sat 5-11, Sun 5-10* **ENTREES:** *$14-$25*
PRE-THEATER DINNER: *Daily 5-7, 3-course prix fixe $25* **CREDIT CARDS:** *All major*
RESERVATIONS: *Recommended* **DRESS:** *Business casual*
CROSS STREET: *8th* **PARKING:** *$10 valet at dinner*
METRO: *Gallery Place-Chinatown*

THE THEME FROM *MISSION IMPOSSIBLE* keeps you company if you get put on hold when you call, and sly design details suggest that the CIA had a hand in this restaurant's blueprint. Notice the windows by the red velvet booths, the ones that allow you to see the kitchen, and vice versa? The declassified intelligence documents sandwiched between Plexiglas?

Yet it would be wrong to paint Zola, a neighbor to the Spy Museum, as a typical theme restaurant. It took some time after its launch for the waiters and cooks to hit their stride, but they're performing with plenty of confidence these days. Most happily, chef Frank Morales, late of the Oval Room downtown, has transformed a mixed American menu into something focused and fresh. A dense and flat-tasting tuna tartare might try to sabotage your meal, and chicken with raisin-tomato sauce is merely OK, but dishes like those are outnumbered by

> **Chef Frank Morales has transformed a mixed American menu into something focused and fresh.**

plates that encourage return engagements: fat prawns draped in sun-dried-tomato sauce and bedded on gingery grits; succulent grilled veal accessorized with crisp green beans, favas and a light wash of jus; a first-class lobster roll that misses only because there's no sand beneath your feet. A sense of humor crops up in "Buffalo" chicken croquettes flanked with blue cheese dip and vegetable sticks—try 'em, you'll like 'em.

Endings have never been better; the kitchen makes it tough to choose among the towering chocolate bombe, the fetching pineapple upside-down cake with a velvety scoop of ice cream, and a cookie plate that blasts much of the competition out of the water with, among other treats, melt-in-your-mouth butter cookies flecked with citrus zest.

The oval wine displays in the center of each small dining room aren't just handsome props but represent serious collections from around the world.

208

The ESSENTIAL GUIDE

GUAJILLO: Shrimp seviche

THE ESSENTIAL GUIDE

A roundup of restaurants to help you find the features and food you want, fast

RANKING BY STARS

★ ★ ★ ★

Laboratorio del Galileo
Maestro
Michel Richard Citronelle

★ ★ ★

Bistrot Lepic
Bob Kinkead's
  Colvin Run Tavern
Cafe Atlantico
Cashion's Eat Place
Charleston
DC Coast
Elysium
Equinox
Gerard's Place
Heritage India
Huong Que (Four Sisters)
Inn at Easton
Inn at Little Washington
Jaleo
Kaz Sushi Bistro
L'Auberge Provencale
Makoto
Marcel's
Nectar
Obelisk
Palena
Sushi-Ko
TenPenh

Tosca
2941
2 Amys
Vidalia
Yanyu
Zaytinya
Zola

★ ★

A & J
Addie's
Al Tiramisu
Andale
Artie's
Ashby Inn
Bacchus
Bardeo
Big Bowl
Bistro Bis
Bistro Francais
Bistrot du Coin
Bistrot Lafayette
Black's Bar and Kitchen
Black Olive
Bombay Club
Bombay Tandoor
Breadline
Cafe de Paris
Cafe Divan
Cafe 15
Carlyle

Caucus Room
C.F. Folks
Charlie Palmer Steak
Circle Bistro
Colorado Kitchen
Corduroy
Costa Verde
Crisp & Juicy
Cuban Corner
Cubano's
David Greggory
Dish
Eat First
88
El Chalan
El Golfo
Ella's Wood Fired Pizza
El Manantial
15 ria
Firefly
Four & Twenty Blackbirds
Galileo
Green Papaya
Guajillo
Han Sung Oak
Harris Crab House
Harry's Tap Room
Hollywood East Cafe
Il Pizzico
Indique
Islander Caribbean
Jimmy Cantler's
Joe's Noodle House
Johnny's Half Shell
Kabob Palace
Kinkead's
Kuna
L'Auberge Chez Francois
Layalina

Le Mannequin Pis
Les Halles
Le Tire Bouchon
Little Fountain Cafe
Lupo's Italian Chophouse
Majestic Cafe
Mandalay
Mantis
Melrose
Melting Pot
Meskerem
Minh's
minibar at Cafe Atlantico
Montmartre
Mykonos Grill
New Fortune
New Heights
Nick & Stef's
Nizam's
Oceanaire Seafood Room
Old Europe
O'Learys
Olives
Oval Room
Palm
Perry's
Pesce
Pizzeria Paradiso
Prime Rib
Rail Stop
Raku
Ray's the Steaks
Sakoontra
Samantha's
SBC Cafe
Sea Catch
Seasons
1789
Signatures

Singh Thai
Smith Point
Sorak Garden
Spices
Sunflower
Sushi Taro
Taberna del Alabardero
Taste of Morocco
Tavira
Thaiphoon
Wazuri
Woodlands
Yechon
Yuan Fu
Zest

★

Addis Ababa
Afghan
Agrodolce
Amma Vegetarian Kitchen
A.V. Ristorante
Bistro d'Oc
Boulevard Woodgrill
Burma
Cafe Asia
Cafe Milano
Cafe Salsa
Cantina Marina
Caspian House of Kabob
Chicken on the Run
Cho's Garden
The Diner
Dukem
Famous Luigi's
Faryab
Hakuba

India Palace
La Fourchette
Local 16
Matchbox
Matsutake
Meiwah
Mon Ami Gabi
Mr. K's
Natta Thai
Nora
Olazzo
Old Ebbitt Grill
Old Glory
Ortanique
Persimmon
Rafagino
Southside 815
Stardust
Sushi Aoi
Teaism
Wurzburg Haus
Yee Hwa
Yoko

O STARS

Morrison-Clark Inn
Taverna Cretekou
Two Quail

TOO NEW FOR STARS
TO BE ASSIGNED

Buck's Fishing & Camping
Ceiba
Gabriel
Logan Tavern
Love Cafe
Roof Terrace

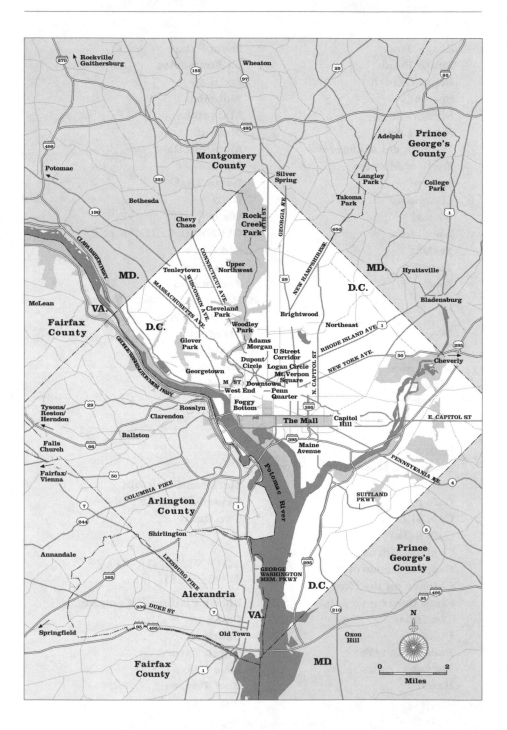

DISTRICT OF COLUMBIA

ADAMS MORGAN

Addis Ababa
Cashion's Eat Place
The Diner
La Fourchette
Little Fountain Cafe
Mantis
Meskerem
Perry's

BRIGHTWOOD

Colorado Kitchen

CAPITOL HILL

Bistro Bis
Charlie Palmer Steak
Montmartre
Two Quail

CHINATOWN

Burma
Eat First
Matchbox

CLEVELAND PARK

Bardeo
Indique
Palena
Spices
Yanyu

DOWNTOWN
16TH STREET AND EAST

Cafe 15
Ceiba
Corduroy
DC Coast
Gerard's Place
Les Halles
Oceanaire Seafood Room
Old Ebbitt Grill
Ortanique
TenPenh
Tosca

DOWNTOWN
16TH STREET AND WEST

Bombay Club
Breadline
Cafe Asia
El Chalan
Equinox
Famous Luigi's
Galileo
Kaz Sushi Bistro
Laboratorio del Galileo
Mr. K's
Olives
Oval Room
Prime Rib
Taberna del Alabardero
Teaism
Vidalia
Yee Hwa

DUPONT CIRCLE

Al Tiramisu
Bacchus
Bistrot du Coin
C.F. Folks
88
Firefly
Gabriel
Johnny's Half Shell
Melting Pot
Nora
Obelisk
Palm
Pesce
Pizzeria Paradiso
Raku
Sushi Taro
Teaism
Thaiphoon
Wazuri

Cafe Divan
Cafe Milano
Michel Richard Citronelle
Old Glory
Pizzeria Paradiso
Sea Catch
Seasons
1789
Smith Point

GLOVER PARK

Heritage India
Old Europe
Sushi-Ko

LOGAN CIRCLE

15 ria
Logan Tavern

FOGGY BOTTOM /
WEST END

Circle Bistro
David Greggory
Dish
Kinkead's
Marcel's
Meiwah
Melrose
Nectar
Roof Terrace

MT. VERNON SQUARE

A.V. Ristorante
Morrison-Clark Inn
Sushi Aoi

PALISADES

Makoto

PENN QUARTER

Andale
Bistro d'Oc
Cafe Atlantico
Caucus Room
Ella's Wood Fired Pizza
Jaleo

GEORGETOWN

Amma Vegetarian Kitchen
Bistro Francais
Bistrot Lepic

minibar at Cafe Atlantico
Nick & Stef's
Signatures
Teaism
Zaytinya
Zola

SOUTHWEST
WATERFRONT

Cantina Marina

UPPER NW

Buck's Fishing & Camping
2 Amys

U STREET CORRIDOR

Dukem
Islander Caribbean
Kuna
Local 16
Love Cafe

WOODLEY PARK

New Heights

MARYLAND

ANNAPOLIS

Jimmy Cantler's
Melting Pot
O'Learys

BALTIMORE

Black Olive
Charleston

BETHESDA

Bacchus
Black's Bar and Kitchen
Chicken on the Run
Faryab
Green Papaya
Jaleo
Mon Ami Gabi

Olazzo
Persimmon
Raku

CHEVY CHASE

Mciwah
Tavira

COLLEGE PARK /
LANGLEY PARK

Lupo's Italian Chophouse
Mandalay
Woodlands

COLUMBIA

Cafe de Paris

EASTERN SHORE

Harris Crab House
Inn at Easton

GERMANTOWN

Agrodolce
Caspian House of Kabob
India Palace

MARYLAND
COUNTRYSIDE

Zest

OLNEY

Le Mannequin Pis

ROCKVILLE /
GAITHERSBURG

A & J
Addie's
Crisp & Juicy
Cuban Corner
Hakuba
Il Pizzico
Joe's Noodle House
Melting Pot
Mykonos Grill
New Fortune
Woodlands
Wurzburg Haus
Yuan Fu

SILVER SPRING /
WHEATON

Cubano's
Crisp & Juicy
El Golfo
Hollywood East Cafe
Samantha's

VIRGINIA

ALEXANDRIA

Afghan
Bistrot Lafayette
Cafe Salsa
Elysium
Majestic Cafe
Southside 815
Stardust
Taverna Cretekou

ANNANDALE /
SPRINGFIELD

A & J
Sorak Garden
Yechon

ARLINGTON

Big Bowl
Boulevard Woodgrill
Cafe Asia
Carlyle
Costa Verde
Crisp & Juicy
Guajillo
Harry's Tap Room
Kabob Palace
Layalina
Matsutake *(3 locations)*
Melting Pot
Minh's
Ray's the Steaks
Singh Thai
Taste of Morocco
Thaiphoon

FAIRFAX / BURKE

Artie's
Cho's Garden
Le Tire Bouchon
Rafagino
Sakoontra
Woodlands

FALLS CHURCH

Crisp & Juicy
Han Sung Oak
Huong Que (Four Sisters)
2941

GREAT FALLS

L'Auberge Chez Francois

RESTON / HERNDON / STERLING

Big Bowl *(2 locations)*
El Manantial
Matsutake
Melting Pot
SBC Cafe
Yoko

TYSONS CORNER

Bob Kinkead's Colvin Run Tavern
Maestro
Palm

VIENNA

Amma Vegetarian Kitchen
Bombay Tandoor
Natta Thai
Nizam's
Sunflower

VIRGINIA COUNTRYSIDE

Ashby Inn
Four & Twenty Blackbirds
Inn at Little Washington
L'Auberge Provencale
Rail Stop

BY CUISINE

AFGHAN

Afghan
Faryab
Kabob Palace

AFRICAN

Wazuri

AMERICAN / CONTEMPORARY

Addie's
Ashby Inn
Bardeo
Bob Kinkead's Colvin Run Tavern
Buck's Fishing & Camping
Carlyle
Cashion's Eat Place
Circle Bistro
Corduroy
David Greggory
88
Elysium
Equinox
15 ria
Firefly
Four & Twenty Blackbirds
Gabriel
Inn at Little Washington
Logan Tavern
Melrose
minibar at Cafe Atlantico
Morrison-Clark Inn
Nectar
New Heights
Nora
Perry's

Persimmon
Roof Terrace
SBC Cafe
Seasons
Signatures
Smith Point
Stardust
2941
Two Quail
Zest
Zola

AMERICAN / TRADITIONAL

Artie's
Black's Bar and Kitchen
Boulevard Woodgrill
Breadline
Cantina Marina
Caucus Room
C.F. Folks
Charleston
Charlie Palmer Steak
Colorado Kitchen
DC Coast
The Diner
Dish
Harris Crab House
Harry's Tap Room
Jimmy Cantler's
Johnny's Half Shell
Kinkead's
Little Fountain Cafe
Local 16
Love Cafe
Majestic Cafe
Matchbox
Melting Pot

Nick & Stef's
Oceanaire Seafood Room
Old Ebbitt Grill
Old Glory
O'Learys
Oval Room
Palm
Pesce
Prime Rib
Rail Stop
Ray's the Steaks
Sea Catch
1789
Southside 815
Vidalia

ASIAN

Big Bowl
Cafe Asia
Mantis
Raku
Spices
Stardust
Sunflower
Teaism
TenPenh
Yanyu

AUSTRALIAN

Inn at Easton

BARBEQUE

Old Glory

BELGIAN

Le Mannequin Pis

BURMESE

Burma
Mandalay

CARIBBEAN

Islander Caribbean
Ortanique

CHINESE

A & J
Eat First
Hollywood East Cafe
Joe's Noodle House
Meiwah
Mr. K's
New Fortune
Yuan Fu

CONTINENTAL

El Manantial

CUBAN

Cuban Corner
Cubano's

ETHIOPIAN

Addis Ababa
Dukem
Meskerem

FRENCH

Bistro Bis
Bistro d'Oc
Bistro Francais
Bistrot du Coin
Bistrot Lafayette
Bistrot Lepic
Cafe de Paris
Cafe 15
Gerard's Place
La Fourchette
L'Auberge Chez Francois
L'Auberge Provencale
Le Tire Bouchon
Les Halles
Marcel's
Michel Richard Citronelle
Mon Ami Gabi
Montmartre

GERMAN

Old Europe
Wurzburg Haus

GREEK

Black Olive
Mykonos Grill
Taverna Cretekou

INDIAN

Amma Vegetarian Kitchen
Bombay Club
Bombay Tandoor
Heritage India
India Palace
Indique
Woodlands

ITALIAN

Agrodolce
Al Tiramisu
A.V. Ristorante
Cafe Milano
Ella's Wood Fired Pizza
Famous Luigi's
Galileo
Il Pizzico
Kuna
Laboratorio del Galileo
Lupo's Italian Chophouse
Maestro
Obelisk
Olazzo
Olives
Palena
Pizzeria Paradiso
Rafagino
Tosca
2 Amys

JAPANESE

Hakuba
Kaz Sushi Bistro
Makoto
Matsutake
Sushi Aoi
Sushi-Ko
Sushi Taro
Yoko

KOREAN

Cho's Garden
Han Sung Oak
Sorak Garden
Yechon
Yee Hwa

LATIN AMERICAN

Cafe Atlantico
Cafe Salsa
Ceiba
Chicken on the Run
Crisp & Juicy
El Golfo
Samantha's

MEDITERRANEAN

Olives
Zaytinya

MIDDLE EASTERN

Bacchus
Caspian House of Kabob
Layalina

MEXICAN

Andale
El Golfo
Guajillo
Samantha's

MOROCCAN

Taste of Morocco

PERUVIAN

Costa Verde
El Chalan

PIZZA

Agrodolce
A.V. Ristorante
Cafe Milano
David Greggory
Ella's Wood Fired Pizza
Famous Luigi's
Matchbox
Olives
Pizzeria Paradiso
2 Amys

PORTUGUESE

Tavira

SEAFOOD

Black's Bar and Kitchen
Black Olive
DC Coast
Harris Crab House
Jimmy Cantler's
Johnny's Half Shell
Kinkead's
Oceanaire Seafood Room
O'Learys
Pesce
Sea Catch
Southside 815

SOUTHERN

Black's Bar and Kitchen
Cantina Marina
Charleston
Colorado Kitchen
Old Glory
Southside 815
Vidalia

SPANISH

Jaleo
Taberna del Alabardero

STEAKHOUSES

Caucus Room
Charlie Palmer Steak
Harry's Tap Room
Nick & Stef's
Palm
Prime Rib
Ray's the Steaks

SUSHI

Cafe Asia
Cho's Garden
Habuka
Kaz Sushi Bistro
Makoto
Matsutake
Meiwah
Perry's
Raku
Signatures
Sorak Garden
Spices
Sunflower
Sushi Aoi
Sushi-Ko
Sushi Taro
Teaism
Yechon
Yee Hwa
Yoko

THAI

Natta Thai
Sakoontra
Singh Thai
Thaiphoon

TURKISH

Cafe Divan
Nizam's

VEGETARIAN

Amma Vegetarian Kitchen
Sunflower
Woodlands
Yuan Fu

VIETNAMESE

Green Papaya
Huong Que (Four Sisters)
Minh's

CHEAP EATS

(DINNER ENTREES
STARTING UNDER $10)

A & J
Addis Ababa
Afghan
Amma Vegetarian Kitchen
A.V. Ristorante
Bardeo
Big Bowl
Burma
Cafe Asia
Cafe Divan
Caspian House of Kabob
Chicken on the Run
Cho's Garden
Costa Verde
Crisp & Juicy
Cuban Corner
The Diner
Dukem
Eat First
El Golfo
Ella's Wood Fired Pizza
Green Papaya
Guajillo
Hakuba
Han Sung Oak
Hollywood East Cafe
Huong Que (Four Sisters)
India Palace
Jaleo
Joe's Noodle House
Kabob Palace
Little Fountain Cafe
Love Cafe
Lupo's Italian Chophouse
Mandalay
Mantis

Matsutake
Meiwah
Meskerem
Minh's
Natta Thai
New Fortune
Old Glory
Pizzeria Paradiso
Sakoontra
Samantha's
Singh Thai
Southside 815
Spices
Sunflower
Sushi Aoi
Teaism
Thaiphoon
2 Amys
Woodlands
Yechon
Yoko
Yuan Fu
Zaytinya

CHEF'S TABLE AVAILABLE

Inn at Little Washington
Laboratorio del Galileo
Le Mannequin Pis
Melrose
Michel Richard Citronelle
Olives
Ortanique
Tosca
2941
Yanyu
Zest

WHERE TO GET BREAKFAST

Bistro Bis
Breadline
Cafe de Paris
Cafe 15
Circle Bistro
The Diner
Dish
Elysium
15 ria
Firefly
Gabriel
Love Cafe
Maestro
Melrose
Michel Richard Citronelle
Old Ebbitt Grill
Seasons
Teaism

OPEN LATE AT NIGHT

24/7
The Diner
Yechon

4 AM
Bistro Francais *(F-Sat)*

3 AM
Bistro Francais *(Sun-Th)*
Eat First

2:30 AM
Local 16 *(F-Sat)*

2 AM
Addis Ababa *(F-Sat)*
Cho's Garden *(F-Sat)*
Dukem *(Sat-Sun)*
Hollywood East Cafe *(F-Sat)*
New Fortune *(F-Sat)*

1:30 AM
Local 16 *(Sun-Th)*

1 AM
Addis Ababa *(Sun-Th)*
Bistrot du Coin *(Th-Sat)*
Cafe Milano
Dukem *(M-F)*
Hollywood East Cafe *(Sun-Th)*
New Fortune *(Sun-Th)*

MIDNIGHT
Artie's *(F-Sat)*
Bardeo *(F-Sat)*
Cafe Asia *(F-Sat)*
Carlyle *(F-Sat)*
Famous Luigi's
Islander Caribbean *(F-Sun)*
Jaleo *(F-Sat)*
Kabob Palace
Les Halles
Logan Tavern *(Sat)*
Love Cafe *(F-Sat)*
Melting Pot *(F-Sat)*
Meskerem
Old Ebbitt Grill
Old Glory
Pizzeria Paradiso *(F-Sat)*
Samantha's *(F-Sat)*
Wazuri *(F-Sat)*

FOR LIVE ENTERTAINMENT OR DANCING *(D)*

Agrodolce
Cafe de Paris
Cafe Milano
Cafe Salsa *(D)*
Cantina Marina
Charlie Palmer Steak
Cho's Garden *(Karaoke)*
Costa Verde
Dukem
88
Four & Twenty Blackbirds
Islander Caribbean
Kinkead's
Le Tire Bouchon
Local 16 *(DJ)*
Lupo's Italian Chophouse
Marcel's
Matsutake *(Ballston)*
Melrose *(D)*
Ortanique
Perry's *(Drag Brunch)*
Prime Rib
Signatures
Southside 815
Taste of Morocco
Taverna Cretekou
Wurzburg Haus

RESTAURANTS THAT OFFER PRIVATE DINING

Addis Ababa
Afghan
Andale
Artie's

Ashby Inn
Bacchus
Big Bowl
Bistro Bis
Bistro d'Oc
Bistro Francais
Black Olive
Bob Kinkead's
  Colvin Run Tavern
Bombay Tandoor
Boulevard Woodgrill
Burma
Cafe de Paris
Cafe 15
Cafe Milano
Cafe Salsa
Caucus Room
Ceiba
Charleston
Charlie Palmer Steak
Cho's Garden
Circle Bistro
Corduroy
David Greggory
DC Coast
Eat First
88
Elysium
Equinox
Famous Luigi's
Firefly
Gabriel
Galileo
Harris Crab House
Heritage India
Huong Que (Four Sisters)
India Palace
Inn at Easton
Inn at Little Washington

Kinkead's
Laboratorio del Galileo
L'Auberge Chez Francois
L'Auberge Provencale
Les Halles
Local 16
Love Cafe
Lupo's Italian Chophouse
Maestro
Marcel's
Matsutake *(Ballston)*
Meiwah
Melrose
Melting Pot
Michel Richard Citronelle
Mon Ami Gabi
Morrison-Clark Inn
Mr. K's
Mykonos Grill
New Fortune
Nizam's
Nora
Oceanaire Seafood Room
Old Ebbitt Grill
Old Europe
Olives
Ortanique
Oval Room
Palm
Pizzeria Paradiso *(Georgetown)*
Prime Rib
Rail Stop
Roof Terrace
Sea Catch
Seasons
1789
Signatures
Sorak Garden
Stardust

Sushi Aoi
Sushi Taro
Taberna del Alabardero
Tavira
Teaism
Tosca
2941
Two Quail
Vidalia
Woodlands
Yanyu
Yechon
Yee Hwa
Zaytinya
Zest
Zola

FAMILY-FRIENDLY RESTAURANTS

A & J
Addie's
Afghan
Agrodolce
Amma Vegetarian Kitchen
Artie's
A.V. Ristorante
Bacchus
Big Bowl
Boulevard Woodgrill
Breadline
Buck's Fishing & Camping
Cantina Marina
Carlyle
Caspian House of Kabob
Colorado Kitchen
Costa Verde
Cubano's
The Diner

El Golfo
Ella's Wood Fired Pizza
El Manantial
Famous Luigi's
Guajillo
Harris Crab House
Harry's Tap Room
Hollywood East Cafe
Huong Que (Four Sisters)
Il Pizzico
Jimmy Cantler's
Joe's Noodle House
Kabob Palace
Layalina
Les Halles
Logan Tavern
Love Cafe
Lupo's Italian Chophouse
Majestic Cafe
Matchbox
Meiwah
Melting Pot
Minh's
New Fortune
Nizam's
Olazzo
Old Ebbitt Grill
Old Glory
Pizzeria Paradiso
Rail Stop
Raku
Ray's the Steaks
Sakoontra
Samantha's
SBC Cafe
Singh Thai
Sorak Garden
Southside 815
Spices

Stardust
Sunflower
Taste of Morocco
Teaism
Thaiphoon
2 Amys
Wazuri
Woodlands
Wurzburg Haus
Yechon
Yuan Fu
Zaytinya
Zest

CHILDREN'S MENUS / PORTIONS AVAILABLE

Addie's
Agrodolce
Artie's
Big Bowl
Black's Bar and Kitchen
Cafe de Paris
Carlyle
Cuban Corner
The Diner
El Golfo
15 ria
Hakuba
Harris Crab House
Harry's Tap Room
Islander Caribbean
Jimmy Cantler's
Les Halles
Logan Tavern
Matchbox
Matsutake
Melting Pot
Mon Ami Gabi
Old Ebbitt Grill

Old Europe
Old Glory
Rail Stop
Seasons
Southside 815
Stardust
Taverna Cretekou
Tavira
Wurzburg Haus
Zest

THE BRUNCH BUNCH

A & J *(Dim Sum)*
Addis Ababa
Artie's
Ashby Inn
Bistro Bis
Bistro d'Oc
Bistro Francais
Bistrot du Coin
Bombay Club
Bombay Tandoor
Boulevard Woodgrill
Cafe Atlantico
Cafe de Paris
Cafe Milano
Cafe Salsa
Cantina Marina
Carlyle
Cashion's Eat Place
Circle Bistro
Colorado Kitchen
The Diner
88
El Manantial
15 ria
Firefly
Four & Twenty Blackbirds

Gabriel
Guajillo
Harry's Tap Room
India Palace
Jaleo
L'Auberge Provencale
Les Halles
Logan Tavern
Maestro
Majestic Cafe
Melrose
Mon Ami Gabi
Morrison-Clark Inn
New Heights
Old Ebbitt Grill
Old Glory
Perry's
Rail Stop
Roof Terrace
Seasons
Southside 815
Taste of Morocco
Taverna Cretekou
2941
Zaytinya

BUFFETS

These buffets are mostly for lunch or brunch

Addis Ababa
Afghan
Ashby Inn
Bombay Club
Bombay Tandoor
Cho's Garden
Gabriel
India Palace
Maestro

Matsutake *(except airport location)*
Old Glory
Perry's
Roof Terrace
Seasons
Taverna Cretekou
2941
Woodlands

PRE-THEATER BARGAINS

Addie's
Bistro d'Oc
Bistro Francais
Bombay Club
Cafe Atlantico
Cafe de Paris
Cantina Marina
Charlie Palmer Steak
Circle Bistro
Indique
La Fourchette
Les Halles
Marcel's
Melrose
Nizam's
Olives
Ortanique
1789
Signatures
Two Quail
Zola

OUTDOOR DINING

Addie's
Agrodolce
Ashby Inn
A.V. Ristorante
Bardeo
Big Bowl
Bistro Bis
Black's Bar and Kitchen
Black Olive
Bombay Club
Boulevard Woodgrill
Breadline
Buck's Fishing & Camping
Cafe Asia *(Arlington)*
Cafe Atlantico
Cafe de Paris
Cafe 15
Cafe Milano
Cantina Marina
Carlyle
Cashion's Eat Place
Caspian House of Kabob
C.F. Folks
Charleston
Circle Bistro
Crisp & Juicy
Cubano's
David Greggory
Dukem
88
Ella's Wood Fired Pizza
Equinox
Famous Luigi's
Faryab
15 ria
Galileo
Gerard's Place
Green Papaya

Guajillo
Hakuba
Harris Crab House
Indique
Inn at Easton
Islander Caribbean
Jimmy Cantler's
Kinkead's
La Fourchette
L'Auberge Chez Francois
L'Auberge Provencale
Le Mannequin Pis
Les Halles
Little Fountain Cafe
Local 16
Logan Tavern
Mantis
Marcel's
Meiwah
Melrose
Michel Richard Citronelle
Minh's
Mon Ami Gabi
Montmartre
Morrison-Clark Inn
Mykonos Grill
New Heights
Olazzo
Old Glory
Ortanique
Oval Room
Palena
Perry's
Persimmon
Rafagino
Rail Stop
Raku
Ray's the Steaks
Roof Terrace

Sea Catch
Seasons
Signatures
Singh Thai
Southside 815
Taberna del Alabardero
Taverna Cretekou
Teaism
TenPenh
Thaiphoon *(Pentagon Row)*
2941
2 Amys
Two Quail
Wazuri
Woodlands *(Fairfax)*
Zaytinya

NONSMOKING RESTAURANTS

A & J
Addie's
Addis Ababa
Afghan
Agrodolce
Amma Vegetarian Kitchen
Ashby Inn
Bistro Bis
Bistro Francais
Bistrot Lafayette
Bistrot Lepic
Black's Bar and Kitchen
Black Olive
Bob Kinkead's
  Colvin Run Tavern
Bombay Club
Burma
Cafe de Paris
Cafe 15

Carlyle
Caspian House of Kabob
Ceiba
C.F. Folks
Colorado Kitchen
Corduroy
Crisp & Juicy
Cubano's
DC Coast
Dish
El Chalan
El Manantial
Faryab
15 ria
Four & Twenty Blackbirds
Galileo
Gerard's Place
Green Papaya
Hakuba
Han Sung Oak
Heritage India
Hollywood East Cafe
India Palace
Inn at Easton
Inn at Little Washington
Jimmy Cantler's
Joe's Noodle House
Johnny's Half Shell
Kabob Palace
Kaz Sushi Bistro
Kuna
Laboratorio del Galileo
L'Auberge Chez Francois
L'Auberge Provencale
Le Tire Bouchon
Little Fountain Cafe
Love Cafe
Lupo's Italian Chophouse
Maestro

Majestic Cafe
Makoto
Mandalay
Matsutake
Meiwah
Minh's
Mon Ami Gabi
Montmartre
Morrison-Clark Inn
Mr. K's
Mykonos Grill
Natta Thai
Nectar
New Fortune
New Heights
Nick & Stef's
Nizam's
Nora
Obelisk
Old Europe
O'Learys
Oval Room
Palena
Persimmon
Pesce
Pizzeria Paradiso
Rafagino
Raku
Ray's the Steaks
Roof Terrace
Samantha's
SBC Cafe
1789
Singh Thai
Spices
Sunflower
Sushi-Ko
Sushi Taro
Taste of Morocco

Tavira
Teaism
2 Amys
Vidalia
Woodlands
Wurzburg Haus
Yanyu
Yoko
Yuan Fu
Zaytinya
Zest
Zola

Morrison-Clark Inn
Perry's
Pizzeria Paradiso *(Georgetown)*
Sea Catch
1789
Stardust
Taverna Cretekou
Tavira
2941
Woodlands
Zaytinya
Zola

RESTAURANTS WITH FIREPLACES

Addie's
Al Tiramisu
Artie's
Ashby Inn
A.V. Ristorante
Bistro Bis
Bistro d'Oc
Black Olive
Bob Kinkead's
  Colvin Run Tavern
Charlie Palmer Steak
Circle Bistro
Dish
Dukem
Elysium
15 ria
Green Papaya
Harry's Tap Room
Inn at Easton
Inn at Little Washington
L'Auberge Chez Francois
L'Auberge Provencale
Matchbox

ROOMS WITH A (SPECIAL) VIEW

Ashby Inn *(outdoor garden)*
Cantina Marina
  (the SW waterfront)
Harris Crab House
  (view of the water)
Inn at Easton *(outdoor garden)*
Inn at Little Washington
  (outdoor garden)
Jimmy Cantler's
  (view of the water)
L'Auberge Chez Francois
  (outdoor garden)
L'Auberge Provencale
  (outdoor garden)
New Heights
  (windows overlooking Rock Creek Park)
Perry's
  (rooftop overlooks Adams Morgan)
Sea Catch
  (balcony overlooks C & O Canal)
2941
  (terrace overlooking lake)

ROMANTIC

Al Tiramisu

Ashby Inn

Bardeo

Bistro Bis

Bob Kinkead's
  Colvin Run Tavern

Bombay Club

Cafe Atlantico

Cafe de Paris

Cashion's Eat Place

Charleston

Charlie Palmer Steak

El Manantial

Elysium

Four & Twenty Blackbirds

Green Papaya

Inn at Easton

Inn at Little Washington

L'Auberge Chez Francois

L'Auberge Provencale

Layalina

Le Tire Bouchon

Little Fountain Cafe

Local 16

Logan Tavern

Maestro

Marcel's

Michel Richard Citronelle

Minh's

New Heights

Nizam's

Nora

Obelisk

O'Learys

Ortanique

Oval Room

Palena

Perry's

Prime Rib

Rafagino

Roof Terrace

Sea Catch

Seasons

1789

Signatures

Taberna del Alabardero

TenPenh

Tosca

2941

Two Quail

Yanyu

Zest

Zola

CRITIC'S PICKS

A & J

Addie's

Al Tiramisu

Artie's

Ashby Inn

Bardeo

Bistrot Lepic

Cafe Atlantico

Carlyle

Cashion's Eat Place

Caucus Room

C.F. Folks

Charleston

Colorado Kitchen

Corduroy

Crisp & Juicy

Cuban Corner

Equinox

Four & Twenty Blackbirds

Heritage India

Hollywood East Cafe

Huong Que (Four Sisters)

Inn at Easton

Inn at Little Washington

Jaleo

Joe's Noodle House

Johnny's Half Shell

Kabob Palace

Kaz Sushi Bistro

Kuna

Laboratorio del Galileo

L'Auberge Provencale

Layalina

Le Mannequin Pis

Little Fountain Cafe

Maestro

Majestic Cafe

Makoto

Mantis

Marcel's

Michel Richard Citronelle

Minh's

Montmartre

Mykonos Grill

Nectar

Nizam's

Obelisk

O'Learys

Palena

Pesce

Raku

Ray's the Steaks

Sakoontra

Samantha's

SBC Cafe

1789

Singh Thai

Sunflower

Sushi-Ko

Tavira

TenPenh

Tosca

2941

2 Amys

Vidalia

Wazuri

Yanyu

Zaytinya

Zest

Zola